iDisrupted:

disruptive technology, changing the human race forever.

By
John Straw and
Michael Baxter

with contributions from Julien de Salaberry and Harriet Green

New Generation **Publishing**

About the authors

John Straw is a leading authority on emerging technologies, a major voice in the digital services industry, and a serial entrepreneur. He is an active early stage venture capitalist, with a particular interest in technology companies. Currently, he is Chairman of Thomas Cook's Digital Advisory Board, Chairman/ Investor in search start-up Cloudfind, Non-Executive Director at personal data start-up CTRLio and principle at the recently formed investment group Thorium Technology Investors.

Michael Baxter is a business/economics writer, entrepreneur and technology provocateur. His writing is entertaining, a tad quirky, often controversial, thought provoking, and never dull. He is the author of several economics and technology books, including *The Blindfolded Masochist*, and *Bubbles and Wisdom*. Many business publications, including several national newspapers, have published his articles. He is currently a freelance writer with a regular column at The Share Centre.

Julien de Salaberry is a globally recognised expert on healthcare and technology. The founder and CIO of The Propell Group, Julien has a keen eye for identifying innovative technologies. He has directed strategy for some of the world's leading healthcare companies, including Eli Lilly, Boston Scientific and Merck & Co.

Harriet Green OBE and CEO of Thomas Cook is considered one of the most powerful women in the UK. Recent winner of the acclaimed Veuve Clicquot Businesswoman of the Year Award for her transformation of Thomas Cook, she is an advocate of technology and continually shows how our economy can reform and embrace with new technology.

Acknowledgements

This is an ambitious book, and would not have been possible without the support of many.

Particular thanks are due to Jane Varley for proofing the book and providing invaluable feedback, not once but twice; Steve Cross for cover design, Neil Strudwick for internal images, Chanelle McGarry and Jessica Draws. Also thanks to Clifford Peat, for your feedback.

Thank you to those who gave up their time to be interviewed: Professors Patrick McAndrew, Peter Scott and Enrico Motta at the Open University, Guy Rigby at Smith and Williamson, Pete Basiliere at Gartner, Adrian Bowyer at Rep Rap, Robin Weston at Renishaw, Rupert Jupp at Princedown Partners, Nir Siegel and Mark Handford.

Contents

8

"Where a calculator like ENIAC today is equipped with 18,000 vacuum tubes and weighs 30 tons, computers in the future may have only 1000 vacuum tubes and perhaps weigh only 1½ tons."
Popular Mechanics March 1949[1]

When   I   in   dreams   behold   thy   fairest   shade
Whose shade in dreams doth wake the sleeping morn
The   daytime   shadow   of   my   love   betray'd
Lends   hideous   night   to   dreaming's   faded   form
Were   painted   frowns   to   gild   mere   false   rebuff
Then   shoulds't   my   heart   be   patient   as   the   sands
For   nature's   smile   is   ornament   enough
When   thy   gold   lips   unloose   their   drooping   bands
As   clouds   occlude   the   globe's   enshrouded   fears
Which   can   by   no   astron'my   be   assail'd
Thus,   thyne   appearance   tears   in   atmospheres
No   fond   perceptions   nor   no   gaze   unveils
Disperse   the   clouds   which   banish   light   from   thee
For no tears be true, until we truly see

Sonnet created by a collaboration between Shakespeare, an MIT PhD student, and an algorithm. It seems unlikely that Shakespeare knew about the collaboration, however.

1

http://www.popularmechanics.com/technology/engineering/news/inside-the-future-how-popmech-predicted-the-next-110-years-14831802

We must do away with the absolutely specious notion that everybody has to earn a living. It is a fact today that one in ten thousand of us can make a technological breakthrough capable of supporting all the rest. The youth of today are absolutely right in recognizing this nonsense of earning a living. We keep inventing jobs because of this false idea that everybody has to be employed at some kind of drudgery because, according to Malthusian Darwinian theory, he must justify his right to exist. So we have inspectors of inspectors and people making instruments for inspectors to inspect inspectors. The true business of people should be to go back to school and think about whatever it was they were thinking about before somebody came along and told them they had to earn a living."

Buckminster Fuller, American neo-futuristic architect, systems theorist, author, designer and inventor.

Some useful definitions to consider

Moore's Law: This is explained in more detail later, but it describes the rate at which computers become more powerful, and is typically seen to suggest that computers double in power every 18 to 24 months.

AI: Artificial intelligence

Innovator's Dilemma: A theory on how business can be disrupted when new technologies emerge that initially had a slightly different application. For example, many disc driver companies went out of business when the leading type of disc drive shifted from nine inch, used in mini computers, to 5¼ inch, used in desktop computers. By the time dominant companies in the nine inch market spotted the new development it was too late, and other companies had achieved too big a technology lead for the previous market leaders to recover their former glories.

Demand: When the word demand is used in this book, the economics definition is being applied, and relates to how much money people are both willing and able to spend at any one time. Demand depends on what people can afford.

Prologue

This time it is different.

Time, that's what it takes. Technology that can change the world in a dramatic fashion does not come into this world fully formed like Athena from the head of Zeus. It can take years, even decades before the new technology grabs significant market share for itself.

Colour TV was first introduced into the US in the early 1950s. It was not until 1972 that sales exceeded those of black and white televisions. Take the story of cassette recorders, VCRs, record players and even of black and white TVs themselves; the story from market inception to dominance was similarly elongated.

While it takes time for new technology to gain market traction, cynicism in its relevance grows. Lee DeForest – self-styled inventor of the radio, and whose inventions it is said made radio broadcasting possible – is reputed to have opined: "While theoretically and technically television may be feasible, commercially and financially it is an impossibility."

Compare this to recent technological developments. Apple launched its iPod in November 2001. By April 2007 the company had sold its one hundred millionth unit.

New technology – so-called disruptive technology, such as the iPod, smart phones, eBooks and tablets – is not subject to the time constraints that dominated the technology market place throughout the 20th century.
Other technologies in the pipeline will see extraordinarily rapid development. The product cycle from early adopter to market maturity is set to become compressed.

Innovations and developments, such as 3D printing, nanotechnology, robotics, artificial intelligence, virtual reality, genetics, stem cell research, new materials, and technology for promoting a sharing economy, are likely to change the world at a pace that has no precedent. This time it is different.

In one key respect, however, it is much the same as always. Cynics continue to abound. In 1876, Sir William Preece, chief engineer of the British Post Office, said: "The Americans have need of the telephone, but we do not. We have plenty of messenger boys." In 1899, the eminent British scientist Lord Kelvin said: "Radio has no future. Heavier-than-air flying machines are impossible. X-rays will prove to be a hoax."

Most infamously of all, in 1943 Thomas Watson, chairman of IBM, is supposed to have said: "I think there is a world market for maybe five computers." [2]
This time it is the same as ever. The doubters are everywhere, and their cynicism will prove costly.

Disruptive technologies may be able to create wealth on an unprecedented scale – and it is certain that many entrepreneurs and their backers will enjoy wealth beyond anything they had expected – but it will also disrupt. Many companies will go out of business. Giant companies that once loomed above the business landscape like Californian Redwoods will fall.

That's evolution – there are winners and losers. Part of the purpose of this book is to shed light on who those losers may be, and what – if anything – they can do to avoid this fate.

---

[2] This quote may be apocryphal.

Then there are economic implications. Boom or bust or both may result from certain technologies. Alas, neither economists nor policy makers seem aware of the perfect tempest coming their way.

Disruptive technology may provide a feast for many. It could even provide a helping of fine living for most of us. But some will lose out. Some will be left asking: "What happened to my company, my investment, my job?"

But it doesn't have to be bad news. If we play it right, the result of the technological innovations that are afoot will be a kind of economic utopia. Poverty will be ended; we will all live longer and have the potential to be healthier. Technology does not have to replace us; it can enhance us. But we first need to understand what is happening, why it is happening, and recognise both the dangers and opportunities associated with it. Then we can adapt and embrace it.

Part one and introduction

We begin with Apple. The story of this company illustrates a key point of this book. When technology isn't quite good enough or powerful enough to offer popular consumer applications, it can look disappointing and over-hyped. But technology progresses, and once it makes that tiny step from being not quite good enough, to being just good enough, things can change dramatically. Technological progress can fall into three phases: the hype phase, the sceptical phase (as we react to what appears to have been unrealistic promises of the previous phase), and then the transformational phase, as previous innovations converge, create wealth, and – in the case of the period we are set to enter – lead to an acceleration in innovation. We are poised to enter the greatest transformational phase ever. Cynics have become fixated, however; they remain stuck in the sceptical phase.

Chapters one and two look at theory and history. We work forward from creative destruction, look at economists such as Robert Gordon and Tyler Cohen, who doubt the significance of technology, and move on to the idea of 'free', into the dream of utopia. In the chapter on history, we tot up how many of the world's largest companies in the early 20th century are still with us today, and look at the most important innovations ever.

Chapter three is a tease, and a bit of fun. Forward wind the clock 30 years, and what will we then say are the most important innovations ever? Here is a clue: many of them are brand spanking new.

Chapter four looks at technologies, and developments that are making new technologies possible; from Moore's Law, to MEMS, robots, graphene and virtual reality. These are the technologies that provide the foundations for the greatest changes ever seen in the story of our species.

Part two

This part looks at the unravelling of technology, the sharing economy, and how the Millennial generation is different.

It looks at the next industrial revolution and the one that will follow. The first will be charged by the internet of things, robotics, 3D printing and innovations in energy. The second will follow so soon, it may even merge into the first, but this will be extraordinarily dramatic. Nanotechnology and artificial intelligence will change the world more completely than all the innovations of the last 200 years put together.

This part finishes with healthcare. Those who are stuck with their sceptical view of technology have a shock coming their way. Technology is set to transform us, making us healthier and longer lived, and even the war against bugs, which antibiotics seem to be losing, may yet be won.

Part Three

In the third part we look at disruption: and disruption in four ways:

Business:	How technology is going to change banks, energy companies, car manufacturers, retailers and media more radically than the people working in these industries dare to contemplate.
The economy:	Will technology make us richer, or create unemployment? Will it create a world of plenty or will we see a kind of *Downton Abbey* economy emerge, with a society comprising the super-rich and the rest of us who wait on them?
On health:	Will we even need doctors?
On us:	Will technology change what it is to be human?

Part four

And finally we conclude: what can we do?

What can businesses do to survive? What can policy makers do to save jobs? What can educators do to ensure we master technology rather than letting it master us? What can we do to ensure we and our children have a job in 20 years' time? What can we all do – that's us, the human race – to ensure there is still a human race in 30 years' time?

Bear in mind

It is human nature. We overestimate how quickly technology will develop, and underestimate its final impact. Technology has and will continue to disrupt business, the economy, workers, our health, and above all what it is to be human. Nothing is more important than understanding these issues.

Introduction

It seems incredible now that the world's largest company almost went bust ten years ago. Before that, it had to seek help from the enemy in order to survive. Apple aficionados said the company had sold its soul when in 1997 it was forced to date and then sleep with Microsoft. On 6 August 1997, their despair was palpable when, on the occasion of an Apple PR spectacular at the Mac World Expo in Boston, the words of a certain William Henry Gates (more commonly referred to as Bill Gates) echoed across the room like screechy brakes, apparently heralding the end of Apple's reign as the world's leading non-Microsoft compatible PC company.

It was a bitter-sweet year. January of 1997 saw the return of the prodigal son, as Apple's co-founder Steve Jobs returned to the fold after years of enforced exile. But the prodigal son becoming the "*de facto* head" was seen as scant consolation on that auspicious day in August, when, as far as Apple fans were concerned, the devil walked amongst them. On one hand, the Apple faithful gave thanks for the return of Jobs; on the other hand they lamented the deal with the giant software company from Seattle. They spat venom at the very idea that MS Office was to run on Apple computers and Internet Explorer was to be the default browser for Mac OS for five years.

The new look Apple (then known as Apple Computers) with its reappointed head, enjoyed something of a recovery. In October 1998, it was able to announce its first profitable year since 1995, but the company continued to dice with failure. In the year 2000, Apple enjoyed a market capitalisation of nearly US $19 billion, but that was the year of the dotcom bust. By the first quarter of 2003, its market cap was $5.33 billion. During the post dotcom boom, investors across the world seemed to give up on the idea of technology companies altogether; Apple was seen by many as yesterday's company, living off former glories.

Ten years and an iPod, iPhone and iPad later, Apple was valued at a fraction over half a trillion dollars (as of 17 December 2013, with a market cap of US $501 billion, according to Yahoo finance). To put that in context, the world's second largest company by market cap was Exxon Mobile, worth US $424 billion.

The speed of the recovery and the turnaround is remarkable enough, but one question lurks: how did the company achieve it?

It appears that at least one factor, maybe the most important factor, is that change in technology made the Apple renaissance possible. This is an important theme of this book. When technology is not up to the tasks we demand of it, it is easy to become cynical, to adopt a dismissive attitude, claiming that it will take years and years before certain ideas become a possibility. But different technologies can converge, and technology's march forward is relentless, and just a few minor developments in technological power mean that dreams suddenly become possible.

You would have expected John Sculley, the man who replaced Steve Jobs at the top of Apple in the 1983 only to be effectively forced out of the company in 1985, to be bitter and twisted about Apple's famous co-founder. Despite the circumstances of his leaving, however, Sculley appears to have nothing but praise for the man who many saw as his arch nemesis. In an interview with Cult of the Mac, while Jobs was still alive, a magnanimous Sculley explained the Apple turnaround as follows:
"For someone to build consumer products in the 1980s beyond what we did with the first Mac was literally

impossible," said Scully, but then he suggested that by the 1990s things began to change. At this point it was at least possible to get an idea of where consumer products were going. Scully said the key to this being possible was "Moore's Law and... the homogenization of technology." It changed with the dawn of the 21st century, when the cost of components, commoditization and miniaturization coincided to make things possible. Scully said: "The performance suddenly reached the point where you could actually build things that we can call digital consumer products."

To try to summarise a very long interview with Sculley in a few words: Jobs was obsessive about design; he loved the way Sony built consumer electronics, and had an idea for turning computer technology into beautiful design – beautiful to look at and to use. However, during the 1980s and 1990s, his ideas were too ambitious. It was not possible to apply his idea of design to technology that was clunky, unwieldy and which frustrated users to the point of despair with its technical short-comings. But as we moved beyond the year 2000, in the aftermath of the dotcom crash, things changed. Technology suddenly became advanced enough to turn Jobs' vision into reality, and a brilliant plan unfolded. However, it was a plan that simply could not have gained traction a few years earlier.

Technology is like that. When it reaches a stage of sufficient power, it can help to promote a sudden explosion in creativity. It can also make ideas of the past that had seemed unrealistic, both possible and practical.

See it like the super cooling of water. It is generally believed that water freezes at zero degrees centigrade. This is not so. Ice melts at that temperature, but if it is pure and undisturbed, liquid water can remain in its liquid form at temperatures as low as minus 40 degrees. But when liquid water is super cooled in this way, something very interesting happens. When the pool of water begins to freeze, it does so immediately. There is no intermediate step; all the water that is being super cooled is either liquid or ice. Relatively speaking it is like that with technology. As long as it is not sufficiently powerful to provide certain key benefits, it appears to be clunky, cumbersome, and predictions of swanky future uses of technology seem to be stupid or naïve. But once the technology gains a certain critical mass in its capability, the applications taking advantage of it can explode onto the market. It seems to be human nature to overestimate how quickly technology will change, but to underestimate the effect it will have. It also appears to be human nature to become disenchanted with technology just before it reaches the transformational stage. During the dotcom boom, the human trait of over-exuberance led to wild forecasts about how rapidly the internet would change the world. You could say this was the exuberant, or hype, phase. In the aftermath of the crash, to many people, investors especially, the words internet or dotcom appeared to be synonymous with hype. You could say this was the sceptical phase. But the extraordinary rise of Apple that then followed showed how such cynicism was misplaced. Apple's turnaround occurred as we entered the transformational phase.

To put it another way, for years many looked on and thought Apple seemed to be crawling into a pool of despair, but when technology converges and reaches a certain level of power, ideas and brilliant applications can shoot out of that pool, like Thunderbird One from the Tracy Island swimming pool.

The sceptical view of technology

We all get frustrated by technology. Indeed, it appears it can test our temper. One in three British computer users admitted that slow-processing PCs put them in a bad mood for the rest of the day, and 29 per cent said they lost sleep over the issue. The research, produced by Sandisk, also found that in Italy 6.8 days a year of productivity was lost due to slow computers, while 4.9 days a year were lost in the US.

Then there's traffic. There may be someone out there who enjoys being stuck in a traffic jam, who deliberately goes out of their way to find one, but on very rare occasions, if there is something good on the radio perhaps, a traffic jam can be a positive thing. However, any kind of delay caused by traffic usually turns our mood foul.

Add poor signals on our mobile phones to the list of gripes about technology. How many conversations have you had that have been repeatedly interrupted by signal failure?

More alarming than technology rage is the view that in some respects it may have gone into reverse. Take the quite terrifying prospect of antibiotics losing their effectiveness. There are some who believe the discovery of penicillin was the single most important discovery of the 20th century, but over-use of antibiotics, especially in agriculture (80 per cent of antibiotic usage is accounted for by agriculture in the US), has led to the evolution of antibiotic immune bacteria – so-called super-bugs. The World Health Organisation estimates that on average antibiotics add 20 years to our lives, so imagine what will happen if they lose their effectiveness. As Gillian Tett wrote in the *Financial Times*: "We are moving towards a world where, within a generation, the drugs simply may not work anymore. Modern medicine could lose the ability to combat many illnesses or infections." She added: "This sounds so horrifying it seems hard to imagine."

Professor Richard Smith and Joanna Coast said in the *British Medical Journal*: "An increase in resistant organisms coupled with a big fall in the number of new antimicrobial drugs suggests an apocalyptic scenario may be looming." They also said: "From cradle to grave, antimicrobials have become pivotal in safeguarding the overall health of human societies."

And just to really terrify us they gave us an anecdote to illustrate the problem. The current infection rates for patients undergoing a hip replacement are 0.5 to 2 per cent, but without antibiotics, infection rates will soar to 40 to 50 per cent, and about 30 per cent of those infections will be fatal.

The idea that antibiotics are losing their effectiveness conjures up an image of us returning to the Victorian age; a time when childhood fatalities were expected, were a regular part of family life, and indeed death. It also makes us question whether we are really any better off.

The economist Robert J Gordon seems to draw similar conclusions, but from a different perspective. He calls it the New Yorker game, after an experiment carried out by the *New Yorker* publication. It commissioned someone to watch TV for a week and then write about it. The commissioned writer said: "I was so struck by situation comedies of the 1950s, the reruns, how similar their lives seemed to today." Gordon asks us to imagine what life was like 30 years ago, and then to imagine it 30 years before that and keep going back in 30 year intervals. He says the changes between now and the early 1980s are not that great. The changes between the 1950s and 1980s, he says were modest too. But between the 1920s and 1950s lifestyles were transformed. The transformation was even more radical, he says, between the 1890s and 1920s.

Or consider it another way, he suggests. Imagine you have two choices. In one option you have technology circa 2002, complete with Windows '98 PCs. In the other you have iPhones, and tablets, and Facebook, but you lose indoor toilets and hot and cold running water. Which option will you select?

The answer is obvious says Gordon, who claims that of all possible innovations, those that can change lives in a profound way have already been invented. We are left with smaller things. iPhones may offer superior functionality to the mobile phones of the late 1990s, tablets may be preferable in many respects to a Windows '98 laptop PC, but the changes are not profound; they are not like they were when we learnt how to deliver hot and cold running water, electricity, the motor car, and air travel.

Another economist, Tyler Cohen, has a similar idea. He suggests we have picked the low hanging fruit of innovation, and from now on innovation is going to get harder. He cites the internet as an example. He says it has been great for satisfying the curiosity, for those who want to fill their brains with ideas, but he argues the internet has done very little to raise living standards.

Both Gordon and Cohen consider the extent to which growth has stagnated in the West in recent years; how living standards in many cases have not risen at all. As the Nobel Laureate Joseph Stiglitz says, median income today in the US is no higher than it was 25 years ago.

Writing in 2011, Cohen hailed what he called The Great Stagnation. The era of rapid growth was over he suggested. The implication was that only countries with scope for technological catch-up could look forward to a growth rate that was anything like the level we used to enjoy in the west.

Both Cohen and Gordon say the golden ages of innovation are in the past. Gordon talks about the innovation of steam, cotton spinning and railroads between 1750 and 1830 and then the second great era of innovation between 1870 and 1900, which saw electricity, the internal combustion engine and running water – thanks in part to the innovations of indoor plumbing.

In contrast, says Gordon, the computer and internet revolution kicked off around 1960, peaked in the late 1990s, but any resulting growth has fizzled out since then.

It is a fascinating, but not commonly understood, matter of fact that economic growth per capita was virtually non-existent until the 19th century. Your average peasant in 1820s Britain was only marginally better off than his equivalent at the time when the Romans left.

Take this chart.

Changes in GDP and growth in West Europe since the year 1 AD,
source: Angus Maddison, Contours of the World Economy 1 to 2030 AD, page 70

	1 AD	1000	1500	1820	1870	1913	1950	1973	2003
GDP per capita in dollars	576	427	771	1,202	1,960	3,457	4,578	11,417	19,912
	1-1000	1000-1500	1500-1820	1820-70	1870-1913	1913-50	1950-1973	1973-2003	
Annual growth	-0.03	0.12	0.14	0.98	1.33	0.76	4.05	1.87	

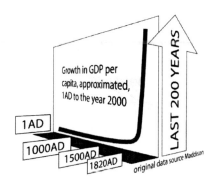

So the question is: will growth from 2003 carry on from the level we saw after 1973, or will it return to the higher level seen post 1950, or will it return to the usual level seen by most of the last 2,000 years?

Gordon and Cohen appear to be suggesting that growth will stagnate, although Cohen only sees this as temporary. He is more optimistic than Gordon is about the longer term.

The essence of their argument is that much of the innovation we have seen in the last few decades have been more fun than useful. iPhones are great, but have they really transformed lives?

They then point to data to back-up their assertions: productivity growth has slowed. How can you explain such a slowdown without suggesting that the benefits of new technology are exaggerated?

The optimistic view

Economics is often known as the dismal science, and Robert Gordon seems determined to make sure that this nomenclature is justified.

Many economists disagree with his diagnosis, however. The most well-known of these is Paul Romer, an economics professor from Stanford University. He reckons we will carry on innovating until the sun explodes. So that means we have five billion years or so of progress ahead of us, which is long enough to outlast even the healthiest reader of this book. Romer says: "Just ask how many things we could make by taking the elements from the periodic table and mixing them together. There's a simple mathematical calculation: it's 10 followed by 30 zeros. In contrast, 10 followed by 19 zeros is about how much time has elapsed since the universe was created."

The law professor Yochai Benkler argues that collaborative projects such as Wikipedia are helping to stimulate a new technological revolution. He says: "By disrupting traditional economic production, copyright law and established competition, they're paving the way for a new set of economic laws, where empowered individuals are put on a level playing field with industry giants."

Stuck in the sceptical phase

The danger that antibiotics may lose their effectiveness is indeed scary, but we are not without hope. Indeed, there are reasons to believe we may be on the cusp of winning a decisive victory over disease, particularly in those conditions previously thought incurable. As Oscar Pistorius showed, it is now possible for a man with no legs to run the 400 metres in 46.25 seconds. As we will read later in the book, cures for cancer, and both Alzheimer's and Parkinson's disease beckon. Some claim that scientists are on the verge of slowing down the ageing process. And that dichotomy – the fear that antibiotic immune diseases may send us back to a Victorian type of existence, versus the hope that technology – will transform medical science, seems typical.

There are dangers in technology. It is indeed possible that its negative effects will outweigh the positives. It is not hard to envisage, as a later chapter will show, circumstances in which technology creates conditions that are even more terrifying than antibiotics losing their effectiveness.

And those who dismiss technology; those who say progress is slowing down, are making a mistake, and furthermore, it is potentially a very dangerous mistake.
The authors and contributors to this book believe that to claim technology peaked in the late 1990s is, quite simply, absurd.

It is true that technology does not always advance in straight lines; sometimes certain applications can be left behind. It is unlikely that motor cars driven by humans will ever travel much faster than they do at present. But that does not mean it will not be possible to travel from one location to another any faster than we do at present.

Those who say technology has peaked are stuck in the sceptical phase of innovation. They are guilty of viewing the world through constricted lenses. It is as if they view the world from the wrong end of binoculars.

Romer and Benkler are right; modern technology is making other technology possible. The rate of technological progress is not slowing down; it is accelerating. Disappointing economic performance and the widening of the gap between the very richest in society and everyone else is not a symptom of technological progress abating. The relationship between technology and wealth creation is complex. On occasions, it can fool us into thinking it's not creating wealth, but never fall into the trap of looking at the present, and projecting forward as though things will not change. It is even possible that a blinkered attitude to technological progress is the cause of much of the world's recent economic troubles.

It is not that Robert J Gordon and Tyler Cohen don't make important points: they do. Many of the problems to which they allude are real; it is just that the overriding theme of each of their respective theses is based on a false assumption.

We have not picked the low hanging fruit; rather technology presents the opportunity to step into an orchard of the ripest and sweetest fruit imaginable. The dotcom boom did not represent the peak of new technology. It was little more than a minor bump in the approach road to the towering mountain that is the technology which is due to follow.

Consider for a moment how technology has accelerated in recent years.

Acceleration

Today, a new automotive design cycle is typically 24 to 36 months, whereas five years ago it was nearer 60 months - or so an automobile consultant quoted in the *Harvard Review* says. 25 years after the launch of the telephone, market penetration in the US was just 10 per cent. It took 39 years to obtain 40 per cent penetration, yet smart phones obtained 40 per cent penetration within ten years. Compare this with the time it took for the televisions to emerge from launch to market saturation.

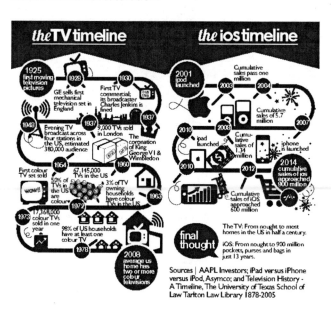

33

Be careful how you interpret this story. The elongated time period related to, say, electricity or the telephone has much to do with infrastructure. Wireless internet access, for example, is growing in popularity more rapidly in part because it needs less infrastructure, fewer roads to be dug up. Google is conducting research into offering internet access via balloons floating high in the atmosphere, sending out bandwidth over huge distances with minimal construction required. The market penetration of the World Wide Web was very rapid. It was developed by Tim Berners Lee in 1989. But the World Wide Web is just one facet of the internet; this was initially developed by ARPAnet in 1969. It took the application of the World Wide Web before the mass market took an interest in the internet. Maybe the introduction of broadband accelerated adoption, and the combination of wireless internet access with smart phones and tablets may have led to a further jump. Further internet adoption may follow as we move towards the internet of things, wearable technology, and - beyond that - interfaces that link the brain directly to the internet.

Disruptive effect

From a certain perspective, technology can be seen to have had a negative effect. Take Eastman Kodak. It was one of the world's largest companies throughout the course of the 20th century. It went on to become a pioneer of digital photography, but within a few years of the 21st century, it went bust.

Take this somewhat unscientifically produced chart:

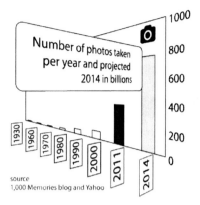

Number of photos taken per year and projected 2014 in billions

source
1,000 Memories blog and Yahoo

According to the 1,000 Moments web site, the total number of photos taken ever is 3.5 trillion. A presentation given by Yahoo predicted that no less than 880 billion photographs will be taken in 2014. According to NPD, "The percentage of photos taken with a smartphone went from 17 per cent in 2010, to 27 per cent in 2011, while the share of photos taken on any camera dropped from 52 per cent to 44 per cent." Actually, it seems quite surprising that the number of photos taken with smart phones is that low, but bear in mind that the research was conducted in 2011. Yahoo's prediction was for 2014, and when it comes to anything digital, three years can seem like a lifetime.

It is Eastman Kodak's tragedy that its own business model imploded just as the markets it had dominated for so long saw levels of usage that dwarfed what we had seen before. If someone in the year 2000 could have somehow got hold of data showing the growing popularity of photography over the next decade and a half, it is surely unlikely they would have forecast the demise of Kodak.

Maybe this is why the link between technology and economic growth is not clear. Technology creates new opportunities, but it disrupts too. Sometimes it can offer new benefits at a fraction of the cost one would have previously paid for inferior benefits.

Cameras in smart phones may be technically inferior to premium cameras, but they are superior in one all-important respect. Most of us have our phone with us all the time, and taking a photograph with our phone is becoming as automatic as checking our watch for the time once was. They are superior to traditional cameras, because of their convenience, yet their cost is tiny. We take more photographs than ever before, yet the cost of developing them and sharing them with our friends is virtually zero. The incremental cost of our smart phone having a camera is small. Consider how much more convenient photography will become with the advent of wearable technology, such as Google Glass and smart watches.

Thanks to smart phones, in one respect we are richer. The story of our lives is now illustrated with more photographs, which are easier to access, and easier to share than ever before. Yet we pay virtually nothing for this benefit. As sales of digital cameras fall, the revenue generated by the photography industry in terms of camera sales and photographic development falls. Maybe it is not so much that new technologies do not generate wealth, but that GDP is no longer an adequate method of valuing our wealth when we receive so many benefits free. Imagine a world in which – thanks to future technology – food, energy, clothes and shelter are so plentiful that they are free. We would surely be better off, but economic statistics may suggest that GDP had declined.

Recent technologies, such as digital music players, smart phones, tablets, e-readers, and – looking forward – smart watches, and other wearable technologies (such as Google Glass) are changing the world. They may well make us better off but this may not be reflected in GDP.

Thanks to smart phones, how many of us still use maps? That is to say old fashioned maps on paper, which are incredibly hard to fold back to their original shape once you have opened them? It is not as if the mapping industry isn't worth big bucks. In 2011, Nokia paid $8.1 billion for NAVTEQ, a provider of Geographic Information Systems, but as far as the consumer is concerned, the market has changed. We used to navigate using paper maps, then the market moved to satellite navigation, but more of us are now using our smart phones, which can give us verbal travel directions. As the technology becomes more sophisticated, imagine how this trend will develop.

The internet and technologies such as smart phones and tablets have in some way disrupted industries across the economy. Despite the way in which they have made photography more popular, they have had a devastating effect on the photographic industry. The expertise that once defined the mapping industry is still in demand, maybe more than ever, but the market for printed maps has collapsed. Smart phones are disrupting the timekeeping industry too; many of us use our phones to tell the time or as an alarm clock. According to research from Pew Research Center, around 83 percent of those aged between 18 and 29 sleep with their cell phones within reach.

In some cases we have seen technology create industries and then destroy them in the relative blink of the eye. Take the video rental business as an example. The first Blockbuster store was founded in Dallas in 1985. By 1992 the company had 2,800 stores, ten years later there were 9,000 Blockbuster stores across the world. In 1994 the company was sold to Viacom for $8.4 billion. However, in 1997 Reed Hastings founded Netflix. This was partly out of frustration when he was fined $40 for the late return of videos. By 1997 16 per cent of Blockbuster's revenue was from fines, amounting to no less than $800 million. In 2011, one year after the company filed for bankruptcy protection, Dish Network bought Blockbuster's assets for $234 million.

But this does not mean the market for watching movies had declined. In the UK, an Amazon subsidiary offers a postal system in which it delivers DVDs to customers once they have returned the previous movies ordered from the company. The company doesn't issue fines and charges by a monthly subscription. In June 2011, PriceWaterhouseCoopers projected that the US movie business would expand by 20 per cent over the following four years, rising from $40.8 billion to $50.3 billion. During the same period, it predicted that worldwide profits would rise from $88.8 billion to $113.1 billion. We keep hearing about how piracy is killing the movie industry; about how the internet is destroying the glamorous world of movie making, yet these predictions of doom are not borne out by the stats. Technology is not killing the industry, but it is changing it. It is being disrupted.

The changes go further. An increasing supply of online video is becoming available. It is surely only a matter of time before we watch the latest HBO show over the internet on our smart phones. But in such circumstances will there still be a need for intermediaries, for TV broadcasters? At the moment, the viewer can watch content via a provider, such as a cable company or a specific TV station, carrying content from various content producers. But why can't content be provided directly to the end user from the content producer? The market may see a new wave of disruption at the same time as our opportunity to observe TV content increases.

Or take the mass media. The internet has had a devastating impact on the publishing industry, but it seems likely that the customer has more choice than ever before. A host of publishers have tried to charge for their content. In the UK, for example *The Times*, *The Telegraph*, *The Financial Times*, and magazines such as *New Scientist*, or *The Economist* charge for premium content. The jury is out on whether premium models can work, but it is doubtful whether publishers can make the money they used to from advertising alone. So we are seeing a situation in which revenue is under threat, but content production is as dynamic as ever.

Now Apple has developed a product called iBeacon, which, amongst other features, can enable managers of certain locations, such as coffee shops, pubs, clubs stadiums, to negotiate directly with publishers so that they can provide certain content to their customers on a premium basis.

To an extent, however, the revenue appears to be accruing to fewer companies – Amazon, Apple and Google for example.

And the conclusion

Technology is changing fast, and for some this may seem like a negative development as their own business or way of life becomes disrupted.

Some economists seem to think that new technology is having a minor effect on the economy; that new technologies are fun, but – unlike the great innovations of the past – don't create wealth.

It may be that technology has made us better off in terms of what we can enjoy from it, but thanks to the way these services are charged – often they are free and distribution costs are negligible – the benefits of technology don't necessarily show up in economic data.

Furthermore, technology is changing rapidly. New technologies are making other technologies possible. We saw this with Apple; thanks to new technology making it more practical to apply its design ideas, the company went from nearly bust to being the world's largest company.

As we await the consequences of further technology disruption, it is easier to become cynical and impatient. Technological progress can fall into three phases: the hype phase, the sceptical phase (as we react to what appeared to have been unrealistic promises of the previous phase), and then the transformational phase, when previous innovations converge, create wealth, and in the case of the period we are set to enter, lead to an acceleration in innovation.

Right now, we are on the cusp of the greatest transformational phase ever. Business, jobs, the economy and society will be disrupted – sometimes for bad, sometimes for good. If we play it right, the benefits will be enormous. Those stuck in the sceptical phase are in danger of losing out, and if policymakers and their advisors are stuck in this phase, there is a danger that the negative will overrun the positive, and the potential feast from technology will be transformed from a gastronomic delight to a pile of rotting opportunities.

Part one: background

Chapter one: From Moore's Law to Utopia: a bit of theory.

Before we continue we need a bit of theory. We also need to step back, and take the helicopter view – or maybe it would be more appropriate to say take the drone view – and try to see the world of disruptive technology through objective eyes.

You will already be familiar with some of the theories discussed in this chapter, while others may surprise you. But all theories are of vital importance, and even the ones you know about may have implications that you have not fully considered.

We will begin with innovator's dilemma, which is a harrowing tale of how established market-leading companies doing all the things that good business text books tell them they should do – namely listen to their customers – can nonetheless go out of business. Innovator's dilemma offers a salutary lesson to all those who dismiss the more quirky and esoteric ideas of engineers as not being commercial.

This chapter then moves on from innovator's dilemma to a threat even more terrifying because of the speed at which it unwinds. This is Big Bang disruption; a kind of turbo-charged version of innovator's dilemma.

We then take a sideways step into the world of Moore's Law, but in the case of this book, Moore's Law is seen as more than its original meaning; rather it is used as a metaphor to describe technologies quite different from the one that just relates to the number of transistors on an integrated circuit.

Moore's Law is important, but it does not support the innovator's dilemma hypothesis on its own. Companies operating in an industry that is seeing the unwinding of a Moore's Law type scenario do not necessarily need to fear the curse of innovator's dilemma. But they do need to fear what happens when we see convergence; when the unwinding of Moore's Law makes new applications possible, and it allows for the possibility of different industries emerging.

Under certain conditions, the combination of a Moore's Law type trajectory into an innovator's dilemma type scenario can affect us all; it can affect our jobs, and the economy. Right now we are at the early stages of seeing precisely these conditions occur.

Returning to business, there is the issue of free. Are we heading for an era when more and more products are given away? How will that hit companies and wages?

And finally we end with some economic theory as we look at how Schumpeter, one of the two great economists of the 20th century, described the conditions we now call innovator's dilemma, with his theory that we refer to today as creative destruction. We end with Keynes – the other man who was surely one of the two great economists of the 20th century – who in a little known paper envisaged a world after the kind of technologies described in this book have had their full impact.

Innovator's Dilemma

According to popular mythology, Henry Ford once said: "If I had asked people what they wanted, they would have said faster horses."[3] One man who did much to add to the

<hr>

[3] Actually it appears Mr Ford did not say these words precisely, although he is widely cited as having said them. Nonetheless, while he may not have

mythology of this supposed Ford quote was none other than Steve Jobs. He loved that saying, and was often heard quoting it. He did so with good reason, because if Jobs and Apple's chief designer Jonathan Ive had listened to the research there would have been no iPhone. Most of us can remember what touch screen phones were like before the iPhone. Most had a stylus, which we invariably lost, and many of us gave up on the idea altogether, returning to our tried and tested push button phones. Most of the early smart phones, such as those based on the Symbian operating system or Blackberry's system, did not employ touch screens, and many of the users of these devices told their phone makers (Nokia in the case of Symbian, and RIM in the case of Blackberry) that they wanted it to stay that way.

On a similar theme, the BBC nearly lost one of the biggest hits in the corporation's history because it listened to market research. On November 2013, the TV show *Doctor Who* ran a 50th anniversary special that was broadcast in no less than 94 counties simultaneously. It was "the world's largest ever simulcast of a TV drama." Yet before the show's re-launch in 2005, surveys had indicated little interest in its revival. As this piece in 'Marketing Week' put it: "When the revival of *Dr Who* is launched despite the negative response from viewers questioned in research we get important evidence that people aren't the best judges of their own future tastes."

Consumers not being the best judges of their own future interests is precisely the reason why we have innovator's dilemma.

---

said it in as many words, the phrase 'If I had asked people what they wanted, they would have said faster horses,' does seem to be an accurate summary of one of his core ideas.

The phrase was coined by Clayton Christensen in his definitive book *The Innovator's Dilemma: When New Technologies Cause Great Firms to Fail*. This is an important theory, and one with which you may well be familiar. Its implications are so important, however, it is worth spending a few paragraphs looking at Christensen's theory.[4]

His concept, as he said in the book's very first sentence, was to look at "the failure of companies to stay atop their industries when they confront certain types of market and technological change." He focused on the disc drive industry, because to quote Christensen again: "Nowhere in the history of business has there been an industry like disc drives where changes in technology, market structure, global scope, and vertical integration have been so pervasive, rapid and unrelenting."

The disc drive business, argued Christensen, was like a fruit fly. Scientists studying genetics don't study humans because the timescales of 30 plus years make such studies impractical. Instead, they study fruit flies because they are conceived, born, mature, and die all within a day.

According to Christensen, of the 17 companies that made up the industry in 1976 all, except IBM, had failed or been acquired by 1995. During these years, 129 firms entered the industry, 109 of which failed. In 1996, the only companies

---

[4] Jill Lapore has recently questioned this theory. See: The Disruption Machine, The New Yorker
http://www.newyorker.com/magazine/2014/06/23/the-disruption-machine?currentPage=all. However, in the view of the authors of this book, Clayton Christensen's response was convincing. See: Drake Bennett, Clayton Christensen Responds to *New Yorker* Takedown of 'Disruptive Innovation' http://www.businessweek.com/articles/2014-06-20/clayton-christensen-responds-to-new-yorker-takedown-of-disruptive-innovation

operating in the industry that had not been start-ups between 1976 and 1995 were IBM, Fujitsu, Hitachi and NEC.

At the time of writing, it rather looks as if the advent of the cloud will make any form of local disc drive storage superfluous, so while the fruit fly continues its short lifespan, the disc drive business for serving users directly, is close to becoming extinct.

The disc drive industry went through a number of key developments. Some of these developments had little effect on the market positioning of key players; if anything they may have reinforced their position. Other developments had a devastating effect on industry players, causing a complete upheaval in how the industry was structured.

At first, Christensen considered an idea he referred to as the mudslide hypothesis. With this theory, technological change is so rapid that for market leaders to hang onto their premier position was akin to climbing up a cliff edge, when the mud that defines the edge is sliding downwards.

But after studying the history of the disc drive industry in more detail, Christensen realised that the mudslide hypothesis was wrong.

What Christensen found was as long as technology was advancing, even if it was advancing very rapidly, the makeup-up of the industry barely changed. This was even the case when new technologies evolved; for example, as ferrite-oxide heads gave way to thin-film heads, or even more radically when the 14-inch Winchester drive replaced removable disc-packs. Christensen said: "In literally every case of sustaining technology change in the disc drive industry, established firms led in development and commercialisation."

The business was disrupted in a quite different way. The disruption occurred when new technology emerged that was initially inferior to established technology in all key respects, and instead only applied to a new and apparently niche market.

For example, the development of 8-inch drives did not appear to offer significant commercial benefits. They had less memory capacity, and the cost per unit of memory was more. Their key selling point was that they were smaller, but at the point of their introduction, the computer market was dominated by mainframe computers. The leading makers of 12-inch drives canvassed the views of their main customers, and the feedback was clear: 8-inch drives offered a benefit that key customers did not consider important.

However, 8-inch drives were of greater relevance to mini computers. You can imagine the views being expressed in marketing departments armed with their exhaustive research into the market place. "Who wants a mini computer?" In reality, the makers of 12-inch disc drives asked their clients what they wanted and the response was the equivalent of saying 'faster horses'. But as the market for mini computers began to take off, sales of 8-inch drives rose. The product was then subject to significant technological progress. 8-inch drives were launched onto the market in the mid-1970s and at that time, their capacity was around 10 megabytes, whereas 14-inch drives had a capacity of around 20 to 30 times more. The 12-inch drives continued to see capacity increase, but the capacity of 8-inch drives grew faster. Demand for 8-inch drives grew faster too, so that by the mid to late 1980s the 8-inch market began supplanting the 12-inch market altogether. By then the companies that had entered the industry focusing on the niche mini computers market had developed such a technological and sales and marketing lead, via their specialisation that the 12-inch players found they were unable to catch up.

The story repeated itself. In fact 5¼-inch drives were launched onto the market just two or three years after 8-inch drives. You can imagine a kind of hierarchy of noses looking downwards. The established dominant players in the 12-inch market, with research to back them up, dismissing the 8-inch markets as little more than toys, while the emerging players in the 8-inch market, targeting the then niche market for mini computers dismissing 5¼-inch drives as toys for kindergarten. The 5¼-inch market did develop, however, because these products were more applicable to the desktop PC market. Bear in mind that, to begin with, 5¼-inch drives were literally little more than toys; at first desktop PCs were bought by hobbyists, with computer games being one of the main applications.

Then the story repeated itself again, with the advent of 3½-inch drives. Once again, the 3½-inch drives were initially inferior in nearly every respect to the 5¼-inch except they were smaller. They did however appeal to a niche a market, which was the new-fangled market for portable/laptop/notebook computers.

Take the story of Seagate, a market leader in the 5¼-inch market. Engineers at the firm had developed a 3½-inch drive very early on in the evolution of this product type. Marketeers at the company tested the new drive, and found little interest in their product amongst their customers, who were companies, such as IBM, which focused on desktop PCs. In response to the lukewarm reaction from customers, Seagate lowered sales forecasts for the 3½-inch drive, and the project was dropped.

Christensen says that actually Seagate executives read the market in which they competed very accurately. What they did not read was the advent of a new market.

It is quite interesting to note that when Seagate did finally launch a 3-½ inch drive, almost none of its products was sold to manufacturers of portable/ laptop/notebook computers. Even when the company began selling 3½-inch drives in a concerted manner, it sold them to existing customers operating in the desktop market.[5]

And here is the warning. Christensen said: "The popular slogan 'stay close to your customers' appears not always to be robust advice." Indeed, says Christensen, feedback from customers can mislead suppliers, sending them down a dead-end as it were.

So that is innovator's dilemma. This is a dilemma that will repeat itself many times over the next few years. It will claim the scalp of many companies, but you may be surprised at the nature of the companies that are vulnerable. Within a few years, major car makers, banks, and energy companies for example, may all fall victim to innovator's dilemma.

Let us end this section with a development that is occurring now: the move from 3G to 4G data. Market research carried out by YouGov SixthSense in the UK found that one in three UK consumers 'can't see the point' of 4G as they believe 3G is good enough for their needs. The survey also found that 55 per cent of consumers believe 4G will be too expensive for them and 66 per cent do not want to spend money on

---

[5] Story has it that Toshiba developed an even smaller drive. They didn't know what to do with it. They showed it to Apple who leveraged it to create the first iPod.

buying any new devices for it. YouGov said: "The findings show that operators face a great challenge in making customers interested in 4G".

This may be an occasion when innovator's dilemma will not strike. In this case, marketeers at the network providers will surely appreciate that once the applications that require 4G become available market perceptions will change. In any case, as demand for data rises, its price will surely fall.

Big Bang Disruption

For companies that are affected, Big Bang disruption can be terrifying.

Usually, when a new product is introduced to the market, the story that unwinds looks a bit like this:

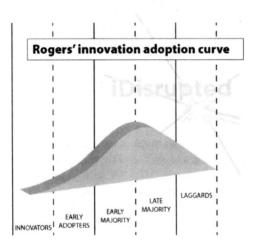

With Big Bang disruption, the story is more like this:

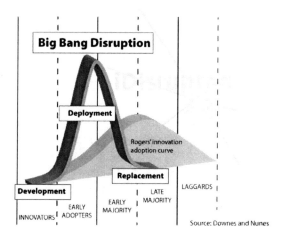

Or to put it another way, the traditional way of thinking about how new products are launched onto the market is collapsing. To quote Larry Downes and Paul F Nunes, who coined the phrase Big Bang disruption, now there are two segments: "trial users, who often participate in product development, and everyone else".

They suggest that the innovator's dilemma theory has a blind spot. The theory assumes that disrupters begin with a product that is inferior to existing alternative in most respects, but by targeting the technology at markets where its benefits are important, such as computers that require smaller disc drives, new entrants can increase their expertise. They can enhance their technology up to the point when it is a viable alternative to established technologies in mainstream markets. But Big Bang disruption, in contrast, assumes new technologies are superior to established alternatives in most key respects at the point of launch. These are technologies that, like

Athena, do come into the world fully formed from the head of Zeus.

Examples of Big Bang disruption include free navigation maps provided with smart phones, which, according to Downes and Nunes, are not only cheaper but better than standalone devices, such as TomTom, Garmin and Magellan.

In fact, not all of these new products they describe are quite there yet. If you have had the misfortune of driving around a roundabout in the centre of a city with which you are not familiar, and the navigation app on your iPhone stops working, you will understand the point. It may be an exaggeration to say these so-called Big Bang disruptions are superior to alternatives at the point of launch. Nonetheless the time it takes for them to achieve superiority is very short.

Downes and Nunes said: "Upstart products and services in a slew of industries have...grown fast enough to leave incumbents gasping." They cite as examples "CampusBookRentals and Khan Academy in education, Pandora and Spotify in recorded music, Skype and Facetime in voice and video calling, and Square in mobile credit processing."

They may exaggerate a tad. It took several years before Skype was sufficiently robust and user friendly for the mass market to adopt it. However, you only need to look at the rise of Facebook, AIRbnb or Uber to appreciate that sometimes the trajectory across the product lifecycle of some recent products/services has been at a pace to leave incumbents gasping.

Downes and Nunes said: "Now entire product lines – whole markets – are being created or destroyed overnight. Disrupters come out of nowhere and instantly are everywhere. Once launched, such disruption is hard to fight." They say that such changes "do not create dilemmas for innovators; they trigger disasters."

But such big disruptions also create opportunity and wealth.

Moore's Law

You can interpret the term Moore's Law in two ways. There is its original meaning, which refers to the speed at which transistors on integrated circuits double. Alternatively, you can use the term as a metaphor to describe any form of rapid technological advancement. Technologists may criticise someone for saying, for example, that solar power is benefiting from Moore's Law. It is not doing so at all in the strictest sense of its definition, but rather using Moore's Law as a metaphor, and as such it makes sense to use it as a description.

And in its metaphorical sense, Moore's Law is one of the most important rules in business and the economy today. They say an economist is someone who when shown that something works in reality, wonders if it works in theory. Moore's Law is only rarely referred to by economists; as such they engineer a triumph of theory over practicality, of fantasy over reality.

The unwinding of the metaphorical version of Moore's Law is changing the world. It is creating dilemmas for innovators, and leading to Big Bang disruptions on an unprecedented scale. It is the reason why this book is necessary.

So let's explain what we mean.

In 1965 Intel's co-founder Gordon Moore said: "The number of transistors incorporated in a chip will approximately double every 24 months." Initially he said this growth would only continue for ten years, but he later extended the time frame for his theory to apply indefinitely. On the whole, this is how it has panned out. It is often said that there is more processing power in an iPhone than the whole of NASA had at its disposal during the moon landings. In fact this is one of those rare occasions when popular mythology may understate the reality. The iPhone, it appears, is far more advanced.

You may be interested to note that if the average family saloon car had seen its top speed increase at the same trajectory seen by computers since 1965, then today, or at least by the end of this decade, it would be able to travel at roughly the speed of light.

Now apply this idea to other industries. Take genetics. To borrow words used by McKinsey: "Today, a human genome can be sequenced in a few hours and for a few thousand dollars, a task that took 13 years and \$2.7 billion to accomplish during the Human Genome Project."

Or to quote one of the leading scientists in the world today Craig Venter[6], in a lecture he gave at the BBC in 2007. He said: "Over a short period of time genome projects, which 10 years ago required several years to complete now take only days." He suggested that within half a decade "it will be commonplace to have your own genome sequence, something that just a decade ago required billions of pounds and was considered a monumental achievement." He said that "our ability to read genetic code is changing even faster than changes predicted by Moore's Law." [7]

---

[6] Craig Venter was one of the first people to sequence the human genome and in 2010 shocked the world when he said he had created the world's first synthetic organism.

[7] In 2014 medical engineer Christofer Toumazou was nominated for the European Inventor Award 2014 in the category "Research." His work has made it possible to analyse DNA within minutes and outside a lab using a

In the field of renewable energy, improvements are not quite occurring at the pace seen in integrated circuits or genetics, but the rate of improvement is impressive nonetheless. Since 1972, the price of solar panels has reduced by 22 per cent for every doubling in installed capacity – this is known as the learning rate by the way. Since 2008, however, the learning rate of solar panels has been 40 per cent. In fact the price of solar PV panels has dropped about 100 times between 1972 and 2012.

While it is not evolving as rapidly as solar power, even wind power has seen sharp falls in cost over the last few decades. In 1984 the installed base of wind turbines in Germany and Denmark – the first countries to adopt wind power on a mass scale – generated 274 megawatts of power at an average price of $2.50 a watt. By 2011, the global installed base was 234,777 megawatts, and the average price was $1.12 per watt. According to a report from Citigroup, wind turbines have a learning rate of 7 per cent, meaning their cost falls by 7 per cent for every doubling in installed capacity.

Looking further forward, in the field of 3D printing one recent development of considerable interest has been 3D printers that can replicate themselves – that is to say 3D printers that can print 3D printers. It does not take a large leap in imagination to conclude that once technologies can replicate themselves, the speed at which costs fall and power increases will accelerate.

Metaphorical Moore's Law may yet prove to be even more extreme in nanotechnology. Within a few years tiny nano based factories, also known as molecular manufacturing, will make products that will change the world. To put this in

USB stick. http://www.mdtmag.com/news/2014/04/rapid-dna-test-usb-stick

context, a nanometre, is one billionth of a metre, so when we say tiny, we understate the reality. We are talking about engineering at the molecular level. But imagine if nano sized factories make nano sized factories.

As James Martin points out in his book *The Meaning of the 21st Century*, nanotechnology also provides the possibility of creating tiny switches, one hundredth the size of today's smallest transistors. This would give us the potential to make computers much more powerful. Thanks to nanotechnology, we may see a sharp acceleration in Moore's Law, as applied to computing capability, within a decade or two.

In fact, James Martin reckons there are three stages of Darwinian evolution. Stage one is "primary evolution", which is the evolutionary process described by Darwin. It relates to the evolution of living species by natural selection. This stage is slow: it requires mutation to DNA to introduce change and is the product of chance. Stage two is secondary evolution, which relates to cultural evolution and of ideas themselves, culminating perhaps in the ability to manipulate DNA. This second stage is faster than the first, because it builds on what we have already learned. It works by selecting and favouring ideas developed through deliberation. The third stage is what Martin calls tertiary evolution, and is a phase we may be entering now. This occurs when intelligent beings learn how to automate evolution itself. To begin with, we see computer programmes built around artificial selection, which follow parameters set down by a human creator; in time this process will accelerate becoming very swift indeed.

And finally, let's return to Moore's Law in its original sense. For some time now, many have been predicting the ultimate end of this law, as integrated circuits become so small, it is impossible for them to reduce further in size. The famous futurologist Ray Kurzweil pointed out in a TED talk that Moore's Law is just one example amongst many of computers gaining power. He said that computing devices have been consistently multiplying in power for more than 100 years. He begins with mechanical calculating devices used in the 1890 US Census, moves on to Turing's relay-based *Robinson* machine that cracked the Nazi enigma code, then to the CBS vacuum tube computer that predicted the election of Eisenhower, to the transistor-based machines used in the first space launches, to the integrated-circuit-based personal computer we use today. He said: "Every time one paradigm ran out of steam another one came from left field to continue the growth. When we see the end of the paradigm it creates pressure to create the next paradigm." He says that when we see the end of Moore's Law we won't see the end of computers becoming more advanced.

Technology creates new technology

Take genetics: would the explosion in the rate of our ability to sequence genomes be possible without advances in computer technology? As McKinsey pointed out, synthetic biology will be a beneficiary of advances in computing. Thanks in part to the power of modern computers, we are on the verge of being able to customize organisms; we can write DNA. The McKinsey report says that advances in genetic science "could have a profound impact on medicine, agriculture, and even the production of high-value substances such as biofuels—as well as speeding up the process of drug discovery."

To put it another way, thanks to the unwinding of Moore's Law used in its original context, we are soon going to see rapid advances in medicine, agriculture and in how we obtain the energy we need to power technology. Those who fall into the sceptical view of technology tend to focus on the direct and obvious use of computers: in office automation, and in entertainment. At their most extreme, they argue that the productive benefits of computers in an office setting have been questionable, and that the fun side of computers – games, Facebook and YouTube for example – is all very nice but has little bearing on output. You may agree or disagree with this diagnosis, but when you factor in the effect that advances in computer technology have had in progressing our knowledge of genetics, with its potential knock-on effects in the medicine, agriculture and energy industries, you realise that the sceptical view is narrow in its perspective.

Then consider the importance of advances in computer technology in enabling 3D printing, or the 3D scanners that are so essential in 3D printing.

To take another example, reconsider one of the first observations in the previous chapter: the ideas of Steve Jobs and Jonathan Ive at Apple. Combining design with computer technology only became possible around the turn of the millennium thanks to Moore's Law and the homogenization of computer technology. Once it was possible however, Apple's ascent up the corporate ladder was meteoric.

One piece of new technology that is currently grabbing headlines is the drone; that is to say flying devices that in a few years may be able to deliver your Amazon online order direct to your door, for example. Each drone will come equipped with computer technology: indeed technology that packs more punch than all the computer power NASA had at the time of the moon landings, but is so light that it does not materially slow the drone down, or reduce its ability to fly.

Sometimes, however, new technology creates other technology, not because existing technology makes it possible, but because it makes it necessary. Take as an example the creation of graphene, one of the new wonder materials that may change the world. The two scientists who won the Nobel Prize for their work on graphene – Andrei Geim and Kostya Novoselov from the University of Manchester – created the material after joking around one Friday afternoon. They used sticky tape to peel off a layer of graphite from a block, and then repeated the process until they were eventually left with flakes just a few atoms thick. No whizzy technology was required in this process, but would the end result – graphene – have captured the imagination of scientists across the world if at that particular time there wasn't the need for such a substance? Had graphene been created by a Victorian scientist, the moment of its discovery may have been forgotten by Saturday morning.

This is an important point. Necessity, as they say, is the mother of invention. It is generally believed that Johannes Guttenberg brought the printing press was brought to Europe in the 15th century. Yet there is evidence that printing technology was available to the ancient Minoans of Crete around 3,000 years before Mr Guttenberg senior had even met Johannes's mother. But the printing press did not take off from Crete to envelope the world, probably because the technology lacked apps that made it viable. Had the Minoans discovered paper and print at the same time then history might have been entirely different. To take another example, you may know that the wheel was not in common use in the Americas before the time of the European settlement/invasion. But as Jarad Diamond pointed out: "Ancient native Mexicans invented wheeled vehicles with axles for use as toys, but not for transport." He says: "This seems incredible to us now, until we reflect that ancient Mexicans lacked domestic animals to hitch to their wheeled vehicles, which therefore offered no advantage over human porters."

There is, however, an even more important point. The internet may yet prove to be the greatest tool ever for promoting innovation. The reason is simple enough, yet often overlooked. Ideas are not developed in isolation. In nearly every example, a new innovation builds upon existing innovations. This is how ideas spread, and lead to other ideas. As a communication tool, the internet is without equal. We can say that many of the innovations of the Victorian age may never have occurred had there been no printing press to encourage the spread of ideas. Similarly, the internet and dissemination of information and ideas that it facilitates are likely to promote a new wave of innovation, the like of which we have never seen before.[8]

Big Bang innovation or singularity

Now we move on to an idea which is beyond extraordinary in it its implications. If the theory is only slightly right, we may be less than a few decades from seeing a new world emerge, which is as different from the one we live in today, as the world of 2013 is different from the one our ancestors knew when they lived in trees.

Think of it in these terms. If Moore's Law is analogous to Innovator's Dilemma, the theory we are now considering is analogous to 'Big Bang disruption'. One of its main supporters is Ray Kurzweil, referred to previously, who these days is Google's director of engineering. To sum up the idea of singularity in a nutshell, it is that innovation is accelerating. In fact we may go further than that, and say it

---

[8] Crowdfunding illustrates this point. It can aid ideas where unknown individuals can pledge funding for research or a new product, instead of an inventor having to visit a bank manager to obtain funding. No company calls the shots about whether a product goes to market, it is the drive of one individual and technically a few people willing to put up a small amount of cash.

is accelerating at an accelerating rate. Such is the trajectory of this acceleration that by no later than the middle part of this century, innovation may be occurring at an infinite pace.

Okay, this conclusion may be a tad unrealistic. But the underlying theory is incredibly important. Even if the theory is only partially right, its implications are about as profound as you can imagine. To suggest innovation may start occurring at an infinite pace may seem a little absurd, but to project that, within two decades, innovation may be changing the world at a pace that has no precedent is not particularly unreasonable.

There is more than one way of looking at singularity.

One approach may be to start with the evolution of RNA, and then DNA. For most of the time in which there has been life on this planet - a total period of some 3.6 billion years - it comprised very simple organisms. Then, around 580 million years ago, nature experienced its own version of Big Bang disruption, and the 70 or 80 million years that followed saw the evolution of all the basic body parts found in nature today. This is the period in natural history when the evolution of animals began. Compared to the pace at which evolution had been working previously, the so called Cambrian explosion occurred in a blink of an eye.

Then forward wind the clock to a period, which in evolutionary terms was just a few minutes ago, and we get the evolution of a hominid species, which, from the point of the first bipedal ape to the evolution of Homo Sapiens, occurred in just a few million years. Moving on, 200,000 years or so ago Homo Sapiens first appeared on earth; agriculture was invented less than 10,000 years ago; the first cities were built around 5,000 years ago; the innovations of Ancient Greece 2,500 years ago; the industrial revolution

300 years ago; the age of electricity 100 years ago; and the internet age less than two decades ago. If you drill down and look at the detail that makes up this story, although you see the odd blip in the trajectory, you see acceleration in the rate of change, right from the moment that RNA first appeared.

So, in other words, history tells us that evolution accelerates and suggests we are less than 20 years or so away from the next leap; 15 years or so away from the one after; and 12 years or so from the one after that. The timing may be out, but not by much, and whether it takes two decades or four before the world is transformed, a good case can be made for suggesting changes will occur at a rate that is in the ball park of the above timings.

One thing about us humans is that we adapt very quickly. Television transformed family life in just a few decades, and for those born in the era when nearly all families in the west had a TV in the living room, the box of moving pictures seemed as normal as wearing clothes. Changes in this very medium have themselves been stunning, but we barely notice them – until that is we watch our favourite TV shows from 20 years ago, and we can't help but notice how production standards have changed; how predictable the jokes were.

Ray Kurzweil says that most of us tend to view the world from a linear perspective, and we just assume that the rate of change follows a steady course. This linear view leads us to greatly underestimate the speed at which technology will change. For example, progress was very slow during the first few years of the human genome project. Critics said that at the rate of progress seen during the first few years of the project it would take thousands of years to sequence the human genome. In fact, the project was completed in 14 years from start to finish, because of the rate at which those advances in technology used to sequence the human genome accelerated.

Take as an example, a story many of us were taught in school. The actual story varies; some have it in Ancient China, others in India and still others in Egypt. Some say the story applied to the inventor of chess, others say a fortune teller. The details do not matter. The subject of our story, let's call him a fortune teller, saves the kingdom in which he lives. Let's call that kingdom ancient Egypt. For his reward, our fortune teller asked that for the first square of a chess board he would receive one grain of wheat, for the second two grains, the third four grains, the fourth eight grains and so on. The Pharaoh, who did not have a good handle on maths, immediately agreed, and watched – encouraged by linear thinking – with glee as the fortune teller was handed first the one grain, then two, and then the four and eight. These were tiny amounts. Even when the number of grains numbered in the lower hundreds, the impact of this reward on his treasury was minuscule. It is just that by the time the number of grains required to correspond with the latter squares on the board were calculated, it turned out that there wasn't enough grain in the whole of Egypt to pay the fortune teller the agreed amount.

That story, of course, expresses the idea of exponential growth.

Apply that idea to Moore's Law, but assume that even as we reach the limit of what can be achieved in computer power using silicon, we see new methods, such as applying graphene instead of silicon, or quantum computing; that instead of slowing we see computer processing power double at a faster rate.[9] Imagine what might happen when

---

[9] By the way, the story about the speed at which computers double accelerating over time is consistent with the history of computer

computers, with processing power which is greater than the human brain, design computers, and we see evolution of this technology follow James Martin's tertiary stage in evolution, when intelligent beings learn how to automate evolution itself.

Singularity may be said to occur when computers are doubling in speed on a daily basis, or when scientists work out how to enable the neurons in our brain to form synapses with neurons in other brains, or simply the point at which scientists learn how to reverse the ageing process. It is possible that singularity may never occur; indeed singularity may be impossible. But it does not seem unreasonable to assume that within one or two decades, technological innovation will have had more of an impact on all our lives than the innovations that have occurred over the past century had on the lives of both our grandparents and parents combined.

Robert J Gordon (see introduction) might argue that if we look back 30 years the world did not feel that much different, but that the next 30 years will see more changes than we saw in the past century and maybe even more than the past millennium.

Some economic and business theory

On the whole economic theory is inadequate for providing us with the tools we require to manage the transformations of the next few decades.

But it does at least supply some starting blocks. And here are some theories: two from the two greatest economists of the 20th century, another produced by the man who – until

---

processing since the mechanical calculating devices used in the 1890 US Census.

recently – was the editor in chief of *Wired* magazine. A fourth is produced by the consultancy Gartner.

Let's begin with Chris Anderson, the former editor in chief of *Wired*. We can sum up his theory in one word: free. Economic theory says price is a function of marginal cost. With many internet and technology related businesses, the marginal cost of production is zero. Therefore, more and more products should be free – at least according to economic theory.

Anderson makes a good point. There is evidence all around us to support this theory. We get our online news (or at least most of it) free; we get our social networking free, we search the internet using Google free, and – thanks to the project called Linux – we can get the operating system in our computers and on our mobile phones free.

Anderson argues that producers of material in which marginal cost is zero need to embrace the free model. Google has proved that it is it possible to make profits of billions of dollars through providing free products.

Yet we also see a fight back. A growing number of publications are providing only a limited amount of free content. Within the Murdoch Empire, both the *Times* in the UK and the *Wall Street Journal* in the US are applying a premium model. The success of iTunes and now of Spotify may demonstrate that the free model does not always hold out. In 2012, 10 per cent of income accruing to UK record sales – which was £103 million – was in the form of streaming subscriptions.

Free may or may not be the future of all products with zero marginal costs, and, by the way, in the future this may include car designs, but it is questionable whether such a development is in the interests of consumers.

Part of the problem relates to the viability of funding via advertising. In the world of internet content, Google and Facebook have massive inherent advertising advantages over content producers such as online newspapers. Google ad words, for example, can be very accurately targeted because of the way ads are only seen by people who first type in relevant search words. Facebook ads, because of the volume of information Facebook has about its users, may ultimately prove to be even more accurately targeted. Contrast that with newspaper publishers, who offer a far more hit and miss form of advertising targeting.

Back in June 2013, it was projected that Google would secure 33.2 per cent of the global online advertising market. Facebook was expected to secure 5 per cent market share, and Yahoo 3.1 per cent. But while Google has around one third of all online advertising, it is wholly reliant on a giant army of bloggers, companies, and publishers providing content. The distribution of online revenue is skewed towards the process of search, away from the manually intensive work of content production.

Furthermore, online journalism that does make money often tends to be very product specific. For example, a finance article about mortgages that are available on the market place may prove to be an attractive place for mortgage providers to advertise, but a more thoughtful, time consuming piece on, say, whether mortgages are good or bad for the economy may not generate any advertising revenue at all.

Frustrating though free models must be for publishers, it is a reality with which they have to grapple. The problem from their point of view is compounded by the fact that for every income earning journalist there seem to be many amateurs who are willing to work free. Like the programmers behind Linux, their motivations are many.

Professional journalists may argue that they provide premium products, and that amateurs can never hope to achieve their level of quality. There is some truth in this, but only some. Most journalists have experienced seeing comments related to one of their online articles, only to note that some of the comments seemed to make better points (and be just as well written) than the journalist him/herself managed.

Some have argued that free has led to a decline in journalistic standards; that editorial has become less objective, less well researched. If such criticisms are valid, this may be an example of free working against the interests of the public.

Hype Cycle[10]

Before we continue it is a good idea to consider one more theory: the Hype Cycle created by Gartner.

Hope is a good thing, but sometimes hope can get in the way of reason. We saw this during the late 1990s with dotcoms. The markets just went mad. The Fed Chairperson at that time – Alan Greenspan – called it irrational exuberance. He was understating the truth.

On the other hand, it is human nature to be too optimist in estimating how quickly new technology will take off. Maybe this optimism manifests itself in hype.

---

[10] See http://www.gartner.com/technology/research/methodologies/hype-cycle.jsp

But then, as hype creates a bubble which then bursts, hope can turn to tears. Maybe we then have a kind of reverse hype; let's call it anti hype. In the aftermath of the dotcom crash, you were lucky if an investor would touch an idea for a dotcom business with the proverbial barge pole. Yet, during this period, the foundations were laid for many of the business ideas that have since transformed business. After all, Apple launched the iPod in 2001, which was the moment when dotcom hype had pretty much turned into total anti-hype.

Gartner has produced a good method for describing this. It calls it the hype cycle.

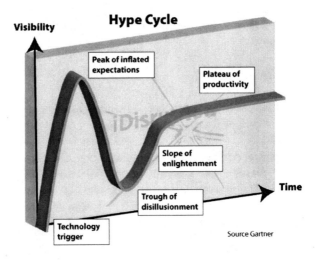

Creative Destruction

One economist did develop a theory that explains innovator's dilemma around half century or longer before Clayton Christensen coined the phrase. The economist was Joseph Schumpeter, who once said he had three aims in life:

to become known as the greatest horseman in Europe, to be the greatest economist in the world in the 20th century, and to be the best lover in Vienna. We can only guess at whether he achieved the first and last of these three objectives, but a case could be made for saying he achieved the second.

These days he is most famous for talking about great gales of creative destruction. Schumpeter was a great believer in the entrepreneur. He also had unorthodox views about monopolies. He argued that the profits made by monopolies were essential to fund investment and innovation. But he also argued that in the long run monopolies collapsed because great gales of creative destruction erode their business model.

It is important to note that some people erroneously interpret Schumpeter as saying destruction is essential to free up space for creativity; that recessions are therefore good things as they create vacuums into which new ideas can grow. In fact Schumpeter has the relationship the other way around. He said destruction was the result of creativity or innovation; that innovation does not need destruction for it to occur, rather that it destroys, in the case of Schumpeter's theory, it can even destroy monopolies.

Utopia

Let's finish this chapter with the view of the man who was Schumpeter's rival for the title of greatest economist of the 20th century: John Maynard Keynes.
Circa 1930 Keynes wrote: "Let us, for the sake of argument, suppose that a hundred years hence we are all of us, on the average, eight times better off in the economic sense than we are today. Assuredly there need be nothing here to surprise us." He said: "Assuming [there are] no important wars and no important increases in population, the

economic problem may be solved, or be at least within sight of a solution, within a hundred years."

So what will this mean? Keynes fretted on how we might cope with a life of leisure. He said: "To use the language of today – must we not expect a general 'nervous breakdown'? We already have a little experience of what I mean – a nervous breakdown of the sort which is already common enough in England and the United States amongst the wives of the well-to-do classes, unfortunate women, many of them, who have been deprived by their wealth of their traditional tasks and occupations – who cannot find it sufficiently amusing, when deprived of the spur of economic necessity, to cook and clean and mend, yet are quite unable to find anything more amusing."

And finally he said: "For the first time since his creation man will be faced with his real, his permanent problem – how to use his freedom from pressing economic cares, how to occupy the leisure, which science and compound interest will have won for him, to live wisely and agreeably and well."

Chapter two: The story so far. From the invention of agriculture to the golden age of innovation

Mark Twain once said history does not repeat itself, but it rhymes. Winston Churchill said: "The further back you can look, the further forward you are likely to see." History does not predict the future, but it can give us hints. We can learn from what it tells us and get a better idea of what the future may bring.

And what better place to start than to ask: what are the most important innovations ever and what impact did they have had on the world?

You may recall from your childhood, King, or Cousin, Louie, the singing ape from Disney's *Jungle Book* who wanted to know the secret of man's red flower – fire in other words. He reckoned that if he could master fire, he would no longer have to content himself with merely being the king of the swingers.

Cousin Louie may have had a point. There is no shortage of scientists who study the evolution of humans and agree that learning how to make fire was the key to our development. Alternatively, to be more precise, they say it was learning what to do with fire that gave us our edge: namely cook. When we learnt how to cook food, the number of plants/animals we could eat increased and, perhaps more importantly, we could digest our food much faster. Humans, once they learnt how to make fire and cook with it, had more spare time. It was time they could perhaps use to enhance their ability at making tools, to engage in social rituals, and in contemplating their lot. In short, fire gave us leisure and time to prepare for the future. The innovation of making fire and cooking had two major impacts. Firstly, it meant early humans with this secret enjoyed a better survival rate than other early hominids, presumably leading to the extinction of our early ancestors' main rivals.

It is hard to say what other early innovations gave us an edge. Anthropologists have found evidence that early man, in particular Neanderthals, had toothpicks, or even toothbrushes. The evidence was found in Cova Foradà, a cave site on the coast of modern day Spain, and dates to between 150,000 and 60,000 years ago. Marina Lozano, one of the scientists who made the discovery, said: "The toothpick was not only used as a primitive method of dental hygiene, but it is associated with a dental disease and with the clear intention to alleviate the pain, and that makes it unique."

Another very early contender may have been the innovation of trade. There is evidence that early Homo Sapiens traded with each other, and this gave us an edge over our main rivals at that time – our cousins with the gleaming teeth – Neanderthals. Dr Jason Shogren and his colleagues produced a computer program in which the Neanderthals and Homo Sapiens were equal in all respects bar one – Homo Sapiens traded. The model showed that the Neanderthals were forced into extinction quite rapidly, once we learnt to trade. The victory of our ancestors didn't necessarily come about through war or conflict with their cousins. If Dr Shogren is right, just by trading we were able to survive, make better use of the limited resources available, and effectively crowd out our ancient rivals. The Neanderthals were disrupted, all right.

Over the next 50 or so millennia, we learnt how to tame animals and then circa 10,000 BC, we learnt how to make the provision of meal times more reliable by inventing agriculture. This has an odd effect, however. The invention of agriculture was closely linked with sharp rises in population; it meant there were more of us, but it did not necessarily mean we were better off on average. The invention of agriculture is also closely linked with the emergence of all kinds of nasty diseases, such as rickets and the archaeological evidence is clear that we shrank – average height began to fall, and only began to rise again when diet improved. Agriculture made bigger populations possible, and the greater number it afforded led to the conquest of often quite healthy tribes by the more numerous and vertically challenged agrarian based communities. The interesting development that occurred from the invention of agriculture is that it may have led to greater supply of food, but perhaps we became less healthy. It is a theme that is repeated throughout history, and may be repeated again in the future. New technology does not always make people better off – not immediately anyway.

You might say that the innovations referred to above were the greatest innovations before the invention of the wheel, but what has been the greatest invention since?

Back in 2013, *The Atlantic* publication assembled a panel of 12 scientists, entrepreneurs, engineers, and historians of technology, and asked them to assess the innovations that have done the most to shape the nature of modern life.

Presented in chronological order, this is the result:

BC	The sailboat, fourth millennium BC
	The lever, third millennium BC
	The abacus, third millennium BC
	The nail, second millennium BC
	Alphabetization, first millennium BC
	Cement, first millennium BC
	Archimedes' screw, third century BC
First Millennium	Paper, 2nd century
AD	Gunpowder, 10th century
Middle Ages	Paper money, 11th century

	The compass, 12th century
	Optical lenses, 13th century
	The printing press, 1430s
Post Middle	The mechanized clock, 15th century
Ages	The Gregorian calendar, 1582
First Industrial	The steam engine, 1712
Revolution	The mouldboard plough, 18th century
	The sextant, 1757
	The cotton gin, 1793
	Vaccination, 1796
	Photography, early 19th century
	The telegraph, 1837
	Anaesthesia, 1846
	Sanitation systems, mid-19th century
	Oil refining, mid-19th century
	Refrigeration, 1850s
	Industrial steelmaking, 1850s
	Oil drilling, 1859
Second Industrial	Pasteurization, 1863
Revolution (age	The steam turbine, 1884
of symmetry)	The internal combustion engine, late 19th century
	The automobile, late 19th century
	The telephone, 1876
	Electricity, late 19th century
	Air-conditioning, 1902
	The aeroplane, 1903
	Radio, 1906
	Television, early 20th century
	The assembly line, 1913
	Nitrogen fixation, 1918
Between the	Scientific plant breeding, 1920s
wars	Rocketry, 1926
	Penicillin, 1928
	The combine harvester, 1930s

	Nuclear fission, 1939
Second half of 20th century	Semiconductor electronics, mid-20th century
	The green revolution, mid-20th century
	The pill, 1960
	The Internet, 1960s
	The personal computer, 1970s

Incidentally, *The Atlantic* list has the printing press as the most important innovation of the lot, followed by electricity, penicillin, semiconductors and optical lenses.

It is an interesting list but has some odd omissions. It failed to mention the invention of plastic, for example, which had a massive effect on the economy, and surely disrupted many existing industries. The list also fails to refer to the world wide web – an innovation that may yet prove to be as significant as the printing press, neither did it mention 3D printing, the sequencing of the human genome, innovations in prosthetics that have made it possible for people with no limbs to walk, advances in robotics, the innovations in new materials such as graphene, the internet of things, or wearable technology. But then maybe some of these omissions are reasonable given that not much time has passed to allow us to quantify their importance. The omission of the world wide web is peculiar, however.

Also missing from the list is crop rotation, selective breeding, and the enclosure of common land. But then again, in the New World where land was more plentiful, and the legacy of the feudal age less marked, the end of enclosures may have been an irrelevance.

Larry Keeley, Co-founder and President of Innovation and Strategy at innovation consultancy Doblin, has also had a go at defining the most important innovations. His list has very different look about it.

1.   Weapons.
2.   Mathematics and the number zero.
3.   Money.
4.   Printing.
5.   Free markets and capital markets.
6.   Domesticated animals and agriculture.
7.   Property ownership.
8.   Limited liability.
9.   Participatory democracy.
10.   Anaesthetics and surgery.
11.   Vaccines and antibiotics.
12.   Semiconductors.
13.   The Internet.
14.   Genetic sequencing.
15.   Containerized shipping.

What is clear is that the innovations of the 18th, 19th and early 20th centuries did not automatically lead to the average person becoming wealthier – at least not for some time. For example, between 1790 and 1820 average wages in the UK, the home of the first industrial revolution, fell. There may have been some bad luck involved here. This period happened to coincide with an era of very poor harvests caused by poor weather, while – and perhaps this was a result of innovation – the population soared.

While living standards did not appear to rise in the UK until 1820, it is quite interesting to note that for a 20 year period from 1850 the average height shrunk from 170 to 165 centimetres amongst newly recruited soldiers. While economic historians seem to agree that wages rose from 1820, even Charles Feinstein – whose estimates of real wage growth were lower than most – calculates that for the 80 year period from 1780, average wages rose by around 30 per cent. During the early stages of the industrial revolution workers often had to work 18 hour shifts. Just as bad for the people of this period was that the move from towns to cities meant that many lost the ability to supplement their income by growing their own food, or operating craft shops. During this period, it was apparently not uncommon for up to 20 people to share one rental property, and sometimes an entire family shared the same bed. It seems that even Charlie's grandparents in Roald Dahl's *Charlie and the Chocolate Factory*, who spent all their time in the same bed, were better off than families during the early stages of the industrial revolution. This was also a period in which overcrowding and poor sanitation led to waterborne diseases, such as typhoid, which had a high mortality rate. It wasn't until the 1850s, when urban planning improved, that the spread of diseases began to lessen.

Another important point is that while the mean average wage began to increase from the 1820s, the median wage may not have done so. The industrial revolution may have had the initial effect of impoverishing many, but it also created wealth. A small number of highly wealthy people when added to a sample can significantly distort the mean average, but barely affect the median average.

That is not to say that innovations did not lead to more wealth in industrialised countries eventually; it just took time. Maybe we saw a repeat of this in the 20th century, when a world war and then a great depression followed the end of the second great era of innovation.

The second industrial revolution, or what renowned historian Vaclav Smil calls The Age of Symmetry – from around 1860 to the start of World War 1 – was possibly the most important age of innovation ever. Yet the period from 1914 to 1945 was not a happy period for humanity. Maybe it is a coincidence, but it seems implausible to say that there was no link. The golden half-century of innovation may have led indirectly to two world wars and an economic depression.

Today, we are witnessing a similar phenomenon. The end of the dotcom boom of the late 1990s encouraged central banks to slash interest rates in response to falling stock prices, and encouraged higher investment into so-called safe assets, such as bricks and mortar. We saw equity investment, which is traditionally seen as high risk, lose popularity, and instead we saw more property backed leverage. Risky investment into innovation was substituted by collateralized debt obligations and the disaster which was mortgage securitisation. In the 1990s and noughties, the combination of new technology and globalisation may have had the effect of pushing down median wages even when mean wages were rising. To an extent, the effect of this was hidden by the combination of rising house prices and leverage (or debt).

Thus it may be possible to draw a line linking recent innovations to the finance crisis of 2008.

But if living standards can be disrupted by new technology, what about business?

In the early 20th century, the famous economist Alfred Marshall argued that the world's largest companies were so impressive, so powerful, that they were effectively immortal – or at least like Californian Redwoods, which, while they did not live forever, lived so much longer relative to humans that they appeared immortal.

In 1995, the economist Leslie Hannah revisited the Marshall study. Hannah drew up a list of the 100 largest companies in the world in 1912, and reviewed what happened to them.

By 1995, 19 of the firms were still in the top 100, 28 had survived and were larger (after allowing for inflation), 29 had experienced bankruptcy or similar, and 48 had disappeared.

Here is a list of the 1912 companies that survived to 1995, or at least those that merged and were still represented in the top 100 in 1995:

Rio Tinto
British-American Tobacco
Eastman Kodak
Guinness – now Diageo
Lever Brothers – now Unilever
Procter & Gamble
Du Pont
Farbwerke vormals Lucius & Bruning (Hoechst) – now a subsidiary of the Sanofi pharmaceuticals group
Brunner Mond (Zeneca) – now AstraZeneca
G Elberfelder Farbenfabriken – now Bayer
BASF
General Electric
Siemens
Jersey Standard (Exxon) – now part of Exxon Mobil
Royal Dutch Shell
Indiana Standard (Amoco) – now part of BP
New York Standard (Mobil) – now part of Exxon Mobil
Burmah Oil (Burmah Castrol and BP)
Texas Co (Texaco) – now part of BP and Chevron
Atlantic Refining (ARCO) – now a part of BP

One company in the list that immediately sticks out is the now bankrupt Eastman Kodak. It was one of the world's top 100 companies in 1912 and 1995, but despite being one of the early pioneers of digital photography, it is perhaps the most spectacular victim of innovator's dilemma.

Some companies survived by shifting into new industries, for example American Can into financial services and the French steel giant Schneider into electrical engineering.

So this begs the question: how can the innovations that have occurred over the last century or so explain the fortunes of the world's top companies?

Industry	Industry mean performance. Ratio of average market cap in 1995, versus 1912 (inflation adjusted) [11]	
Textiles and leather	0.1	Materials science, for example plastic and nylon, would have ripped the heart out of the old natural textiles businesses with heavy overheads. Cotton pickers of America were killed by man-made fibres that would have been nothing to produce comparatively. The biggest player in 1912 in this sector was J&P Coats. It was the world's third largest company, and today Coats plc is the world's leading industrial thread and consumer textile crafts business, but is much smaller today than in 1912.
Coal Mining	0.2	Too capital intensive to extract it in comparison with the real disruptor – oil fuel.
Mechanical engineering	0.4	Electronics may have played a key role.
Nonferrous metals	0.4	Disruption by manmade materials.
Iron/steel/ heavy industry	0.6	Move toward services industry may have impacted. The largest player in 1912 was US Steel, then the biggest company in the world. Today it is the world's 13th largest steel company.

[11] : A reading of 1.0 means no change, 2.0 means twice the size in 1995, 0.5 half the size

Branded products	1.3	The survival here may be a testament to the ability of some brands to survive.
Chemicals	2.4	Good track record in the 20th century, but this may be a sector which is about to see significant disruption.
Electrical engineering	2.7	Benefits from Moore's Law, but how will graphene affect it?
Petroleum	3.7	The 20th century may have been the century of oil, but will the 21st century follow suit?
All 100 giant firms	1.4	

Innovation is like a rapacious beast. As long as there is a demand for the products it makes possible, it seems unstoppable.

Some technologies, such as the printing press and electricity, made other advances possible.
This pattern is set to repeat itself.

But innovation does not always make people better off, or if it does there can be a significant time delay.

Business today needs to learn the lesson of Marshall's Californian redwoods. A company that does not innovate can be left to dwell in the corporate graveyard in the sky.

Individuals need to learn the story of past innovation to start getting a feel for what they can do to benefit from the next phase.

Policy makers need to ask whether there is anything they can do to mitigate the negative effects of innovation.

These topics will be reconsidered towards the end of this book.

But next we need to take a look at what innovations are out there, what new technology is developing, and what is likely to develop over the next few years.

In the middle section of this book we will build on the lessons of this chapter and the previous one to show which companies and business sectors are at risk of new entrants disrupting their business.

Chapter three: The most important innovation of all time circa 2044

Introduction

Imagine it is the year 2044. Looking back, how different will the world be? We cannot answer this question for sure, but we can digress for the duration of this chapter, and ask ourselves: what are the most important developments, innovations and discoveries – let's call them advances – of the modern era.

By looking at this list of advances we can perhaps start to get a handle on how profound the changes afoot are.

We shall finish the chapter with a quick look back from the year 2044, and ask how important recent advances are compared to the advances of the 20th Century, the Victorian era and before.

By doing this it is hoped you will be persuaded about an important point. The story of innovation has not, contrary to the view of sceptics, peaked; we have not picked the low hanging fruit. In fact, the next 30 years will see more changes than the past 1,000 years combined.

This is both an optimistic and scary conclusion. Later in the book we will be looking at the implications of some of these advances. And towards the end of the book we will be looking at what can be done to try to ensure the final outcome is positive, and not negative.

The next 30 years will be exciting, and indeed terrifying. It is good if you find it frightening, because only then can we make the kind of choices we need to make to increase the chances of the best possible outcome emerging.

83

To deny the significance of the changes that are occurring is dangerous, because then a negative, even horrendous outcome, becomes more likely. To deny the significance, without at least examining the evidence, appears to be almost irresponsible.

The key advances of our times

Excuse the Quentin Tarantino nature of this book. Most films, like books, have a clearly defined beginning, middle and end. Tarantino has often played around with that conventional order. The last chapter was about history and goes back centuries; the next chapter is about recent history, the present and the next few years. This chapter, however, is about the future, around 30 years from now.

Why this rather odd take on chronology? Because to understand the significance of what is happening now, we need to imagine where it is going. To grapple with the sceptical view of innovation, we need to take a leap forward. We need to do the kind of thing that Robert J Gordon, from the book's introduction, invited us to do, and look at the world in 30 year intervals. He says that if you look back 30 years not much has changed. Look back from 30 years ago to a period 30 years before that, (so we are talking mid 1950s) and not that much has changed either. Look back over the previous 30 years, however, and change is far more significant, and from the 1920s to the 1890s, change would be even more marked. Gordon says this exercise proves innovation has slowed down.

Well, let's play that game, and imagine the world in 30 years' time, circa 2044.

Imagining the future is usually a mug's game, but the innovations that are afoot are so dramatic, and the changes they will bring will be so profound that we owe it to our children, or indeed ourselves 30 years hence, to start imagining. The changes that are set to occur will happen so rapidly that if we leave it much longer to prepare, we will be leaving it too late, with consequences that may be too alarming to even contemplate. The rationale of this book is an attempt to help us prepare.

In any case, to understand the significance of what is happening now we need to imagine its full implications.

We are only human, and drawing up a detailed 30 year plan is not feasible. We can only deal in vagaries – albeit important vagaries. We can plan for ten years' time, however, and the process of doing this is what the middle section of this book is about.

For now you are just invited to imagine.

One way to get a feel for the impact that current innovations and those in the pipeline will have is to imagine it is the year 2044, and then ask yourself: what were the most important innovations of the previous few decades? Then compare those innovations with the most important advances of the previous 1,000 years or so.

In 2044, when we look back, what will we consider to be the most important innovations of the modern era? Here is a very subjective attempt at listing them and also at putting them in some kind of order of importance.

	Innovation	The whys and wherefores
1	Nanotechnology	A purist might say we are cheating here. Nanotechnology is not one piece of technology; it is many and will develop from a myriad of different developments, including advances in new materials such as graphene. But it is included here because it is so

incredibly important. A nano metre is one billionth of a metre. Nanotechnology is any technology that works at the nano scale. Within 30 years, nano sized robots will make nano sized robots, nano sized factories will make nano sized factories. Nanotechnology will lead to computers thousands of times faster than the current state of the art, and will revolutionize manufacturing, medical science, robotics and artificial intelligence.

| 2 | Genetics, the decoding of the human genome, synthetic biology, and stem cell research | This will be covered in more depth in the next chapter. Suffice to say for now that advances in our knowledge of genetics, DNA and beyond that into synthetic biology (the creation of living forms by humans/computers) and stem cell research are already leading to breakthroughs in medical science, energy and food science. Such advances will make us healthier, live longer, provide us with cheaper and healthier food, and go some way to fulfilling our energy needs in the 21st century. |
| 3 | The internet, collaborative learning, and open standards. | Like the printing press, and before that the invention of writing, the internet has been a key medium for spreading knowledge. Ideas build on ideas, inventions come from other inventions, open standards – in which the crowd can contribute towards the innovation process without the encumbrance of patents and rules over ownership – will be the means by |

		which the rate of innovation accelerates. For more, see the next chapter.
4	Artificial Intelligence (AI)	The field of artificial intelligence has been subject to massive advances in recent years. Whether AI supplants humanity itself, or rather enhances it, will be one of the key questions of this century. Depending on how AI develops it is possible that it should instead be in number one position in this chart.
5	3D printing/end of offshoring and labour cost arbitrage	The fact that 3D printing sits only midway in this chart, is testament to how important other technologies are, and not meant to downplay its significance. Even those with a sceptical view of technology acknowledge the importance of 3D printing in helping the development of prototypes and in providing finished goods for industries that require small production runs, such as in providing components for the aircraft industry. But 3D printing is evolving. Recent 3D printers have been used to print metals, cars, pizzas and more recently a 3D printer was even used to build a house in 24 hours. Most spectacularly of all, 3D printers have been used to print body parts. At some point in the next decade, 3D printing will be responsible for a revolution in manufacturing at least as important as the development of assembly line production. It will change the shape of industry, and affect the geo-political

		map of the global economy.
6	Robotics	The fact that Google bought eight robotics companies in 2013 probably says all you need to know. Robotics is no longer restricted to the field of science fiction. The industry has seen significant advances in recent years, and the age of the robot economy beckons.
7	Network economy	Some might ask: what is the difference between the internet and the network economy? Truth be told, the latter builds upon the former. The network economy, be it the internet of things, big data, the cloud, and ultimately a huge nebulous mass of information which we may be permanently connected to via interfaces linked to our brains, it may change the very nature of what it means to be human.
8	Vertical farms/smart cities	Vertical farms potentially solve one obvious problem, but are more likely to solve many others. By creating space for growing crops vertically, like a block of flats but with crops instead of people, vertical farms have the potential to increase the world's capacity for growing food. But even setting that potential benefit aside, it is clear they provide the potential to supply more locally grown food for cities, to make more efficient use of water, to eliminate the need for pesticides, or indeed tractors. Linked to vertical farms is the concept of smart cities. In smart cities, data will be processed, and by data we mean

massive amounts of information on traffic flow, electricity and water usage, even waste. The result is that smart cities will be more efficient.

9	Water desalination	This will be re-considered in the next chapter. As the world's population grows, and the development of emerging markets leads to an even more rapidly growing global middle class, it will lead to a greater appetite for a more varied and healthy diet. Water may prove to be the most valuable commodity in the world. It may even be, as it were, the bottle neck in the development of current technologies. Water desalination that would involve us tapping into the massive water reserve that is the oceans and is many times bigger than we need, may provide the answer. As yet, not one technology has emerged to create a cost effective solution to water desalination, but recent advances, especially in materials science, provide the hope that such advances are less than two or three decades away.
10	Energy storage	Energy storage has been called the holy grail of physics. An extremely efficient form of energy storage already exists; it is called oil or gas. But as we all know, the supply of oil is not unlimited, and it's being linked with climate change. In contrast, the supply of energy from the sun, either directly in the form of solar, or indirectly in the form of wind or waves, is unlimited.

We can use solar energy to provide the world with its energy needs without in any way reducing the Sun's own ability to generate energy. [12] However, solar power cannot generate energy when it is dark; wind power is similarly limited when it isn't windy. That is why energy storage is so essential.

| 11 | Prosthetics/ exoskeletons | You would have thought the fact that prosthetics have enabled Oscar Pistorius, despite having the handicap of having no lower legs, run the 400 metres in 46.25 seconds, says all you need to know. Prosthetics does indeed provide the potential to change the lives of people who in any other age would be rendered incapable of walking or picking things up with their hands. But prosthetics and exoskeletons may also be used to make healthy people stronger, faster, and a bit like the TV character in the 1970s: the bionic man. |
| 12 | Virtual reality | Will virtual reality replace the need for TV, holidays and even face to face meetings? By providing an immersive experience that surrounds us with video and sound, and beams computer graphics to us that are so realistic that they look real and then combined with |

[12] There is a theory, far from proven, that wind power is not renewable however. It says that if we were to fill the land and sky with wind turbines so that we generate all the energy we need from the wind, the Earth's ability to create wind may be reduced. This doesn't mean, by the way, that wind power is a bad idea; merely that it may be a mistake to try to generate all our energy from this source. Since, for other reasons, it is generally agreed that attempting to generate all our energy from the wind wouldn't be efficient, this is not likely to prove to be an issue.

technologies that can fool our brains into perceiving smell, and touch and taste, it is hard to know whether VR should make us feel excited or scared. However, it should definitely elicit one of those emotions.

So much for the most important innovations of the present, the near future and the last few decades. But how do these stack up against the innovations of the last thousand years or so?

Let's look at the most important innovations in the past two thousand years, excluding the very recent ones, and in the opinions of the authors.

1:      Printing press.
2:      Vaccines and antibiotics.
3:      Advances in energy, from steam, oil and
        electricity.
4:      Internal combustion engine.
5:      Mass production.
6:      Communication: telephone, TV and radio.
7:      Flight.
8:      Agrarian revolution.
9:      Anaesthetics and surgery.
10:     Containerisation.

And now let us compare the innovations of the past with recent and current ones.

Printing press versus
the internet: The printing press played a key role
                               in making many of the innovations
                               of the last 150 years possible. The

internet works in much the same way, but exaggerates this effect. Indeed, in the age of the internet, printing itself is looking increasingly redundant.

Mass production versus 3D printing: Mass production revolutionised manufacturing, drove down cost, led to much greater capacity, and decreased the emphasis on craftsmanship. 3D printing, because it will enable local manufacturing, will slash the cost of transporting goods; it will increase the variety of goods that can be produced; it will give customers more say over the products they buy, lead to more bespoke designs for no more money and may lead to the return of craftsmanship. It will also lead to less waste. Like mass production before it, 3D printing will revolutionise the manufacturing of products.

Communication: telephone, TV and radio versus the internet and Virtual Reality (VR)

The telephone made instant communication possible; the internet has made it possible to communicate complex ideas and to communicate with several people at once. TV and radio are entertainment media that changed how we spend our evenings, and VR may change what it is to be human.

Advances in energy, from steam, oil and electricity versus robotics and nanotechnology

The energies of the industrial age made industry possible. Robotics and nanotechnology will change industry more profoundly than anything in history has done before.

Vaccines, antibiotics, medication and surgery versus genetics, the decoding of the human genome, synthetic biology, stem cell research, and prosthetics

The medical advances of the last 100 years or so have led to greater longevity, improved health and have cured diseases and disabilities that were once thought to be impossible to cure. Genetics and stem cell research will lead to even greater longevity, improved health, and will eradicate conditions once thought incurable, such as cancer, Parkinson's disease and diabetes. Medical and technical advances will provide effective artificial limbs for amputees, will enable people who are blind to see again, will enhance the vision of those with normal eyesight, and will augment limbs making us stronger.

Internal combustion engine versus energy storage and the internet of things

The internal combustion engine made the motor car possible. Advances in energy storage in combination with other technologies will change the nature of cars profoundly. The combination of the internet of things and robotics, will lead to self-driving cars,[13] and the internet will combine self-driving cars with the ethos of sharing to reduce the number of cars required to fulfil our needs. The internet of things will lead to more efficient traffic management, which could remove traffic jams.

Flight versus the internet and VR, and vertical farms

Flight made it possible to travel the world. It revolutionised the concept of holidays, and facilitated international trade and the transportation of perishable goods from long distances. Modern technology may not be able to come up with a superior means of travelling long distances, but the internet and VR may facilitate effective communication over long distances. VR may in time be able to provide users with an experience not dissimilar from holidaying abroad (albeit some may describe this as a scary alternative). Vertical farms and stem cell research (such as growing meat in petri dishes) may remove the need to transport perishable food over long distances.

---

[13] Indeed, self-driving cars are already legally operating on the roads of California.

Agrarian revolution versus vertical farms, water desalination and stem cell research

The agrarian revolution came in waves, from the end of enclosures, crop rotation, the combine harvester, and pesticides and antibiotics, it led to the production of more food from fewer resources, but in the process and in many cases may have led to damage to the environment as well as increasing resistance to antibiotics. Vertical farms and stem cell research will once again increase production of food from fewer resources. But they will come with lower external cost in the form of environmental damage. Water desalination may yet be able to reverse the process of desertification caused at least in part by unsustainable agriculture practices.

Containerisation versus the internet

An essential lubrication to the process of globalisation was created by a new standard in how goods are stored when they are shipped abroad. It is hard to argue, however, that the internet has not been an even greater force behind the process of globalisation.

Artificial Intelligence   In the above comparisons, AI was not mentioned. This is because there has been no equivalent in the history of homo sapiens. AI may represent the most significant single change yet in the story of evolution from the moment RNA first appeared. In combination with the networked economy, robotics, and VR may change what it is to be human.

And finally let us draw up a new list, circa 2044; a list of the most important innovations of the previous 1,000 years.
First, here is a rule.

We look at the direct consequences of innovations, and ignore their role in innovations that preceded them. It has to be thus.

When we talk about the most important events in the story of our lives, we ignore the moment when our parents met or conceived us. We have to, otherwise the most important innovations will always be the oldest by definition. The big bang will always be the most important event in natural history, probably followed by the formation of the solar system, the Earth, the evolution of RDR, DNA, the Cambrian explosion and then the first bipedal ape.

But to make that argument is not in keeping with the spirit of this book. You could argue about which is the most important innovation ever: the printing press or the internet? A sceptic might say the printing press, because without it there would be no internet, but to say that is akin to saying the most important event in the story of the world wide web is when Mr and Mrs Berners Lee had a child called

Tim, or the discovery of gravity was thanks to the union of Mr and Mrs Newton Senior.

Given this, we have a dilemma. How important will the printing press be when we consider that the internet will have made printing largely unnecessary? How important will the internal combustion engine be? Will mass production be disrupted out of significance? It seems that some of the great innovations of the past may have to be relegated.

Here is an attempt at describing the most important innovations ever, circa 2045.

1	Nanotechnology.
2	Antibiotics – although as we shall see in this book's conclusion, even antibiotics may lose their importance.
3	Genetics, the decoding of the human genome, synthetic biology, and stem cell research.
4	The internet, collaborative learning, and open standards.
5	Printing press.
6	Artificial Intelligence (AI)
7	Advances in energy from steam, oil and electricity.
9	3D printing.
10	Robotics.
11	Communication: telephone, TV and radio.
12	Flight.
13	Network economy.
14	Smart cities and vertical farms.
15	Water desalination.
16	Energy storage.
17	Prosthetics.
18	Virtual reality.
19	Anaesthetics and surgery.
20	Containerisation.

You may disagree on the order, and you may think we have been harsh in the way we have treated some of the older innovations, nonetheless advances such as nanotechnology, AI, robotics, the internet, genetics and stem cell research, and VR will change us in a way that nothing has changed us before.

The world in 2044 will be more different from the world in 2014 than the world today is different from 1894.

The next chapter will drill down into recent technologies and open up the net, considering other advances that didn't quite make our list here.

Chapter four: The technology behind disruption.

This chapter is about technology and what makes new technology possible. It looks at the present and the next few years. But to tell the story we must first indulge in a little bit more history; this time looking at the last few years. By doing this we can focus on some of the key technologies and developments that have made a new innovation revolution possible.

Let's start with a few reasons, not so much technologies, but a way of doing things; a way of working, that the internet has made possible.

Why the devil is an inadequate explanation of the innovation that makes us scream and jump all in rhythm and in tune?

In the list of the great innovations of the 20th century outlined in previous chapters there is a glaring omission. Popular mythology has it that this omitted innovation was given to us by the devil.

According to mythology, when Robert Johnson met the devil at the intersection of Highways 49 and 61 in Clarksdale Mississippi, he sold his soul. In return Johnson was granted extraordinary ability at playing the guitar. He "played his instrument with an unearthly style, his fingers dancing over the strings. His voice moaned and wailed, expressing the deepest sorrows of a condemned sinner." The story of that meeting has become so ingrained in the story of rock, that we have countless songs referring to the devil, from the Stones classic *Symphony of the Devil* to the *Highway to Hell*, and then we hear stories of how you hear the voice of Satan himself when you listen to certain rock songs backwards. [14]

The reality, however, is quite different; the reality is uplifting where the myth is frightening, and provides a lesson to those who are watching innovation unwind today.

The real story of how rock'n'roll was invented lies with convergence. It developed after two cultures were mixed: European music culture, with its emphasis on mathematical precision, and African music culture, with a more rhythmic emphasis. Via Baptist music and blues, we finally got the development of rock'n'roll. Mythology also lists the names of the music artists who followed Johnson in dying at the age of 27. Did Jimi Hendrix, like Johnson, die at 27 because the devil finally claimed his prize, or were their deaths merely examples of how great innovation often comes out of turbulence and angst?

We can take another less noisy, but still important innovation that also developed out of convergence: the discovery of DNA. The double helix was identified when the American biologist James Watson and the English physicist Francis Crick built on experiments with x-rays – supplied by the biochemist Rosalind Franklin – using tools from multi-disciplines: biochemistry, genetics, information technology, and mathematics, or so says Steven Johnson in his book: *Where do good ideas come from?*[15] It turns out that the convergence goes further, and that the physicist George Gamow studied the work of Watson and Crick and, drawing upon the knowledge of his own discipline, explained how the four bases in the double helix of DNA could control the synthesis of protein from amino acid.[16]

---

[14] They say if you play Led Zeppelin's Stairway to Heaven backwards you can hear the words "here's to my sweet Satan" at one point.

[15] Where good ideas come from, page 68

[16] http://en.wikipedia.org/wiki/George_Gamow

As the famous Hungarian-British author Arthur Koestler once said: "All decisive events in the history of scientific thought can be described in terms of mental cross-fertilization between different disciplines."[17]

So if cross fertilisation is the means by which innovations occur, consider the impact the internet might have. No medium in history has even come close to the internet for promoting cross fertilisation of ideas. The power of the internet to create cross fertilisation is reason enough to contradict the views of those who say innovation has peaked; that is to say those whose take on the world falls into the category we might call the sceptical view of innovation.

Open standards

There is another, possibly even more important, driver of innovation, and once again it relates to the internet.
Contrary to popular belief, innovations are not developed in isolation. Just about every great idea in history has built upon someone else's idea. Or maybe that understates it. Just about every great idea in history has built upon a raft of ideas developed by a host of different people.

Take the industrial revolution. History books focus on the individuals: John Kay and his flying shuttle or James Hargreaves and the spinning jenny, for example. The history books mislead us. In fact, each innovation was the work of an army of engineers, tweaking here and tweaking there, and in each case building upon existing technology. Robert Stephenson once said: "The locomotive is not the invention of one man but of a nation of engineers." And the

---

[17] This quote was referred to by Steven Johnson, in his book Where Good Ideas Come From, Penguin, 2010

industrialist A J Mundella said: "Every invention we have made and patented (and some have created almost a revolution in the trade) has been the invention of overlookers, or ordinary working men, or skilled mechanics, in every instance."[18]

As an uncharacteristically humble Isaac Newton once said in trying to explain where his ideas came from: "I stand on the shoulder of giants." Actually even in saying that he was building on the words uttered by someone else – Bernard of Chartres said: "We are like dwarfs on the shoulder of giants."

Henry Ford once said: "I invented nothing new. I simply assembled the discoveries of other men behind whom were centuries of work. Had I worked fifty or ten or even five years before, I would have failed. So it is with every new thing. Progress happens when all the factors that make it are ready and then it is inevitable. To teach that a comparatively few men are responsible for the greatest forward steps of mankind is the worst sort of nonsense."

But if ideas build on older ideas, think how the internet can revolutionise this.

No medium in history comes close to the internet in enabling ideas to develop. Innovators using the internet to develop their ideas are like hobbits standing on the roof of the world's tallest building. But there is nothing wrong with that. It is quite simply how innovation happens.

The internet, however, has created a new innovation which enhances this very process; a new innovation which ranks up there with the most important innovations of all time –

---

[18] Stephenson and Mundella quote taken from Terence Kealey, Sex, Science and Profits, William Heinemann: London, 2008

and indeed was referred to in the previous chapter – and it is the development of open standards and open learning.

There is Wikipedia, which is possibly the greatest source of collective reference ever created, or Linux, an open standard that may yet define the way in which we operate computers.

In the field of healthcare, Open Source Drug Discovery (OSDD) has established an open source platform for both computational and experimental technologies with 2000+ members, who are students, scientists, academic institutions & companies worldwide.

GSK, in collaboration with Path Malaria Vaccine Initiative, opened up its research data and labs to external scientists who are using GSK's massive collection of data on 13,500 other compounds that seem to offer promise in the fight against malaria. It is likely that GSK will launch a malaria vaccine soon, after very positive trial data in Africa. Such an approach can help address preventing diseases, such as malaria, which have a huge medical need but offer little in the way of profitability.[19]

As we shall read in the next few pages, the human genome project was an open programme, and an open standard in 3D printing has emerged.

In learning we have seen the development of Open Education Resources (OER), in which a growing number of universities put the learning material they have developed in-house on the internet free of charge. We also have the MOOC (Massive Open Online Course.)

---

[19] Lori Mehen Is the future of Pharma open source? Opensource.com 21 April 2011 Dr Joe Cohen, An effective vaccine against malaria may at last be in sight, FT 24 April 2014,

Free open standards do not make it impossible to generate revenue. IBM engages actively in the development of Linux, and receives no remuneration for this, but in so doing it also creates expertise for itself, which it can then sell on a consultancy basis. Some universities put their course material on the internet free of charge, but this does not stop students from enrolling with them, and paying to take their courses, with the support of the university's experts and the reward of a degree proving to be just as important to the student as free learning material. [20]

But if the internet is the great medium for lubricating the mechanism by which innovation happens, and if the internet has helped to create open standards, there is a devil in the way.

The devil may not have been responsible for the invention of rock'n'roll, but there is a hindrance to innovation that is so pernicious its personification would surely be the devil.

So what is this evil?

It is the patent.

Did you know that sunspots were discovered by four different scientists, each living in a different country, in 1611? Molecular theory was invented independently in 1811 and 1814. In 1869, the Frenchmen Louis Arthur Ducos du Hauron and Charles Cros independently invented colour photography. Joseph Swan demonstrated an incandescent light bulb in Britain in 1878; Edison patented his lamp in 1879.[21] Alexander Graham Bell and Elisha Grey filed patents for the telephone on the same day, Charles Darwin and

---

[20] Interview with between Michael Baxter and Professor Patrick McAndrew at the OU conducted on 16 January 2014.

[21] Steven Johnson, Where do good ideas come from?

Alfred Wallace independently developed the theory of evolution.

In fact the story of innovation is littered with simultaneous and almost identical discoveries made quite independently. There is a phrase for it: it is called multiple discovery.

So if inventions that have occurred in history were going to be invented by someone else soon anyway, what possible justification is there for patents?

If it can be shown that without patents companies would not invest in R&D and they would not make discoveries, then maybe patents could be justified, but the story of innovation appears to show that this is rarely the case.

But there are many occasions when the innovation process was slowed by patents. The evolution of the aeroplane was delayed by patents filed by the Wright Brothers, and – as we shall read shortly – the revolution we call 3D printing accelerated when certain patents in the field expired.

In 1996 Steve Jobs said: "We have always been shameless about stealing other people's ideas." He was not wrong. Apple didn't invent windows, Xerox did. And Apple didn't invent the computer mouse, but it was the first to apply the double click. In 2012 Steve Jobs said: "I am going to destroy Android because it's a stolen product. I'm willing to go thermonuclear war on this." Some might say double standards there.

It has been estimated that the value of wealth lost thanks to patents is ½ trillion US dollars.[22]
We will now devote a few pages to some of the key innovations that have provided the building blocks for today's innovation revolution.

---

[22] Everything Is A Remix,

Computers

This chapter is not about ancient history, it is about recent innovation, but to begin the story it may be worth starting with the innovation of the integrated circuit. The development of this device owed much to cross fertilisation. In 1959 Jack Kilby of Texas Instruments filed a patent for miniaturized electronic circuits, meanwhile Robert Noyce and the Fairchild Semiconductor Corporation received a US patent for a silicon based integrated circuit.

There have been occasions in the story of innovation when two rival companies working on complementary technologies engaged in a patent war, and in doing this slowed down the innovation process. The detailed story of Texas Instruments and Fairchild Semiconductor Corporation is not one we need to go into here, but the important point is that the two companies agreed to cooperate, and once silicon based miniature integrated circuits had been developed, we saw the emergence of the force we now call Moore's Law – which of course was named after Noyce's co-founder at Intel: Gordon Moore.

The advances in speed and power of computers, as the number of transistors that could be squeezed on an integrated circuit increased year on year, has been the most important building block for today's innovation revolution.

Data

The Internet
This was first created by ARPAnet in the late 1960s, which was part of the US government, in an attempt to create a network of computers that would be impervious to nuclear attack. If the story of the origin of the internet tells us anything, it is that wonderful things are often used for quite a different purpose than that intended by their inventors. In

fact ARPAnet was launched in the 1950s by President Eisenhower, in the midst of the cold war, in response to the news that the Soviets had launched Sputnik, mankind's first foray into space.

World wide web

It took the invention of the world wide web by Tim Berners Lee, an employee at CERN, before the internet began to penetrate mass consciousness. Berners Lee finished the first web site using hypertext in 1990 and posted the project on the alt.hypertext newsgroup on 7 August 1991.

It is quite extraordinary how rapidly the internet took off from there. The dotcom boom began and crashed all within ten years. The world's first and third largest companies by market cap [23] owe their success to the internet and the world wide web in particular. At no time in history had such a simple idea as hyper-texting had such a radical change on the world so quickly.

Fibre optics and Butter's Law of Photonics

It is not clear when the phrase Butter's Law of Photonics first crept into popular usage. Gerald Butter, one of the icons of the communications industry, formed the Optical Networking Group while he worked at Lucent Technologies. At Lucent's Global Media Day in the late 1990s, Bell's Lab made a presentation in which they referred to Butter's law of Photonics. In the context of this presentation it described a phenomenon in which the cost of transmitting a bit over an optical network decreases by half every nine months. More often, however, Butter's Law of Photonics is said to suggest that the amount of data that can be transmitted down a fibre optic cable doubles every nine months. [24] Related to that is Nielsen's law, named after Jakob Nielsen, author and former engineer at Sun Microsystems, which

---

[23] Apple and Google
[24] Tehrani, Rich; As We May Communicate

says: "network connection speeds for high-end home users would increase 50 per cent per year."

It may be worth bearing in mind that when it comes to Fibre Optics, the key is not so much the cables themselves as the technology at the sending and receiving ends.

Fibre optic technology itself is old. Back in 1880 Alexander Graham Bell invented a 'photophone', which transmitted a voice signal on a beam of light. But who needs to make phone calls using that technology when they can be made using much simpler technology? And so fibre optics did not take off until there was a need for them. Fibre optic wire, which carried up to 65,000 times more information than copper wire, was invented in the 1970s. In 1975 the US government linked computers in the NORAD headquarters at Cheyenne Mountain using fibre optics to reduce interference. [25]

Inventions are not much use when no one needs them. The printing press may have existed in Ancient Crete, wheels may have been a part of toys in Ancient Mexico, but without paper on Crete and horses in Ancient Mexico, the innovations were of no great moment.

With the innovation of the internet and then the world wide web, there was now a need for fibre optics, and it was that which spawned its innovations.

Data, computer processing power and healthcare

The veracity, variety, velocity and volume of healthcare related data combined with the processing power of

---

[25] The Birth of Fibre Optics, Mary Bellis

computers, such as IBM's Watson, will revolutionise healthcare as we know it now.

Compression technologies

Linked with sending data is innovation relating to compression, an example is JPEG, a compression technology for still images, and MPEG (Motion Picture Expert Group) used for compression of moving images (video).

Compression technologies are a combination of clever software and processing power. Thanks to computers gaining in power at a speed described by Moore's Law, modern computers can decompress compressed data on the fly, whereas it might once have taken several hours.

Lasers

Lasers were first theorised by Albert Einstein in 1917, but controversy surrounds the occasion when the first optic or laser light was generated. Candidates for this honour are Theodore Maiman, who invented the ruby laser in 1960 and Gordon Gould, the first man to use the word laser, and who began building an optical laser in 1958.

Laser stands for light amplification by stimulated emission of radiation. A laser light is produced when an excited electron (one with added energy), which is orbiting its atom's nucleus in a higher than normal orbit, returns to its lower (normal) orbit and releases its energy in the form of electromagnetic radiation (light). There are several types of lasers:
- Solid-state which can emit infrared light.
- Gas lasers – some forms can be used for cutting hard materials.
- Excimer lasers, which produce ultra violet light.

- Dye lasers and semi-conductor lasers – used in laser printers or CD players.

Applications of lasers:
- Medical usage. Lasers can be focused to a microscopic dot of high energy and intensity, making the technology useful as a cutting and cauterizing instrument. Lasers are also currently being used in ophthalmology for the correction of detached retinas. Looking into the future, we should expect to see lasers used more frequently in: surgery[26], diagnosing diseases such as cancer[27], and also in the treatment of diseases such as cancer.[28] Lasers will also be applicable in the field of nanoscale surgery.[29]
- Welding and Cutting.
- Surveying and ranging – thanks to lasers we now know the range from Texas to the moon within an accuracy of 15 cm.
- Garment industry– can cut garments in mass quantities.
- Communication – can be used in fibre optic cables to maintain signals over longer distances.
- Heat treatment, such as hardening of automobile camshafts.
- Barcode scanners.
- LiDAR – measures distances by illuminating a target using lasers, and analysing the reflected light – relevant to self-driving cars, and drones.

---

[26] Due to their greater accuracy and the need to reduce impact on the patient during surgery – quicker recovery.
[27] Where the laser is being exploited in the field of spectroscopy with a view to reducing reliance on x-rays. This could eventually replace the gold standard mammogram.
[28] Where the laser will be used to treat at a cell level.
[29] Lasers can operate at femtosecond pulses and be tuned to exact wavelengths.

- Laser power beaming can send energy into space, ie to power a rocket, or from space onto earth, in the forms of highly concentrated light that be converted via solar power into electricity.

As a cursory look at the history of lasers shows, this is relatively new technology, but what makes lasers truly exciting is how they can be applied to other technologies.

LiDAR

LiDAR, sometimes referred to as Light Detection and Ranging and LaDAR, which is said to stand for Laser Detection and Ranging[30], was invented by nature many millions of years ago, because this is the technology used by bats as they navigate with uncanny accuracy. The idea is simple enough, shine a light at an object and measure the time it takes for that light to be reflected back. The technology itself was first developed in the 1960s, but what is especially interesting, is that while the technology here is helping to propel the wider advances that are occurring today, to begin with it was used by the military, by the police (in speed guns) and in surveying. It seems unlikely that its original inventors – that's human inventors, not the bats – had robotics or self-driving cars in mind when they developed it. This is a pattern that is repeated over and over in the story of innovation. After all it is unlikely that the inventors of the internet at ARPAnet were thinking about the possibilities of social media, or video on demand, or crowd sourced funding, when they began linking computers together.

---

[30] Actually, it appears that neither the words LiDAR or LaDAR are acronyms at all, and simply combine the words light/laser and radar. It appears that the words Light Detection and Ranging and Laser Detection and Ranging crept into usage after the word LiDAR was first used.
http://en.wikipedia.org/wiki/Lidar

Wireless data

Bluetooth	Bluetooth is an example of what's called a wireless personal area network. It was invented by Ericsson in 1994. It offers a maximum throughput of 1mbps over a maximum range of about thirty metres. Its benefit is that it is very low energy intensive, and the data are more than sufficient for many applications envisaged for the internet of things.
ZigBee	Can be used to connect devices at a very low cost and with very little energy consumption. It has transfer speeds up to 250kbs, and a maximum range of 100 metres. ZigBee was conceived in 1998, standardized in 2003, and revised in 2006. [31]
Infrared connections	Can transfer up to a few megabits per second over a few metres, and is particularly useful for applications such as TV remote controls.
Wifi	Uses radio waves transmitted between 2.4 and 5 GHz to provide wireless internet access.

---

[31] http://en.wikipedia.org/wiki/ZigBee

Micro electromechanical systems (MEMS)

"There's plenty of room at the bottom," said Professor Richard Feynman in 1959. Many see that statement as marking the beginning of MEMS. The technology builds on the technology behind integrated circuits, and is used to make sensors, actuators, accelerometers, switches, and light reflectors. Transistor and MEMS technologies originated from the pioneering Bell Labs' work in the late 1940s and early 1950s.[32]It combines a mechanical component with electronic elements, and the first example of this technology was created in 1964, by Harvey Nathanson from Westinghouse.

MEMS are critical for the successful working of the internet of things, and their power and sophistication grows, in part as integrated circuits grow in power at a trajectory described by Moore's Law.

In 1999 Lucent technologies developed the first optical network switch.

RFID

RFID stands for radio frequency identification device. It's a form of smart bar code that can communicate with a network system, or indeed with smart phones or tablets. RFIDs can be used, for example, to communicate the nature of every item in your shopping trolley, while in a supermarket, so that when you pay for your shop, the store's network immediately knows what products you are buying.

---

[32] Roadmap to a $Trillion MEMS Market,
http://meptec.org/Resources/Roadmap%20to%20a%20$Trillion%20MEMS%20Market,%20Meptec.pdf

RFID tags can be used to track products through the supply chain; they are what makes the internet of things possible.

In a healthcare context, RFID is contributing towards patient disease management, where patients, through their handsets, are able to gain access to relevant information. For example, caring for the elderly, where a person is able to continue living in his or her own dwelling and be monitored whilst there,[33] or in hospital care management, where a hospital is able to track all staff, equipment and patients. [34]

RFID technology in a healthcare supply chain context is enabling pharmacists and patients to verify that the medicine is non-counterfeit and therefore safe to take. Counterfeit medicine is a significant problem in both mature and emerging markets. In the latter, a large proportion of the counterfeit medicine is poisonous leading to many deaths - up to 15 per cent of drugs in developing nations are counterfeit.

Software defined radio or SDR

SDR in one form or another has been in existence for 30 years, but it has only been quite recently that it has taken off – thanks to new technology and the emergence of potential new applications. SDR is another massively important step. Before its widespread use, a mobile phone may have required one chip for radio communication, another to talk to cell towers, another for Wifi and yet

---

[33] This prolongs the life of the aged person through better quality of life and reduces the burden on the healthcare system.

[34] RFID / NFC technology in a healthcare supply chain context is enabling pharmacists and patients to verify that the medicine is non-counterfeit and therefore safe to take. Counterfeit medicine is a significant problem in both mature and emerging markets. In the latter, a large proportion of the counterfeit medicine is poisonous leading to many deaths - up to 15 per cent of drugs in developing nations are counterfeit.

another to facilitate Blue tooth. By using software, all these function can be provided by a phone core processor. Because the technology entails software, it is highly flexible, which offers a major benefit. SDR technology can tune into different wavelengths simultaneously. To quote Timothy B Lee who penned an article about SDR for Ars Technica: "The widespread adoption of software-defined radio hardware could undermine the FCC's control over the electromagnetic spectrum itself. "On the other hand, SDR opens up the prospect of millions of people being able to experiment in this area, whereas previously it was dominated by industrial labs with strong backing. Mr Lee said that while "hobbyists [may] pollute frequency bands... it's also likely to usher in an era of unprecedented radio innovation." [35]

GPS

Here we go again! Global Positioning Satellites are vital technology for making driverless cars, robotics, and many applications of the internet of things, such as tracking products, and they were developed for quite a different purpose. The US military first created them during the height of the cold war, and, just like the internet, the initial impetus came after the launch of the Soviet spacecraft Sputnik.

The technology works via the interaction of satellites and GPS devices on Earth. The satellite broadcasts radio signals containing information providing their location, status and precise time, calculated using an atomic clock. These signals are then sent at the speed of light towards the earth. A GPS device receives signals from at least four satellites, and by measuring the time it took for the signals to reach the device, it is able to calculate its precise distance from each

[35] Timothy B. Lee How software-defined radio could revolutionize wireless

of the satellites, and then, by the magic of geometry, can calculate precise distance.

3D printing technologies: Stereolithography, Fused Deposition Modelling, Selective Laser Sintering, and RepRap

It is often said that the story of 3D printing began with Stereolithography, which was patented by Charles Hall, the founder of 3D systems, in 1986. Of course, in those days the process we now refer to as 3D printing, was called additive manufacturing. Stereolithography entails the process of creating solid objects from liquid plastic.

Other forms of 3D printing include Fused Deposition Modelling, which was developed in the late 1980s (and commercially in the 1990s) and Selective Laser Sintering, also developed in the 1980s.

A number of people in the 3D printing business believe that innovation has accelerated with the expiry of certain key patents.

2005 saw the foundation of RepRap, an open source initiative to build 3D printers. In 2008 RepRap launched Darwin, which was the world's first self-replicating 3D printer. One of the key patents in Fused Deposition Modelling expired in 2009, and with that the innovation cycle led by RepRap with its emphasis on open source appears to have accelerated.

Over the next few years a number of patents in 3D printing will expire, and it has been speculated that this will spark off rapid price reductions, and further innovations.

Decoding of Human genome

In June 2000 the then US President Bill Clinton said: "Today, we are learning the language in which God created life. We are gaining ever more awe for the complexity, the beauty, the wonder of God's most divine and sacred gift. With this profound new knowledge, humankind is on the verge of gaining immense, new power to heal. Genome science will have a real impact on all our lives – and even more on the lives of our children. It will revolutionise the diagnosis, prevention and treatment of most, if not all, human diseases." He was speaking on the day that the human genome project had completed the task for which it was set-up: the decoding of the human genome.

As is so often the case in the story of innovation, it is not easy to find the start point. Was it 1911, when Alfred Sturtevant created the first Drosophila gene map? Was it 1953, when Francis Crick and James Watson discovered the helical structure of the DNA molecule? Or was it the mid-1970s, when Frederick Sanger developed techniques to sequence DNA? The human genome project itself was begun in 1990 and by June 2000 it was announced that the majority of the human genome had been completed. In February 2001, the Human Genome Project (HGP) published its results to that date: a 90 percent complete sequence of all three billion base pairs in the human genome.[36] The genome was fully sequenced in 2003.

Here are some important considerations:
- From the outset the human genome project was envisaged as being open, with the full results of its research rapidly made available on the internet.
- Progress in the project followed an exponential curve. At the halfway point of the project a tiny

---

[36] http://www.genome.gov/12011239

fraction of the human genome had been sequenced, and many suggested it would take decades, even centuries before the project was complete.

- Once completed, the project did not automatically solve the riddle of how we are made. Although the media often talks about specific genes relating to specific diseases, the reality is that several genes forming a kind of sub-network within the human genome network create certain functions or susceptibilities.

- Since the genome project has been completed, the cost of sequencing a human genome has fallen by a remarkable extent. The original project cost 2.7 billion US dollars and took 13 years, but today any human genome can be sequenced in a few hours for a cost of a few thousand dollars. It has been projected that within ten years it will cost $100 US dollars and take just one hour to sequence a human genome.[37]

The human genome has been sequenced but the research continues. In 2005 the HapMap project was begun. This is an example of international collaboration, [38] and is attempting to create a kind of international database cataloguing "similarities and differences in human beings." HapMap says its "researchers will be able to find genes that affect health, disease, and individual responses to medications and environmental factors."[39]

---

[37] Derek Thompson, IBM's killer idea: The $100 DNA-sequencing machine, The Atlantic, November 16, 2011.

[38] Scientists and funding agencies from across the world have worked together on this project, including from Japan, the United Kingdom, Canada, China, Nigeria, and the United States.

[39] http://hapmap.ncbi.nlm.nih.gov/thehapmap.html.en

Genome sequencing goes beyond the genome. It is increasingly referred to as Panomics and will revolutionise disease treatment including drug discovery and delivery. Panomics refers to the range of molecular biology technologies, [40] and is the equivalent of the GoogleMap for the human body.

Once this information is known for each individual, you can start to imagine how customised or personalised medicine could and will become.

Synthetic biology

On May 2010, Craig Venter announced the world's first synthetic cell. To quote Venter: "It began with digital code in a computer, building the chromosome from four bottles of chemicals, assembling the chromosome in yeast, transplanting it into recipient bacterial cell, and transforming that cell into a new bacterial species." Critics say it is overstating things to say Venter created the first man made life form, because without the initial bacterial cell Venter's project could not have completed its experiment. Nonetheless, Venter does not exaggerate when he says he and his team had helped to create the first replicating species that we have had on the planet whose parent is a computer.

Given what we have learned already about how innovation often accelerates as technology advances, it is hard to understand how the idea that innovation has peaked can be taken seriously in the same decade that has seen the first ever synthetic organism.

---

[40]Including bionics, proteomics, metabolomics, transcriptomics, etcetera.

Stem cell research

The biology online dictionary defines a stem cell as: "an unspecialized cell characterized by the ability to self-renew by mitosis while in undifferentiated state, and the capacity to give rise to various differentiated cell types by cell differentiation."

It has an alternative definition: "A cell that has not yet acquired a special function." [41]

You could say a stem cell is to living things what letters are to books. You can take the 26 letters of the alphabet, but one wonders if even an infinite number of chimpanzees with an infinite number of typewriters could ever produce the complete works of Shakespeare.

But from a stem cell taken from a living thing, scientists could theoretically create any part of that living thing; its eyes, mouth, heart, liver, or maybe even its whole.

A particular form of stem cell research, entailing the creation of stem cells from embryos, has given rise to the hugely controversial use of human embryonic stem cells. More recently the creation of stem cells from adult cells, in a process called induced pluripotent stem cells has gone some way towards overcoming ethical concerns.

The story of stem cell research begins in 1962, when Sir John Gurdon removed the nucleus of a fertilized egg cell from a frog and replaced it with the nucleus of a mature cell taken from a tadpole's intestine. This modified egg cell grew into a new frog, proving that the mature cell still contained

---

[41] http://www.biology-online.org/dictionary/Stem_cells

the genetic information needed to form all types of cells.[42] In 1978 the first stem cell was discovered in human blood, the first human embryonic stem cells were created from a hamster in 1988, the cloned sheep – Dolly – was born in 1997, and also in that year a haematopoietic stem cell was found to be the origin of Leukaemia, leading some to say that this proves there are cancer stem cells.

In 2000 it was discovered how to produce different cells from adult cells. In 2012 Shinya Yamanaka from Kyoto University in Japan won the Nobel Prize. To quote the Nobel organisation, his achievement was "in identifying a small number of genes within the genome of mice...When activated, skin cells from mice could be reprogrammed to immature stem cells, which, in turn, can grow into all types of cells within the body." It said that these discoveries may lead to new medical treatments.

Stem cell research is driving a new science called regenerative medicine, which will enable us to replace or regenerate human cells, tissues or organs in order to restore or establish normal function.

Prosthetics/bionics

The work done at MIT Media Labs in this field is amazing. Bionics not only includes prosthetics, but also exoskeletal devices. The Six Million Dollar Man TV series with Lee Majors or even Marvel's Iron Man no longer seem so far-fetched!

One particular innovation in prosthetics, which is very new, is known as targeted muscle reinnervation. It was developed by Dr Todd Kuiken at the Rehabilitation Institute of Chicago.

---

[42]

http://www.nobelprize.org/nobel_prizes/medicine/laureates/2012/yamanaka-facts.html

Targeted muscle reinnervation entails redirecting nerves that had connected a limb, which has since been amputated/lost to another portion of the body, such as the chest. When this part of the body moves, the motion is picked up by electrodes that can then provide signals to a prosthetic limb. In other words, targeted muscle reinnervation enables a patient to move his or her artificial limb by thinking about it just as they did before with their natural limb.

Vertical farms

Vertical farms have one obvious advantage and several other more subtle benefits.

The obvious advantage is that they save land. See a vertical farm as being like a block of flats, but instead of housing people it houses crops. Dickson Despommier, professor of public and environmental health at Columbia University in New York, says that 80 per cent of land suitable for growing crops is in use, therefore the key to growing more crops lies in going upwards.

Vertical farms also offer the benefit that they can make very efficient use of water, since the water in vertical farms can be more easily recycled; vertical farms are not dependent on the weather, and can also be situated near the place of consumption.

Vertical farms may solve the problem of how to provide locally grown food to cities. They also eliminate the need for tractors, and limit the requirement for pesticides.

The big drawback is that farming needs light. Back in 2012, *The Economist* looked into the question of vertical farms and quoted one expert as saying: "Generating enough electricity using solar panels requires an area about 20 times larger than the area being Illuminated." So if that is right, the obvious benefit of vertical farms – that they make better use of land available – might be cancelled out.[43]

However, advances in technology may overcome this disadvantage, and in any case the problem of light does not nullify the benefits of vertical farms making efficient use of water, and in providing a local source of food supply.

Smart Cities

Smart Cities are not an innovation; they are something that other innovations have made possible. But the result will be truly significant. In a smart city, massive amounts of data will be collected and processed. This will result in demand meeting supply in a way that was never possible before, and in reduction of waste. In a smart city, sewers, the electricity grid, water supply, transport, and even rubbish bins, will generate data that can be processed, and used to make cities operate more efficiently. For example, traffic light systems will be updated on the fly to ensure traffic runs as smoothly as possible. Buses will be diverted to meet demand. It will be possible to order self-driving cars, or a taxi, in such a way that optimises efficiency. So, for instance, the car that collects you may be the nearest available one in the city. Electricity from intermittent sources may be channelled into non-time sensitive tasks, such as overnight charging of electric cars, mobile phones or fuelling storage heaters.

Water desalination

Water is possibly the most valuable resource on this planet. As the population grows, and if the climate warms up, water supply may prove to be the single biggest impediment to

---

[43] Does it really stack up?, The Economist, December 9th 2010

123

feeding the world. It may even trigger wars. Consider, for example, how fresh water originating in Tibet supplies water via the flow of rivers to the world's two most populous regions. Tibet holds the third largest depository of fresh water in the world, behind the Arctic and Antarctic. The Indus, Brahmaputra, Irrawaddy, Salween and Mekong rivers all flow from Tibet, as well as the Yellow River, Yangtze Kiang, and Sutlej.

The obvious solution to a potential global water shortage lies with taking a small percentage of the water that lies in the Earth's oceans, and turning it into fresh water via desalination.

As you will discover shortly, some of the new materials currently under development do have potential as a means of cost effective water desalination.

Energy storage

Renewable energy technology is becoming more efficient. Neither wind nor solar power are seeing their efficiency progress at a rate commensurate with Moore's Law, but solar panel costs in the US fell 60 per cent between Q2 2011 and Q1 2013. Indeed the solar industry has its own Moore's law equivalent, known as the Swanson Effect,[44] which says that the cost of the photovoltaic cells needed to generate solar power falls by 20 per cent for every doubling of the cumulative number of units shipped.

The cost of energy generated by photovoltaic cells per watt has in fact fallen from $76.67 in 1977 to $0.74 in 2013.

But the problem with most forms of renewable energy, especially wind and solar, is that the source of energy is

---

[44] Named after Richard Swanson, the founder of SunPower,

unreliable. Wind turbines do not work when there is no wind, and solar panels do not work at night.
Renewable energies could be transformed by advances in energy storage.

Advances in energy storage are also crucial to the development of drones, wearable technology and the internet of things.

As was stated in chapter two, necessity is the mother of invention. It has been a relatively new development for energy storage to be so vital, and with this necessity, innovations will surely follow.

Last year, Tesla's CTO and co-founder JB Straubel said: "Battery innovation is improving around 5 to 8 per cent per year." In fact, Straubel said: "The impact of battery innovation on the design of the car can be even more significant than Moore's Law has on some computing products." Maybe we can call this Straubel's Law. [45]

In summary, the key technologies in energy storage are:
- Flywheels. We all know that if you spin certain objects, they can keep spinning for a few moments. Flywheel's state of the art is spinning wheels in a vacuum. Formula one fans may be familiar with the concept, because KERS, which can provide racing cars with a sudden injection of pace, uses fly wheel technology.
- Superconducting magnetic energy storage.
- Batteries, including lead acid – which appears to be technology that has limited potential to advance, lithium ion batteries, lithium air batteries, and liquid sodium sulphur batteries.
- Pumped storage hydroelectricity.

---

[45] How battery improvements will revolutionize the design of the electric car

- Compressed air storage.
- Electrolysis of water and mechanization.
- Thermal storage.
- Hydraulic energy storage.

As we shall see shortly, there are other developments in energy storage, in their early stages, that may yet revolutionise the evolution of this technology.

We will return to the issue of renewable energy and storage in chapter eight: Be warned that some of the developments afoot are mind blowing!

Materials

In the previous chapter, it was suggested that nanotechnology may prove to be the most important innovation of the lot, and yet, nanotechnology is not really one thing. It is the technology of dealing with substances on a very small scale – a nanometre is one billionth of a metre. Thanks in part to advances in computers, and in part thanks to technology developed for computers, in recent years and indeed recent months, we have seen extraordinary advances in new nanomaterials, also called wonder materials.

Here is a brief account.

The highest profile of the new wonder materials is **graphene.** The material was first isolated by Andre Geim and Kostya Novoselov at the University of Manchester in 2003. In 2010 they were both awarded the Nobel Prize for physics. Take a second glance at those two dates: isolated in 2003, and awarded the Nobel Prize in 2010. A time interval of just seven years between discovery and being awarded the Nobel Prize is itself unprecedented. The fact that the prestigious award was made so soon after the initial breakthrough illustrates two points. Firstly the importance of graphene, and secondly it underlines one of the key hypotheses of this book: namely that the rate of innovation is accelerating.

In fact graphene had been discovered before; it is just that no one had appreciated its significance.

Graphene is made from a single layer of carbon atoms. They are arranged in a honeycomb or chicken wire structure. According to the University of Manchester web site, graphene "is the thinnest material known and yet is also one of the strongest. It conducts electricity as efficiently as copper and outperforms all other materials as a conductor of heat." It "is almost completely transparent, yet so dense that even the smallest atom helium cannot pass through it."

Its applications include flexible computer displays, faster microprocessors, stronger and lighter composites such as tennis rackets or bikes, more efficient solar cells, sensors, medical imaging, flexible batteries and water desalination.

Sceptics say the cost of manufacturing graphene is prohibitively high and indeed, as an article on GigaOM pointed out: "In 2010, it cost tens of thousands of dollars to manufacture a piece of graphene smaller than a postage stamp." Back then it was made using very slow processes, such as splintering off slices of graphene from graphite – that's the same material used to make the lead in pencils. It was also made from synthesizing it in a furnace. But then things have since advanced. The same article adds that these techniques "have given way to room-temperature, large-scale methods that promise to be much cheaper." [46]

---

[46] How do you manufacture huge amounts of graphene for a fraction of the cost?

Graphene has rivals, a material called **silicene**[47] and another called **graphyne** are said to be potentially more super than super graphene, the material world equivalent of Superman without the allergy to kryptonite.

Other wonder materials include **ionic liquids**, which have potential applications as a green cleaning solvent, fuel cells for cars, solar cells, and perhaps most important of all in energy storage.

Also of potential high impact are **DNA hydrogel** (scaffolds for tissue engineers, drug-filled wound plugs, water-activated switches), **Self-healing concrete** (large structures, such as viaducts), programmable matter (self-assembling robots), and **metamaterials**. The last one on that list is especially interesting. Metamaterials can be used to manipulate electromagnetic waves. Among the functions they offer is invisibility. What with graphene being described as a wonder material, metamaterials creating invisibility, LADAR using the same principles that bats use to navigate, it conjures up that image of Superman chatting to Batman about how he tried to give a naked Wonder Woman a surprise, only to discover that he gave the invisible man a much bigger surprise instead. But metamaterials do more than provide invisibility. These materials were only discovered in 1999; they are not found in nature, and are made from clusters of atoms. When light passes through certain substances such as water, it is bent. When it passes through a certain metamaterial, it is bent in the opposite direction – a reaction known as negative refraction. Invisibility aside, metamaterials have the potential to create ultra-powerful microscopes, which in turn may lead to

---

[47] More recent research has questioned whether silicene exists. See:
Silicene: To be or not to be? Justin H S Breaux, Argonne National Laboratory
http://www.anl.gov/articles/silicene-be-or-not-be

further discoveries. They also have applications in advanced solar energy generation.

Imagine you are watching a movie, and you pop out for a few minutes, and put the movie on pause. The images freeze. A similar thing happens with the wonder material called **light memory crystals**, which is coated by yttrium silicate. It was able to stop light, the fastest thing in the universe, which normally travels at 300 million meters per second, for one whole minute. This trick was pulled off by scientists at the University of Darmstadt in Germany back in July 2013. The material may have applications in building long range quantum networks – a quantum network being a network that can deliver sub-atomic particles; in other words a very fast way of transmitting data.

Other wonder materials include self-healing **oleophobic coatings** – which could lead to screens on smart phones that can repair themselves if damaged, and **carbon nanotubes** – which have the potential to enable the creation of tubes hundreds of times stronger than steel, but six times lighter. These may have applications in safer buildings, cars and aircraft, and with the added benefit of improved fuel efficiency.

Then there are **liquid metals**. Metal materials that are liquid at room temperature can be manipulated to form an almost infinite number of shapes, and form a thin skin layer that can enable these shapes to keep their integrity. Strictly speaking we are not talking nanotechnology, but we are talking wonder materials. Many wonder materials may be compared to 'Superman', or 'Wonder Woman', or 'The Invisible Man', whereas liquid metals may be more analogous with the T1000, the shape changing android from *Terminator 2*.

As we shall read shortly, liquid metals will come in very handy in another area of innovation. All will be revealed before the end of this chapter.

What are the implications of recent technology?

The technological revolution has already begun. The technology already exists. The applications of this technology, however, are only just emerging.

This section of the chapter looks at these applications.
The last section asks you to once again imagine.

McKinsey, a global consultancy, recently produced a report on disruptive technology.[48] And it very helpfully waved a dollar sign at us. The company put in an estimate of the disruptive effect of certain new technologies. The headline figure seems pretty startling. The consultancy took 12 technologies and worked out that the combined economic impact of these technologies in the year 2025 will be between $14 and $33 trillion.[49] To put that in perspective, global GDP in the year 2012 was roughly US $85 trillion. So, according to McKinsey, this means that these technologies will have quite an impact.

There is a caveat however. They are not saying that these technologies will increase GDP by between US $14 and $33 trillion; rather they are referring to economic impact. So let's say new technology leads to the collapse of a $1 trillion industry, but the industry that replaces it adds $1.1 trillion

---

[48]Disruptive technologies: Advances that will transform life, business, and the global economy, McKinsey May 2013
[49] Note, McKinsey went to lengths to suggest its estimates were not comprehensive.

to the economy. In this example, GDP was boosted by $100 billion.[50]

There is another point. It is possible that McKinsey did in fact underestimate the impact of these technologies. It is possible that some of the technologies referred to in the report may lead to even greater changes. If technology advances progress at a steady rate, even at a rate commensurate with Moore's Law, its forecasts may prove right. But as Apple showed with its triumvirate of products – the iPod, iPhone and iPad – once technology reaches a certain level, a tipping point if you like, things can change rapidly. In the case of Apple it went from nearly bankrupt to being the world's biggest company in around ten years. There is another complementary point. When technologies converge, the result can be a sharp acceleration in innovation and a whole raft of applications that no one had previously anticipated.

Even so, McKinsey's study is impressive. It is human nature to overestimate how quickly new technology will emerge, but then to underestimate its impact. During the dotcom collapse, no one could have forecast the rise of Google, or the turnaround at Apple.

Many technologies that are developing are likely to become game changers. As was pointed out in the introduction, between 1950 and 1973 the GDP of Western Europe grew by an average 4.05 per cent a year. This suggests that by 1973, GDP for the region was 249 per cent of the level in 1950. In 1960, it was 149 per cent of the level in 1950. It is not unreasonable to assume, providing policy makers don't

---

[50] McKinsey didn't actually do that GDP calculation, this example is given just to make it clear that impact and GDP contribution are not the same thing.

mess things up, which they might, that global GDP will grow at a similar pace over the next 25 years thanks to new technology. This might suggest that in 2025 global GDP may be $126.4 trillion, an increase of around $37.9 trillion per annum from 2012, and by 2037 $211 trillion, an increase of $126.8 trillion. But even that understates the potential. Today rapid growth across much of the world, in China and other emerging markets for example, is occurring anyway as countries representing at least two billion people close the existing technological gap with the West. The economic impact of new technologies will be incremental to this. McKinsey's forecast of an economic impact of between $14 and $33 trillion in the year 2025 seems to be on the low side – and significantly so.

Here is a summary of the McKinsey findings.

Disruptive technologies McKinsey

Technology	Economic impact, according to McKinsey
Mobile internet	$1.7 trillion
Automation of knowledge work	$9+ trillion
The internet of things	$36 trillion
Cloud technology	$1.7 trillion to $3 trillion
Advanced robotics	$6 trillion
Autonomous and near-autonomous vehicles	$4 trillion
Next-generation genomics	$6.5 trillion
Energy storage	$2.5 trillion
3D printing	$11 trillion
Advanced materials	$1.2 trillion
Advanced oil and gas exploration and recovery	$800 billion to $3.4 trillion

Renewable energy	$3.5 trillion $80 billion

During the middle section of this book we will dig deeper, and look at examples of how new technology may disrupt business and jobs but create wealth.

But before we do that you are invited, once again, to imagine.

Sure, technological advances of recent years are impressive. Once applications for these advances come on stream, the impact on our lives will be dramatic.

However, this is just the beginning of the story. The technological revolution that is set to unfold will make the speed of change and innovation seen in the last few years feel like snail's pace. And this is why.

The next phase

Ask yourself how the inventions of recent years have been able to occur.

This question was partially answered at the beginning of this chapter. Ideas build upon ideas. The key to innovation lies in cooperation; in innovators standing on the shoulders of giants. And no medium in history can match the internet for taking entrepreneurs and inventors, and yanking them - perhaps by the lapels or by the scruff of their necks, or even by the neurons in the brain that can create a can-do too attitude - onto the virtual shoulders of giants. The internet also makes it possible to crowd source ideas. Thanks to the internet, brainstorming is possible whereby hundreds, even thousands, can feed off each other's ideas in forums, chat rooms, via comments on blogs, or just by passively reading the huge weight of content that now exists.

But in other cases, new technology has made even newer technology possible.

Graphene may have been isolated after two academics from Manchester University were messing around on a Friday afternoon, but the technology that may make it possible to mass produce graphene entails a chemical vapour deposition process developed for the manufacturing of the silicon chip. Lithography, a process that has evolved for applications in tracking billions of transistors on a chip, has been used to create metamaterials. The scanning tunnelling microscope developed by IBM in the 1980s has made it possible to observe carbon bonds in graphene. New technology has made advances in new materials possible, and the advances are occurring now because other technologies have only just made this possible. [51]

Likewise, the decoding of the human genome accelerated as computer power became more powerful. The reason it is now possible to sequence a genome so much more quickly lies in part with the fact that computers are many times more powerful than they used to be.

And now, just to tease you, let us finish with a near nano-sized whistle-stop tour of some of the most exciting developments that are occurring:

Computers: As and when graphene or another wonder material takes over from silicon as the building block of computer chips, expect a substantial jump in the power of computers. Coupled with this, we may see the development of spintronics, which is a nanotechnology that uses the spin of an electron to potentially produce significantly more powerful computers, and a faster and bigger memory. When an electron spins, it can do so in one of four directions, effectively up right, up left, down right and down left. Digital

[51] The wonderful world of wonder materials

computers work in zeros and ones. Spintronics is an order of magnitude more powerful because it can use four sets of instructions, instead of digital's rather limiting two sets. It works at the nano-scale, which also means spectacular possibilities.

Spintronics is an example of quantum computing – it works at the atomic level. Quantum computers have the potential to be millions of times faster than current computers.

Data: Two recent developments could have a radical effect on bandwidth. Firstly, there is 5G. In 2013 Samsung announced it had developed what it called adaptive array transceiver technology. Samsung described the technology this way: "It transmits data in the millimetre-wave band at a frequency of 28 GHz at a speed of up to 1.056 Gbps to a distance of up to 2 kilometres." What does this mean? According to Samsung, by 2020 they will be able to provide data at speeds of 1.056 gigabits, or around 100 times faster than 4G, and 1,000 times faster than 3G at commercially available rates. This is an incredible bandwidth.

Another technology that may enhance data speed is known as LiFi. Unlike WiFi, which transmits data using radio waves, LiFi uses visible light. It works via lights, which go on and off at speeds that cannot be perceived by the human eye. Data speeds are said to be around 250 times faster than superfast broadband. LiFi is not perfect; it can transmit data, but it is much harder for users to send data using the technology. And since it works by light, it cannot travel over long distances or through walls. But LiFi, in combination with fibre optics, can be used to supply ultra-fast internet speeds in large buildings, such as shopping malls or offices.

Back in 2013, researchers at the Fraunhofer Institute for Applied Solid State Physics and the Karlsruhe Institute for Technology broke the world record for the length of wireless data transmission. They transmitted 40 Gbit/s (over 4,000 times faster than 4G) at 240 GHz over a distance of one kilometre.

3D printing: Up to now, most have focused on 3D printing applications for building prototypes. This is an important application, but things are moving on. One of the benefits of 3D printing is that it can make structures that would be very difficult to create using normal production methods. Now 3D printing is used to manufacture finished products with a high value used in low production runs, such as components for aircrafts. Beyond that we have what is called 4D printing, which involves printing nano-designed programmable matter that can change shape after it is printed. One application might be furniture that assembles itself. It may also be possible to use this technology to create nanoscale robots that can fight diseases such as cancer. Beyond that we have 3D printing combined with stem cell research to print out body parts to order.[52]

In 2013 researchers in China were able to print a small working kidney. Research is underway that involves not only printing non-human cells, but merging human cells with non-human cells.[53] Other recent announcements related to 3D printing include a NASA sponsored project to print a cheese pizza, and a 3D printed house, created in 24 hours.

Then there is the Mark One 3D printer from Mark Forged which can print carbon fibre. The company says it can print objects that are 20 times stiffer and five times stronger than existing plastic printing technologies. A company called American Graphite Technologies is working on a 3D printer can that print graphene. A new open sourced metal printing technology has been launched costing less than $1,500,

[52] Biology's Brave New World. Foreign Affairs Magazine
[53] 3D Printers Could be Banned by 2016 for Bioprinting Human Organs, *IB Times*

while a company called Electroloom is working on a 3D printer that can print clothes. Finally, the world's biggest company has filed five patents related to liquid metals, and some of these patents describe how the applicant – Apple – plans to tie the technology in with 3D printing.

Health: Nanotechnology, genetics and stem cell research are all being applied to advanced medicines and other health related treatments. Amongst technologies under development are nano-particles wrapped in material taken from the membranes of red blood cells that could become the basis for vaccines against a range of infectious bacteria, including MRSA.[54] The 2012 Nobel Prize in medicine was awarded to Shinya Yamanaka and her team, who worked out how to make stem cells from adult patients' cells. More recent technology has simplified the process, enabling the possibility of creating stem cells by bathing adult cells in acid. Israel's Bar-Ilan Institute for Nanotechnology and Advanced Materials is developing early DNA nano-machines to carry and deliver precious molecular cargo—a drug, protein, enzyme, or nano-molecule, for instance. These DNA nano-machines remain shut tight until a special circumstance, like a collision with a cancer cell, induces them to open and release their cargo. One revolutionary application of DNA nano-machines may be selective drug therapy.[55]

Renewables: These will be discussed in more depth later, but two new developments in the field of energy storage are incredibly exciting. A company called LightSail is developing a system for energy storage using compressed air. One of the problems with compressed air is that it gets very hot, and the hotter it is, the harder it is to store in a tank. As it cools down it loses pressure. A part of Lightsail's cleverness

[54] Vaccine for Bacterial Infections, *Biomedicine News*
[55] Dorrier, Jason DNA Origami to Nanomachines: Building Tiny Robots for the Body and Beyond, Singularity Hub, 27 January 2014

involves applying water to the air as it is being compressed, thereby reducing the rate at which it heats up, and then using the heat that has been transferred into the water to slow the rate with which it cools down.[56] Two other interesting examples of technology involve new forms of batteries. Batteries consist of two metals, traditionally zinc and graphite, immersed in an electrolyte, traditionally ammonium chloride. MIT Professor Don Sadoway has created a battery consisting of liquid magnesium (which is an exceptionally light metal) and liquid Antimony (a heavy metal) making up the electrodes, with molten salt sandwiched between, forming the electrolyte. Batteries using this technology appear to be just one year from going into mass production thanks to a company called Ambri, set up by Professor Sadoway, and backed by, amongst others, Bill Gates. The professor claims that the batteries will be able to offer huge improvements in efficiency over traditional batteries, and will work on a large scale so that they can form a part of the electricity grid, providing electricity when solar or wind power for example is not working effectively.

Finally, researchers at Stanford have developed a rechargeable battery, which uses a combination of fresh and salt water combined with electrodes made of nano-rods of manganese dioxide (so that's nanotechnology) and silver. The battery works by using the difference in salinity between fresh and sea water (salt water being a good conductor of electricity). To begin with the battery is filled with fresh water, and when it is charged the fresh water is then replaced with salt water, making a battery. The team at Stanford, who have developed the technology, calculate that 13,000 gallons of fresh water per second could produce up to 100 megawatts of power, enough electricity to support 120,000 households. Yi Cui who headed the team at

[56] Making Economical Clean Energy at Planet Scale

Stanford says that it's possible that sewage water could be used.

And now we will move away from large scale **energy storage,** suitable for the grid, to **electric cars.** Santhakumar Kannappan at the Gwangju Institute of Science and Technology in Korea has worked out how to produce batteries for electric cars that use graphene. Not only are these batteries as effective at storage as lithium batteries, they can re-charge almost immediately. Meanwhile, a company called Wysips Connect has developed a transparent panel that can be fitted in front of smart phones to generate electricity from solar energy, as well as receive data transmitted using LiFi.

NEMS
Earlier in this chapter, we read about micro electromechanical systems (MEMS), technology that is used to make sensors, actuators, accelerometers, switches, and light reflectors. This is vital technology for the internet of things, self-driving cars, and perhaps even robotics. A new iteration is now being developed called **Nano-electromechanical systems** or NEMS, which uses switches at the nano-scale. This may prove to be critical for making other forms of nanotechnology practical.

Robotics
In the autumn of 2013 Amazon announced a product called Prime Air: a system for delivering packages by drone. The company hopes to have the system working by the end of the decade and claims that it will be able to deliver packages to millions of customers within 30 minutes of them ordering. In 2013, Google bought eight robotics companies, including Boston Dynamics, a contractor to the US military. In an interview with the *New York Times,* Andy Rubin, who is head of Google's robotics division, said that the main purpose of its robotics acquisitions in the short run is to

provide a delivery system. In other words, Google's robot 'posties' may go head to head with Amazon's drones for the right to deliver our shopping. Looking forward, but not that far forward, robotics is set to begin realising the predictions of science fiction writers of the 20th century.

Virtual Reality
The story of virtual reality fits in almost perfectly with one of the key themes in this book. A new technology can offer much in theory, but the reality can be disappointing, leading to a growing feeling of scepticism. But then, as different technologies develop in tandem, the bold, but ridiculed predictions of the earlier days start to look realistic. The sceptics dismiss the talk; they cannot see beyond the first stage in the innovation cycle. Virtual reality headsets are shortly to become available to offer functionality and at a price that will enable the technology to revolutionise computer and video games. We now know that once technology falls to a price that makes it acceptable to the mass market, we see acceleration in innovation. The higher the audience, the greater the investment; investment leads to falling price and greater functionality, and this leads to a growing audience leading to more investment. And so on. It was thus in the story of PCs, and is it about to be thus in the story of virtual reality.

Virtual reality itself was first referred to in 1987 by Jaron Lanier. The hype began almost immediately, but the reality was not quite good enough. Prices were way too high; virtual reality headsets offered a very small display, so that images looked as if they were a long distance away, and then there was the problem of latency with a time lag between the movement of a wearer's head and the corresponding movement in graphics. With that hiatus in the development of technology, we moved into the sceptical phase of new technology. Even the virtual reality web site, presumably set-up as a tool for promoting the medium, but in need of an update, says: "Virtual reality development has really slowed in recent years and progress is not exactly recent."

But the evolution of various technologies, such as sensors, new materials, screen technology and above all in the raw processing power of computers have converged in a kind of perfect storm. A company called Oculus Rift has been drawing rave reviews for its virtual reality head set, and during the period when this book was written it was acquired by Facebook. Combine its technology with other advances, such as Leap Motion, which enables users to control their computers by the wave of their hand, and the original dream of virtual reality – the one that has been ridiculed and apparently debunked – is set to become reality. These words were written in January 2014. The next four to five years will see virtual reality begin to change the way we watch movies, look at web sites, and – beyond that – the way in which we communicate over long distances. It will be a perfect example of what happens when advancing technologies converge. What makes the Oculus Rift story even more compelling is that its initial funding came via Kickstarter, a platform for crowd sourced funding made possible by the internet.

Within the healthcare sector, virtual reality has many potential applications including: [57]

- In surgery, including surgical navigation, IGS, CAS, AR surgery, and robot-assisted surgery.
- Medical data visualization, including multi-modality image fusion, advanced 2D/3D/4D image reconstruction, and pre-operative planning and other advanced analytical software tools.

---

[57] As a post script to this chapter, which was written before the purchase of Oculus Rift by Facebook, at the time of purchase Facebook's CEO specifically referred to virtual reality's application in healthcare.

141

- Education and training, including virtual surgical simulators and other simulators for medical patient procedures.
- Remote care / surgery including battlefield surgery.
- Rehabilitation and therapy, including immersive VR systems for pain management, behavioural therapy, psychological therapy, physical rehabilitation, and motor skills training.

Brain interfaces

In August 2013, researchers at the University of Washington claimed to have performed a human-human brain interface via the internet. Two researchers at opposite sides of the university campus were hooked up to the internet via a machine involving electrical brain recordings and magnetic stimulation. The experiment appeared to show that one researcher was able to move the other researcher's finger, just by thinking about it. University academic Andrea Stocco was one of the brains behind the research in more than one sense of the word. He was one of the researchers behind the experiment, and one of its subjects. He said: "The internet was a way to connect computers, and now it can be a way to connect brains. We want to take the knowledge of a brain and transmit it directly from brain to brain." Chantel Prat, assistant professor in psychology at the UW's Institute for Learning & Brain Sciences, said: "We plugged a brain into the most complex computer anyone has ever studied, and that is another brain."

In the field of **artificial intelligence**, various technologies worth watching include pattern recognition and machine learning. Google has teamed up with NASA to create a Quantum Artificial Intelligence Lab to study how quantum computing might advance machine learning. Google says machine learning will help us to build better models of the climate and disease. A company called SwiftKey has employed machine learning techniques with pattern recognition with an algorithm which focused on the sonnets of Shakespeare. The result was a kind of three way collaboration, between Shakespeare (not that the bard knew about the collaboration), J Nathan Matias, a staff member at SwiftKey, and an algorithm. Mr Matias produced a sonnet using words chosen from 'next words' generated by the algorithm. The resulting sonnet is shown in the preface to this book. Google has recently bought UK AI company DeepMind. According to Professor Larry Wasserman from Carnegie Mellon, the company is trying "to build a system that thinks." It seems more likely that DeepMind algorithms will initially be of use within Google as it develops pattern recognition to help image searches (searching for similar images) in robotics, and self-driving cars. [58]

Artificial intelligence will play a significant role in the development of diagnostic tools. The continuous addition of patient data in a healthcare diagnosis tool will enrich it and improve the standard of care delivered. Such diagnostic tools will have a disruptive impact on the way in which medical care is delivered these days. Increasingly, the individual will be able to self-diagnose. Vinod Koshla of Koshla Ventures is quoted as saying that 80 per cent of what doctors do now will be done via technology in the future.

The shape of things to come

Critics of the idea of superfast internet ask: why is it necessary? "4G is fast enough," they say. They are not applying imagination. Consider the possibilities of an internet with quantum computers as servers with data transmitted more than 100 times faster than current broadband speeds to devices perhaps in the form of

[58] The Future of Machine Learning and the End of the World?
http://normaldeviate.wordpress.com/2012/10/30/the-future-of-machine-learning-and-the-end-of-the-world/

wearable technology that give us constant access to the internet; maybe even interacting with the internet via brain interfaces. Artificial intelligence may create new search functions of an order of magnitude more advanced than what we are used to. Add to that the possibilities that come with virtual reality. All the information on the internet, language translation, superfast calculations and complex analytical tools could be made available to us instantly, and presented to us so that all our senses feel the information. Communications across long distances will also take on a new meaning. That might sound scary, but it most certainly is not trivial.

Part two: the unravelling of technology

Chapter five: The next industrial revolution

How many industrial revolutions have there been? There was the revolution that began in the mid-18th century, which saw the development of steam, a revolution in textiles, and the great exodus from the country into towns and cities. Arguably, there was another one during the Victorian era that Smil Vaclav[1] in his book *Creating the Twentieth Century*, calls the Age of Symmetry. The early years of this momentous era began with the discovery of dynamite, followed swiftly by the telephone and photographic film. The 1880s alone, says Vaclav, gave us "electricity – generating plants, electric motors, steam turbines, the gramophone, cars, aluminium production, air-filled rubber tires, and pre-stressed concrete." And in the early 1900s we saw the first "airplanes, tractors, radio signals and plastics, neon lights and assembly line production."

Smil says this Age of Symmetry began in 1867 and ended in 1914.

The second half of the 20th century saw the digital age; the era of computers. Was that a third revolution?

The precise names matter not. It is not like the natural borders of some countries. Asia is divided from Europe by the Ural Mountains. The limits of Australia or Great Britain are defined by the oceans and sea that surround the land mass.

We can label revolutions as first, second or third, but it is just shorthand? If the computers and the internet

---

[1] Smil, Vaclav. Creating the Twentieth Century: Technical Innovations of 1867-1914 and Their Lasting Impact. Oxford: Oxford University Press 2005

heralded a new revolution, when did it begin? Was it with the invention of the World Wide Web, the formation of Moore's Law or with Alan Turing's Enigma machine in World War 2?

The technologies that are developing today and the convergence that is accelerating their development is creating changes in industry so that it feels very different from that which we have witnessed over the previous few decades.

The description may not be precise, but it is close enough to say that a new industrial revolution is underway. It is being created by more than one technology. There is even more than one contender for the title 'technology at the heart of the new industrial revolution', but it is unravelling, and it is incredibly important.

This chapter looks at the next industrial revolution and leaves you with a thought. Another revolution, quite different in character from the one that is about to occur, may follow close behind. Together, these new industrial revolutions will create more change in the world over the next few decades than the previous few centuries combined.

The Internet of Things

It has been estimated that no less than 75 billion devices will be connected to the so-called internet of things by 2020. But in January 2013 it was revealed that the internet of things had 320 new members that were a tad different from what one might have expected, and indeed a lot more frightening. At the same time Twitter gained itself 320 new users, again quite different from your normal tweeter. So who or what were these 320 mysterious new additions to the virtual world?

The 320 additions were in fact sharks, swimming off the coast of Western Australia. It works like this: the sharks were fitted with internal acoustic devices, which in turn transmitted to local lifeguards in the form of a tweet every time the sharks were within a kilometre or so of certain beaches. The tweet provides information on the size, breed and approximate location of the shark.

In doing this scientists managed to fulfil three quite distinct tasks. Firstly, they made it safer for surfers, who could now be given early warnings if sharks were in their vicinity. Secondly, scientists were able to acquire a whole new set of data on the habits of sharks, and thirdly they provided a possible storyline for a future *Jaws* movie. Imagine the potential for a kind of 4D movie, creating a more immersive form of Hollywood. Via the magic of wearable technology sitting on the rim of a surfer's ear, the tweets could be converted into audio signals so that when the shark is still some way off, the surfer might hear der dum. If the shark swims closer it may play the sound der dum, der dum, and then if it gets really close, the surfer might hear dum dum dum dum da da DUUUM.

So that's the power of modern technology and in particular the internet of things. It can directly provide us with services that make our lives easier or safer. It provides data with all kinds of ramifications for the advancement of scientific knowledge, marketing, manufacturing and security, and it provides new opportunities in the field of entertainment. The above example of the theme from *Jaws* being tweeted to surfers was a touch facetious, but there are other examples that we will come to.

The implications are both exciting, and yet more terrifying than the scariest thing Hollywood can conjure up.

The above method to provide lifeguards with information on the whereabouts of sharks has been made possible by various technological advances. First of all the internal acoustic devices were only made possible thanks to advances in energy technology. The devices are equipped with tiny batteries that can last for up to ten years. But without the advances in computers, processing power and software tools, the technology would have been of no use anyway. The ability to tweet information about the whereabouts of sharks to lifeguards comes thanks to the different technologies converging.

Here is another example of the internet of things transforming lives. Imagine a mechanic working on a helicopter. When he packs up work, and examines his tool box he discovers there is a screwdriver missing. It must be found. Travelling in a helicopter when there is a chance that there is a screwdriver lurking somewhere in its mechanical parts is not usually considered a good move.

But supposing that screwdriver had been fitted with an RFID device. These devices could perhaps best be described as being like bar codes that can transmit very simple information, but – unlike a barcode – this information can be transmitted over longer distances – up to 100 metres – and the information they transmit can be sent over the internet. They primarily consist of an aerial and a small chip; most of the device is in fact aerial. The devices can be tiny, and thanks to consumers buying products within this market, their cost has plummeted in recent years, so that it is almost inconsequential. RFID chips can be embedded into clothing, tools, the packaging of products sold in shops, onto components that are assembled in the manufacturing process and into drugs or even tiny, nano-sized surgical robots that could be used to fight diseases.

The mechanic who has lost his screwdrivers and fears it may have dropped into the engine of the helicopter he had been working on, could ascertain the precise location of the missing screwdriver, via the combination of the RFID chip and his smart phone. That, in part, is the wonder of the internet of things.

Suddenly it is possible to know where things are. The production process can be transformed with precise information on the positioning of each component, robot and even humans being involved in the production process. Warehouses will have a precise record of stocks and components in store, updated each and every time there is a change.

Domestic lives will be transformed. If you are on your way home, and can't remember if there is any milk in the fridge, and you don't know whether you need to stop off at a shop, all you need do is to check your smart phone.

We have all had the experience of ringing our mobile phones to find out where they are. But supposing it had fallen out of your pocket while you went for a walk earlier in the day. Ringing it won't help. The RFID chip on the phone can tell us, via our tablet or PC, precisely where the mobile phone is.

But this is not the whole magic of the internet of things. It is just one tiny part of what makes it so compelling.

Opinions vary on how many devices will be linked to the internet of things. Morgan Stanley has estimated 75 billion devices by 2020. It is estimated that at the end of 2012, there were eight to ten billion devices connected. Cisco predicts there will be 15 to 25 billion connected devices by 2015, and 40 to 50 billion by 2020.[59]

These are massive numbers, and represent a huge opportunity for those who build, or indeed design, the chips that make the internet of things possible. It is a massive opportunity for those who provide the hardware and software power possible to process the huge amount of data that will be generated, and it is a phenomenal opportunity for those who can make use of the data generated.

The internet of things will make it possible for you, while returning home from work perhaps, to seamlessly turn the heating on, switch on lamps, warm up the oven, or even run a bath, before you reach your home.

Ovens and fridges, vacuum cleaners, light switches, and water tanks will be connected to the internet of things. We may find that one day the fridge refuses to open because it knows, from our wearable, that we haven't done enough exercise!

Water companies will know precisely how much water each of us needs, the electric grid will have better advance knowledge about how much power it needs to provide at any one moment. Bus companies will know in advance how many passengers are planning to take a particular bus, and may be able to divert to another route where a group of people may be waiting for a bus not due for another 45 minutes. The internet of things will transform the process of taking a bus, so that it becomes akin to calling for a lift.

---

[59] Since each item connected to the internet of things needs a unique address the world has run out of IPv4 addresses and has built a new protocol called IPv6 to provide more addresses.

Demand can meet supply with a degree of precision and efficiency once thought impossible.

But above all, the combination of advances in RFID technology and greater processing power that has made the internet of things has created the intriguing opportunity to solve one of life's great mysteries. No doubt you have already guessed what it is. It is of course the puzzle of missing socks.

How is it possible for there to be so many missing socks in the world? Is there a secret conspiracy between washing machine manufacturers and aliens, who provide secret black hole technology to suck out odd socks, and transport them via a worm hole to another side of the universe in a place where odd socks have enormous value, and are used in much the same way that we use gold, or is there is a more prosaic explanation? Alas, Google maps does not yet chart the Andromeda Galaxy so if the former explanation is true, we may remain in the dark. If, on the other hand, the odd socks still exist somewhere on Earth, the internet of things will tell us where.

Enter stage right: MEMS

But the story of the internet of things becomes even more intriguing when we add to the mix MEMS, and beyond that NEMS.

MEMS, as was explained in the previous chapter, stands for Micro Electromechanical Systems. They are tiny computers combined with some form of mechanical ability. NEMS and smart dust are similar, but even smaller.

Imagine trying to develop a mechanical device for working out whether an object is standing the right way up, upside down, or on its side. And then if it is on its side, which way it is pointing. One way of obtaining this information is by putting ball bearings on a thread inside.

Turn the object upside down, and a vertical ball bearing moves.

Turn it on its side, and the ball bearing in the second device moves.

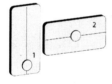

Now imagine that principle, but applied on a tiny scale, and with a slightly more high tech implementation inside a smart phone, using silicon and an electric circuit instead of ball bearings on thread. That, in a very crude form, is what an accelerometer is. And an accelerometer is an example of a MEMS.

The first iPhone had MEMS inside that provided precisely this function. That's how, when you are looking at a smart phone's screen, the display is able to adjust itself into a vertical, or a horizontal screen view, with the images always going from left to right.

MEMS is not new technology. The technology inside a MEMS device is similar to the technology inside a transistor or an integrated circuit. Because they are so similar, our ability to produce MEMS has progressed at roughly the same rate as our ability to produce integrated circuits. It is just that until the iPhone, the market was limited.

In 2011 the semiconductor industry was worth around $300 billion and the MEMS component market around £10 billion.

This appears to be set to change, because – thanks perhaps to the iPhone – the MEMS genie is out of the bottle. It may be only a small exaggeration to say that the combination of MEMS, RFID tags, the internet, and the power per square inch of modern processors, that whatever business wishes, the internet of things can command it. As Dr Janusz Bryzek says: "Within just 4 years from iPhone introduction, mobile devices absorbed several billion MEMS/sensor components."[60]

Sensors will give applications in health; in measuring blood pressure, glaucoma diagnosis, and blood analysis. They may provide micro needles, or insulin pumps. A proposal has been submitted for fitting toilets with MEMS, so that your faeces and urine can be regularly checked for infection or blood.

MEMS can provide tiny oscillators and sensors, microphones and optical displays. They can gauge the temperature, wind speed and air pressure. They can measure your insulin

---

[60] Roadmap to a $Trillion MEMS Market, Dr. Janusz Bryzek, VP MEMS Development, Fairchild Semiconductor, Mancef, Board Member

levels, the speed of your heartbeat or blood pressure, or the pressure in your car's tyres, feeding the information through to your car's computer, along with details about the average speed of traffic on the road you are about to travel along, as well as measurements detailing how close you are to the nearest empty parking place.

In 2010 Hewlett Packard presented a vision for what it called a central nervous system of the earth, using MEMS for climate monitoring, oil exploration and production, assets and supply chain tracking, smart highway infrastructure, tsunami and earthquake warnings, smart grid and homes, and structural health monitoring.

At an individual level, MEMS form an important part of wearable technology. To date the most well-known examples of this technology would be Google Glass and Samsung's smart watches, although funnily enough the rumour that Apple is working on a smart watch has garnered almost as many headlines as Samsung's actual smart watches.

But wearable technology includes wrist bands worn by runners, which check their pulse and heartbeat, as well as keep a record of their training while running.

Transparency Market Research has projected that the global wearable technology market will grow in size from being worth $750 million in 2012 to $5.18 billion in 2018.[61]

It breaks wearable technology down into:
- Fitness and wellness, including smart clothing and smart sports glasses, activity monitors, and sleep sensors.

---

[61] Wearable Technology Market - Global Scenario, Trends, Industry Analysis, Size, Share And Forecast 2012 - 2018
http://www.transparencymarketresearch.com/wearable-technology.html

- Infotainment, including smart watches, augmented reality headsets, and smart glasses.
- Healthcare and medical, including continuous glucose monitors, drug delivery monitors, and wearable patches.
- Industrial and military use: hand worn terminals and augmented reality headsets.

Other research predicts that by 2017, there will be 169.5 million wearable and health and fitness devices worldwide.[62]

The data produced by wearable technology can form part of the internet of things. It will provide individuals with a record of their personal lives, but could also be supplied to carers or medical staff in patient care, or to large industry concerns and government.

MEMS making up the internet of things will enable us to turn our oven on or switch on lights at a remote distance. This may seem trivial, but if such technology is applied to aid carers, then it suddenly takes on a level of extreme importance. Such technology can tell the carer if the person they are looking after has got out of bed, or it could be used to automatically turn on hallway lights to prevent a fall. It has been estimated that remote monitoring technologies could save the US health care system $197 billion between 2010 and 2013.[63]

Back in 2010 Horst Muenzel, regional president of Robert Bosch LLC, predicted that by 2017 there will be 1,000 sensors for each person on this planet (that's on average).

---

[62] ABI Research as cited by Technology trends to watch, CEA.

[63] According to A Brookings Institute analysis by economist Robert Litan, source: Technology trends to watch CEA.

But perhaps most importantly of all, the internet of things has applications in industry.

Take this as an example taken from Dr Janusz Bryzek's report *Roadmap to a $Trillion MEMS Market*.

"At the BSAC meeting on 9/22/11, Vijay Ullal, VP of Maxim, referenced three major technology based revolutions:

1st revolution increased productivity by bringing steam, electricity, internal combustion, radio and aeronautics.

2nd revolution further increased productivity through transistors, computers and internet, propelling the semiconductor market to $300 billion.

3rd emerging revolution based on fusion of computing, communication and sensing, freeing humans for creative work and enabling MEMS market size to catch-up with semiconductor market,"

In other words, the internet of things with MEMS at its heart is a candidate for creating a new industrial revolution. As we shall see shortly, the internet of things. is not unique in having this description applied to it.

So how much will the internet of things be worth?

McKinsey estimated that in 2025, the internet of things could impact upon business, consumers and government in areas worth around $36 trillion a year.

Dr Janusz Bryzek projects that the MEMS component market on its own will be worth $20 billion in 2016.

It is all exciting stuff, but it comes with caveats and catches.

Dr Bryzek reckons that "processing the sensor information would require increasing the size of the internet 1000 times."

This means the expansion would require more processing power with a corresponding rise in demand for energy.

Others are cynical about the internet of things.

Gartner suggests that it may be 10 years yet before the internet of things achieves mainstream adoption, and yet it suggests the hype related to it is out of proportion to the time frame in which it may affect our lives.

In fact, it has the internet of things, along with its close cousins big data and wearable technology, sitting near the top of its hype cycle.

There are specific reasons why the internet of things may yet prove to be a disappointment. One gripe relates to the nomenclature. Let's face it, the phrase 'internet of things' is very clumsy. The phrase also applies to such a wide cross section of ideas and possibilities, that it seems once the technologies referred to here are adopted, the generic term 'internet of things' will be dropped, in much the same way that we don't have a generic term for technologies that keep us warm for example. The current hype relating to the internet of things may be analogous to an early hominid academic – for example Professor Australopithecus, from the third tree on the right, next to the big hill – producing a report circa two million years ago predicting the economic impact of new technologies designed to keep us warm, including shelter, fire and clothing. Such a report may have included references to research from early hominid scientists, who had discovered a way to use animal skin to cover up their more delicate organs. But these days, we see shelter, fire and clothing as distinct. Likewise the term internet of things is applied to quite disparate activities.

An article in *Computer World* by Mike Elgan,[64] however, also raised concerns about the adoption of common standards. The beauty of the internet, as we currently know it, is its openness. The World Wide Web, or languages such as HTML, follow conventions that were adopted before the internet was seen as a money making tool. But the 'internet of things' in contrast seems to be more subject to commercial interests, and there is a real danger that companies, working to their own commercial agenda, filing patents, and promoting their own vested interests, will result in the internet of things becoming a hotchpotch of clashing technologies. This may end up providing short-term profits, but holding back economic development and in the process sucking billions, even trillions, of dollars out of potential GDP.

The *Computer World* piece suggested that in the past, when new technologies were merging, the big companies were in on the act; standards such as HTML had already been established. The article stated: "This is not the case for the Internet of Things. The phenomenon is arising in an industrial environment of powerful companies that each want an unlevel playing field in their favour, or that have strong and mutually exclusive ideas about how industry should work."

These are legitimate concerns, but the combination of the internet of things with big data presents extraordinary commercial possibilities.

As we stated earlier, McKinsey estimates that what it calls the automation of knowledge will have an economic impact in the year 2015 of around $9 trillion.

---

[64] Why the Internet of Things may never happen, Mike Elgan

The combination of both internets – that is the one we are used to and of things – will generate information that, thanks to the power of modern computers, can be processed creating information at a level for which there is no precedent.

New businesses are starting up in the field of data mining. Marketers and production managers, retailers and sports organisations, security forces and governments, educational institutions and scientists, hospitals and climatologists will have access to information that, in one stroke, will make the production and delivery of products more efficient. It will ensure that supply meets demand to a level that was once impossible. It will theoretically create a safer environment, but in the process we may sacrifice our privacy, abdicate control of our lives to authorities, and subject ourselves to a level of scrutiny among security forces that many may say is in direct contravention of the very characteristics that makes us human.[65]

Robotics

But if some say the internet of things is the means by which the next industrial revolution may occur, others say there is another contender for the description of main protagonist in creating the next industrial revolution and that is robotics.

When we think of robots, we tend to think science fiction and mechanical men with metallic voices lacking in emotion. Some robots we consider may be benevolent, such as the robot in the 1960s TV series *Lost in Space*, which was similar in form to the robot in the classic science fiction movie *Forbidden Planet*. Others might think of Arnold

---

[65] We are all already giving up significant chunks of our privacy through our digital exhaust. For example, Google is able to tell when we might buy a house some 6 months before we actually do!

Schwarzenegger, not famous for his acting talents, and yet his voice seemed almost perfect for his famous role in *Terminator*. Others still may think of Isaac Asimov, and his book *I Robot*. Asimov created the three rules of robotics, which was a set of rules that may be appropriate in reality in the next few decades. It was designed to ensure robots only ever serve us.

Few people, however, think of washing machines when the word robot is mentioned. Yet a robot is precisely what a washing machine is.

And while some applications of robots in the pipeline may have a humanoid feel about them, drones designed for a single purpose, such as delivery of post and products offered over the internet, seem to be the most immediate area in which the new generation of robotic technologies are likely to have an impact on our lives.

However, in the second decade of the 21st century, it appears that a handful of technologies are transforming robotics, so that the dreams – or indeed the nightmares – of science fiction writers are beginning to look both possible, and close to realisation.

The new robot revolution is partly being made possible by MEMS.

And the future generation of robots, which may be minuscule in size, may have NEMS[66] at their heart.
Battery technology is also a key to robot development, especially mobile robots such as those in the business of delivery. Battery technology, which was initially developed for laptop PCs using lithium ion technology, has advanced like a rocket into the stratosphere as the market for smart

---

[66] See previous chapter for more on MEMS.

phones and tablets has grown. Now that same technology is being applied to electric cars and robotics.

Future developments in battery technology, perhaps employing graphene, will create new applications and opportunities.

But robotics also requires a form of locomotion. For washing machines, this wasn't necessary, and the movement of most vacuum cleaners, which are also a form of robot, is directly controlled by their operators.
In factories robots may be stationary or move on rails, but components of the robots, such as robotic arms, must be able to move.

In contrast, the next generation of robots, may be bipedal, move on four or more legs, have wheels, or, as in the case of drones recently described by Amazon, may fly – like tiny robotic helicopters.

One interesting application of robots was described by Andreas Raptopoulos, CEO of a company called Matternet, for TED. [67] He described a form of drone that can carry urgent supplies or deliver critical supplies to people who are cut off from transport infrastructure. He said that no less than one billion people are cut off from roads at some point during the year. Mr Raptopoulos said it is possible to deliver an object by flying drone over a distance of 10 kilometres at a cost of just 24 cents per 2.5 kilogram object.

Amazon itself revealed its idea for delivering products by drone in December 2013. It announced what it calls Prime Air, a service that Amazon expects to be able to deliver objects up to 2.3 kilograms in weight ordered from its web

---

[67] Andreas Raptopoulos: No roads? There's a drone for that
http://www.ted.com/talks/andreas_raptopoulos_no_roads_there_s_a_dro
ne_for_that.html

site, within 30 minutes of order – depending on how close the delivery address is to the nearest Amazon warehouse. Amazon claims the service could be up and running within four years.

Amazon refers to the drones, by the way, as octocopters. No matter what we call them, Amazon's octocopters or Matternet's delivery drones are robots, complete with MEMS, processors and wireless communication.

In his TED talk, Mr Raptopoulos said: "At the inception of the internet, who would have anticipated the explosion of social networks, of machine-to-machine awareness, of distributed workflows, of the disruption of the music, video, photography and TV markets, Bitcoins or Snapchat? The internet connects information, but it hasn't connected all people. We're designing the very edge of the web that can reach every unnavigable place where there's human need."

In short, converging technologies have made the recent advances in robotics possible. These are advances in processing power, in the size of computers; advances in battery technology and in MEMS – not to mention lighter materials, such as carbon fibre, and advances in mechanical parts that have given dexterity to some robots. McKinsey said that recent advances in robotics are thanks to accelerating advances in machine vision, artificial intelligence, machine-to-machine communication, sensors and actuators. And that is the point. Different technologies, in some cases developed for quite different purposes, are coming together to make advances in robotics possible.

One of the world's more famous robots (actual as opposed to fictional) is Roomba, a vacuum cleaner that can learn the layout of the area it is supposed to clean, and get on with the job, unaided. iRobot, the company behind Roomba, says it has sold nine million units of the device.

Roomba looks like a disc. One version is 34 centimetres in diameter, nine centimetres high, and iRobot claims it is "so intelligent he can tell when the room is clean, will detect and adjust between carpet and hard floor, and will even take himself back to base when it's time to charge."

Other robots already in use include the Husqvarna Automower, which – at least in theory –can cut your grass, while you soak up some rays on your sun lounger.

But robots need more than MEMS; their moving parts need mechanical technologies. No less than 100 sensors, 26 joints and 17 motors make-up the Modular Prosthetic Limb, developed by researchers at John Hopkins University. The limb has been described as a bionic arm. It is designed to be worn by humans and is controlled by the nerve impulse of the person wearing it.

This takes us to one of the more compelling ideas of robotics. Science fiction has installed in us the idea that robots are to be feared; that they may replace, or even destroy us. There remain dangers. But it appears a more likely scenario is that robots will enhance us. We will be able to control robots either remotely, or directly attached to us, giving us super human strength, vision, or the ability to manually manoeuvre objects on a tiny scale.

Just as the internet of things will ultimately become a disparate range of products and functions, with only vague links, the same might be said for robotics.

Some robots will be engaged in the field of human augmentation, while others will work autonomously; some will be massive, others tiny. Some robots will be like friends or pets, others will be devoid of any sense of humanity; they will be designed to fulfil very specific and mundane tasks.

It may ultimately be the robots on a micro scale that will have the most radical effect.

Amazon's idea for drones that can deliver packages over the air is exciting, but perhaps more intriguing are tiny flying drones developed by engineers at Delft University of Technology. They have created what they call a Micro Air Vehicle. The press have christened the device robotic dragonflies.

One such device, called the DelFly Explorer, weighs just 20 grams, but comes with two cameras, and a tiny computer that controls navigation. So what will such a robot do? Its inventors talk about detecting ripe fruit, or streaming video footage from a live concert, or even taking on the persona of fairies at a theme park.

Meanwhile scientists at Harvard have also been working on a tiny, insect sized drone. But in this case, they see the drones as taking on the role usually played by insects. You may know that the bumble bee has been dying off in the millions. No one is quite sure why, but scientists have agreed that this is a very serious problem because bees play a vital role in the pollination of plants. The idea is for these drones, which weigh 80 milligrams, to mimic the bumble bee, and take on the role that nature's workers may not be able to complete for much longer. They can also help scientists better understand why the bees are dying by simulating being a bee.

Scientists studying the field of emergence understand that the communication required for a swarm to form and act in a certain way is actually quite simple. Likewise ants from the same nest may appear to behave as if they are following commands laid down by control. In fact they are not. Ants interact with each other via compounds called pheromones.

Studies appear to show that there are just ten signals that allow ants to communicate with each other, providing such messages as: "I am foraging," "There's food over there," and "Run away." Furthermore, they change their behaviour depending on the volume of messages being issued. During the course of an hour, if an ant perceives ten others foraging, it responds one way. If it perceives more than 100, its reaction is different. Steven Johnson, in his book *Emergence*, puts it this way: "The colonies take a problem that human societies might solve with a command system (some kind of broadcast from mission control announcing there are too many foragers) and instead solve it using statistical probabilities."

In other words, by following simple rules, each ant contributes to an extremely "well managed" system.

Similar ideas can be applied to tiny robots, but they communicate via the internet rather than by using pheromones. Swarming robots could perform different functions, depending on how they swarm, or work together without the need for central control. For example, scientists at The Swiss Federal Institute of Technology in Lausanne have been able to get tiny robots working independently to construct shapes, such as pyramids. They use sensors to detect other robots, and react following a certain set of rules, such as when to lay down a brick, and when to follow traffic rules.

Professor Radhika Nagpal of Harvard University is also using nature as an inspiration for organising complex but unsupervised group behaviour. This time, the inspiration was taken from termites, which instinctively modify the environment in which they work. He said: "Normally, at the beginning, you have a blueprint and a detailed plan of how to execute it, and the foreman goes out and directs his crew, supervising them as they do it. In insect colonies, it's not as if the queen is giving them all individual instructions. Each termite doesn't know what the others are doing or what the current overall state of the mound is."

But drill down, and what does it mean in terms of greenbacks? McKinsey estimates that by 2025 advanced robotics will have an impact on the economic value of manufacturing to the tune of approximately $6 trillion a year, and up to $3 trillion on healthcare. According to ABI Research, the market for consumer robots was $1.6 billion in 2012, and is predicted to be worth $6.5 billion by 2017.

Additive manufacturing

In February 2011, the *Economist* magazine ran an article with the headline: 'Print me a Stradivarius'. It said: "A new manufacturing technology will change the world." And concluded: "Just as nobody could have predicted the impact of the steam engine in 1750...—it is impossible to foresee the long-term impact of 3D printing. But the technology is coming, and it is likely to disrupt every field it touches."

So that's 3D printing; it rivals the internet of things and robotics for the title: 'technology at the heart of the next industrial revolution'.

But where the last industrial revolution saw the emergence of mass production, and tumbling prices as economies of scale were exploited, 3D printing may represent the opposite: technology that makes the concept of economies of scale redundant.

Yet, look within the 3D printing industry itself, and there is a degree of cynicism about the role it may play, and a feeling that, while the technology is exciting as far as it goes, much of the hope placed on 3D printing is little more than hype.

Is that right? Will 3D printing change the world and revolutionise manufacturing, or will it never be any more than just an important tool, a part of the toolkit used by manufacturers?

3D printing, or additive manufacturing as it is more formally known, is not new.

Indeed, additive manufacturing is as old as industry. Take the potter's wheel, for example – that's additive manufacturing.

To explain the idea even further, consider another form of manufacturing – subtractive. This involves taking an object, such as metal or wood, and banging and bending it and sawing it into an appropriate shape.

Additive manufacturing starts off small, and creates an object by building it up, layer by layer. So in the case of the potter's wheel, an object can be formed by adding clay and water, a small bit at a time, until the vase, cup or desired shape, has been created.

A similar principle applies to 3D printing, although the raw materials are typically liquid plastics or metals, that can be laid down layer by layer, with each layer printed on top of the previous layer, like a printer laying down ink.

You could say that the potter's wheel is a robot, albeit one that requires intensive human intervention for it to work effectively. A 3D printer is a robot too, albeit one that is an order of magnitude more powerful and sophisticated than anything a traditional potter might use.

So it may be misleading to list 3D printing and robots separately. In fact 3D printing is a subset of robotics.

Critics of this form of manufacturing look at the current limitations, and suggest that future applications, while exciting, are limited.

Maybe they are, but the combination of 3D printing with other robot technology that can work in tandem with it, advances in materials, and changes within the 3D printing industry itself present opportunities. This will mean that the advances to 3D printers of 2030 compared to those of 2014 can be likened to a comparison between the 3D printer of 2014 to that of a potter's wheel circa 2000 BC.

Five distinct areas come together to make the prospects for 3D printing so compelling.

Firstly, there is demand. The market is increasing in size rapidly. This is analogous with the computer industry. As computers fell in price, demand grew, investment rose with it, the pace of innovation accelerated, prices fell, and so on.

Secondly, there is the development of an open standard, and in association with that, the imminent expiry of a number of key patents.

Thirdly, there are advances in new materials.

Fourthly, there is the potential for the industry to evolve rapidly thanks to the innovation of 3D printers that can print 3D printers.

Fifthly, and perhaps most important of all, 3D printing gives a unique tool to innovators. Those sceptics who say that 3D printing is over-hyped may have a point, but what they may be underestimating is the scale of human ingenuity.

And returning to the third point, bear in mind that nature itself produces via an additive process. A tree, for example, starts off small and grows – although the analogy with 3D printing may not be precise. The individual cells that make up a tree change once they are formed. Maybe nature is closer to 4D printing.

3D printing, over-hyped or not?
So let's look at the arguments that say 3D printing is over-hyped.

There are many negatives associated with 3D printing. And those in the know, those who work in the industry, the gurus of the 3D printing world seem to agree, or at least most of them do. They say 3D printing is a great technology and is an important part of the manufacturing process – if you will it's a tool, a powerful tool, but no more than that. The sceptics say it is useful for sure, but when you ask: "Will it power a new industrial revolution?", they stop in their tracks, look at you with a hint of amusement, or in some cases exasperation, take a deep breath, and then launch into one reason after another why 3D printing can never do that.

One analogy they draw is with conventional paper printing. Laser and inkjet printers may have revolutionised the production of low run documents, and newsletters, but when it comes to large print runs – the type of print run for a magazine or a newspaper – the printer on your desk loses its relevance. Sure, modern day printing presses are wonders of technology, but they are as different from the printers that sit next to our computer as Burj Khalifa – the world's tallest building – is from the mud huts in which our ancestors lived ten thousand years ago. Innovations in desktop printers have been important, but the dream of being able to print magazines or newspapers from your back bedroom, using an off the shelf printer is just that – a dream, one fit only to fill the pipes of 18th century opium smokers.

The scepticism continues, but rather than go into the arguments in detail, let's list them, briefly.

The rationale for scepticism on 3D printing:

- There is a parallel between objects made using a 3D printer and Lego buildings. A wall made of Lego is not strong; the higher it goes, the more likely it is to tumble. Nick Allen, founder of 3D printing company 3D Print UK, in an article for *Gizmodo*, put it this way: "In something like injection moulding, you have a very even strength across the part, as the material is of a relatively consistent material structure." But he said that in 3D printing, construction occurs in layers, which means weaknesses. Mr Allen compared the issue to building "a Lego wall." We all know, that if you press on such a wall from the sides it can come tumbling down.[68]
- The process is slow, and energy intensive.
- Raw materials are expensive. According to Wohlers Associates (as cited in Morgan Stanley, 2013), thermoplastics used in 3D printing may cost as much as $175-250/kg compared to $2-3/kg for plastics used in injection moulding.[69]
- Finished products made by 3D printers often have a coarseness about them; they just don't have the quality that products made using traditional methods possess.
- 3D printing is not new technology. It has been around since 1984, so why has the media suddenly seized on it? The argument says that once the

---

[68] Why 3D Printing Is Overhyped (I Should Know, I Do It For a Living) http://gizmodo.com/why-3d-printing-is-overhyped-i-should-know-i-do-it-fo-508176750

[69] http://marscommons.marsdd.com/3dprinting/tech-trends-new-applications/#sthash.jP1I66mY.dpuf

realisation that 3D printing is old technology sinks in, the media fad will fizzle away.

- They add to that another impediment to the innovation process. Regulation and safety concerns. The argument continues: cars or aircraft will never be primarily 3D printed on a mass scale, because safety regulations will prove to be an insurmountable hurdle.

Alternatively, we can look at the world's famous consultancies and research companies. In a report published looking at disruptive technologies, McKinsey listed 3D printing at number nine in its list of technologies. Gartner has 3D printing riding neat the top of its hype cycle.

Or take these words, stated by Nomura's James Kim: "Recent market optimism about the 'Third Industrial Revolution' potential of 3D printing is overdone, given uncertain growth potential in the consumer market, limited pragmatic applications, and a lack of mass-production ability." [70]

Or consider these words stated by Jim Woodcock, group editor and conference director at Rapid News Communications Group[71]. He said: "The mainstream media have just discovered 3D printing and they are totally in love with it." He added: "The trouble is that because the mainstream media, by-and-large, must appeal to the lowest common denominator, the resulting coverage is at best hugely over simplified and at worst out and out lies."

---

[70] http://www.3ders.org/articles/20131209-3d-printing-hype-overdone-says-nomura-kim.html

[71] http://diginnmmu.com/opinion/3d-printing-dont-believe-the-hype-704

But then again, it is perhaps unfair to call Mr Woodcock a sceptic. He also suggested sticking with the technology. He says there is more to the technology than you see in the news and suggests it could become very important.

Or, returning to Nick Allen he drew an analogy between 3D printers and bread making machines popular in homes in the 1990s. For a while it all seemed great, cooking enthusiasts were delighted with the wonderful bread, with its tantalising aromas, that they created by dint of their own efforts. Yet, suggests Mr Allen, a few weeks later the bread maker was back in the cupboard and the former advocates of making bread at home returned to buying it from a shop. He suggested that most of us would rather go out and buy our bread for say $1, than make it at home for a cost of say $3.

Given what the sceptics say, what is 3D printing good for?
Turkeys don't, as a rule, vote for Christmas, and neither are those who work in 3D printing related areas writing the technology off; they are simply saying they think it is over-hyped.

So, given this more sceptical view, in what ways is 3D printing useful?

- For making prototypes, which in turn may accelerate the speed at which new products are developed.
- For making objects of certain complex geometrical shapes, which would be very hard or even impossible to make using traditional methods.
- For making low run, highly valuable components, such as parts for aircraft. Boeing, for example, uses 3D printers to make 200 parts for ten different types of aircraft. [72] Lockheed Martin is

[72] http://www.mckinsey.com/insights/manufacturing/3-d_printing_takes_shape?cid=other-eml-nsl-mip-mck-oth-1402

implementing 3D printing technology to print titanium satellite parts [73] In the UK, a company called Renishaw has combined with a firm called Empire Cycles to make the world's first bicycle frame made from titanium. The resulting product is impressive, but niche. In an interview, Robin Weston, marketing and applications manager at Renishaw, said that the resulting bike is relevant to "elite cyclists in team GB, or at Manchester velodrome, where squeezing fractions of a second for added performance is a key requirement." [74]

- Customisation: where each product is unique, for example in the case of Renishaw/ Empire Cycles a rider's name can be built into the bike's frame.

- Medical applications: perhaps one of the more interesting, and important applications of 3D printing is in the area of printing parts for the human body such as hip replacements, or even more spectacularly in merging with stem cell research in technology known as bio-printing. However, an article in *Nature* suggested that 3D printed organs are still decades away from reality. The piece stated, however, that "a more immediate benefit of 3-D printing embryonic stem cells might be the ability to make tissue samples that could be used to accurately test drug compounds for toxicity in humans, without the need for animal testing, according to the researchers."[75]

Glancing at the above list, the Renishaw/Empire titanium bike frame is a good case in point. Renishaw says that there

---

[73] http://www.lockheedmartin.co.uk/us/news/features/2014/1-15-3dmanufacturing.html

[74] Interview conducted by Michael Baxter with Robin Weston 4 March 2014

[75] http://www.nature.com/news/scientists-use-3-d-printer-to-speed-human-embryonic-stem-cell-research-1.12381

are several advantages created by making the frame in this way:

- Rapid iterations: the flexibility to make design improvements right up to production.
- Complex shapes: making it possible to have internal strengthening features.
- Hollow structures.
- Built-in features, such as the rider's name.

In an interview conducted with Robin Weston, he cited a fuel nozzle produced by GE for use in aircrafts made by the 3D printing process as an example of 3D printing being effective.

He says: "GE is looking at producing the nozzle in this way because it gives it cleaner quieter more efficient engines... With traditional manufacturing you can only drill in a straight line, with additive manufacturing you can go around corners." That is the key point. 3D printing enables you to produce complex shapes that would be very hard to produce using traditional methods. The GE fuel nozzle produced by 3D printing is far more expensive than the traditional nozzle, but it benefits in terms of fuel saving enabled by the new shape, which outweighs the extra component costs. He said: "Only in the last 3 or 4 years have people looked at using additive manufacturing because it can make more efficient components."

Mr Weston also emphasizes the relevance of 3D printing in areas such as facial reconstruction, where it can be used to make components used in surgical procedures to ensure the components fit properly. He also cites, as an example, dental implants, such as small crowns, as being a perfect example of where 3D printing could be used.

So, the emphasis is one of subtlety. Because 3D printed objects can be made to shapes that may very difficult or even impossible to make using traditional methods, and because such shapes can be tailor made, they can be more expensive than the product they replace, but offer benefits that can provide long term cost savings.

As for the idea of a 3D printer shop on every street corner, making objects for the public as and when there is a demand for them, he is not so sure. That does seem to be the general attitude within the industry.

To encapsulate what the 3D printing industry appears to be saying on one sentence: "3D printing is useful technology as far as it goes, but it is over-hyped."

The transformational phase of 3D printing
In the introduction, we stated that there are three phases in the technology cycle: the exuberant phase, the sceptical phase, and the transformational phase. Right now, it appears that 3D printing is migrating from the exuberant phase to the sceptical phase.

The history of innovation is replete with such scepticism. The supposed words of Thomas Watson, chairman of IBM, saying in 1943: "I think there is a world market for maybe five computers," illustrates the problem.

Such scepticism explains, at least in part, why we have innovator's dilemma. Pragmatic business people, focusing on what the client wants and looking realistically at the state of technology, make pronouncements about how new technology is over-hyped; how expectations have got ahead of themselves; how in the real world things are different. Yet within a few years, these same pragmatic business people find they no longer have a business to run.

That is the nature of technology. We overestimate how quickly it will develop, but underestimate the impact it will eventually have.

Consider this possibility. The 3D printing sceptics are wrong. The technology will, in fact, prove to be the key driver of the next industrial revolution. Business leaders who embrace the sceptical view of 3D printing may find they lead their companies into bankruptcy.

The sceptical view of 3D printing may be wrong for several reasons.

Their error may be perfectly described by the idea behind REP RAP, the open standard in 3D printing, founded by Bath University's Adrian Bowyer in 2005.

The idea of an open standard is important because it enables mass participation in the innovation process. This is a game changer.

The latest iterations of the REP RAP 3D printer can partially re-print themselves. In an interview, Mr Bowyer said that about half of the components are printable by REP RAP machines and that the components you cannot make with a 3D printer are easy to obtain, and can be bought in DIY stores. [76]

It is easy to be critical, and postulate that if REP RAP machines can only print half the components required to make another unit, that is not the same thing as saying 3D printing can now create 3D printers themselves. But instead, see the REP RAP project as a work in progress, and you can start to envisage how this story will change.

---

[76] Interview with Adrian Bowyer conducted by Michael Baxter on 17 February.

Mr Bowyer feels that much of the scepticism aimed at 3D printing is indicative of a lack of imagination. He gave an ear of wheat as an example, saying: "This is fabulously complicated, but costs virtually nothing to make." But Mr Bowyer emphasized that wheat is self-replicating.

So, rather than comparing the 3D printing industry with existing manufacturing processes, compare it with the most sophisticated manufacturing factory ever – nature. The sophistication of nature lies with self-replication, and with evolution.

Nature has made materials with a manufacturing process that modern day manufacturing techniques can only envy.

Evolution is not a predictable process in the sense that you can never say what it will produce. However, it is predictable in the sense that you know it will produce something remarkable – you just don't know what.

With the development of 3D printers that can make 3D printers, the ingenuity of humankind will be given the freedom to express its creativity like never before. 3D printers will enable individuals, working from their home, their garage, or their shed, to experiment and improvise ideas, like never before in history.

Bill Gates and Steve Jobs started in this way. They changed the world, because the technology made it possible back in the 1970s. 3D printing provides similar opportunities, but more so. The result will be unpredictable, but predictably innovative.

Adrian Bowyer says the view that 3D printing is not applicable to the mass market is "completely mistaken." While it is the case that we have our newspapers delivered to us, rather than printed on our own desktop top printer is not the point. The benefit to the end user of printing his or her own copy of a newspaper is not particularly significant. That's why the technology has not been developed.

He said that most engineers by their nature are conservative and they see things from a technological point of view, but perhaps they should be considering how nature constructs things. He takes as an example wood. Wood is essentially made from cellulose (the main structural fibre of the plant kingdom) hemicellulose, lignin and pectin. He says: "Wood works because evolution has arranged the components in a fabulously clever way." The process is analogous to 3D printing, with cellulose arranged like a fibre, and lignin the glue.

He says: "3D printing is the first technology which allows us to organise materials in three dimensions at the microscope level and means you can get different materials from polymers of sugars and create anything that nature can create, from a leaf to a tree trunk." He says it will theoretically be able to make anything nature can make with the exception of bones, which have added complexity.

Pete Basiliere is a research director at Gartner, and is also the company's 3D printing guru. He doesn't deny that right now the technology is over-hyped, but he sees that as a short or medium term issue. In an interview,[77] he said: "Within ten years, our view is that it will be widely accepted, widely used." He says that we are about five years away from "the technology [being] readily used by consumers." On the enterprise side, he says: "This is already on its way," and "the only thing holding it back is low adoption rate." He predicts widespread adoption within three to five years.

---

[77] Interview with Pete Basiliere conducted by Michael Baxter on 11 March 2014.

He cites the hearing aid industry as an example of an industry already heavily influenced by 3D printers. "The hearing aid is pretty well saturated," he says and predicts that the "dental industry is not far behind, because it lends itself to customisation."

Where Gartner gets really interesting is in its prediction that by 2016 it is likely that there will be a new consumer application that will create what it calls a 'compelling need' for 3D printing; one that will drive market growth. Furthermore, Gartner believes that for the market to take off in earnest, it needs to be propelled by "something that the consumer can only acquire by producing it on a 3D printer at home."　There are currently some consumer applications that use 3D printing - personalized and unique toys and gifts, jewellery and avatars, school projects and hobby items, but these aren't sufficient to make that much difference at the moment.

Gartner says: "Our thinking is that [the compelling application] would arise from work done by makers and other enthusiasts who push the envelope of consumer 3D printing uses and be enabled by manufacturers who develop "plug-and-print" devices." [78]

Or to put it another way, 3D printing needs its killer application. We don't know what this app will be. We don't know for sure whether it will emerge in 2016, 2017, or 2026, but 3D printing gives scope for the human imagination to make things like no technology before has done. We cannot predict what the imagination will invent, but we can predict that the human imagination will do wonderful things when given the tools to make it reality.

Mr Basiliere said: "3D printing enables companies to move from design for manufacturing to manufacturing of the

---

[78] Basiliere, Pete, The Future of 3D Printing, Gartner, February 26 2014

design. We are very good at taking an idea and figuring out how to mass produce it. In order to do that we employ a technique called design for manufacturing. With 3D printing, because you can print one-off items, you can make the design that the consumer wanted in the first place. This is a major shift, because now you can manufacture in units of one, or at least very small volumes."

Before we close on the topic of 3D printing, there is another point.

Sceptics point to the idea that the technology is not new.

It is odd that they should make this argument. Computer technology was not new when Apple launched the iPod or iPhone. But that is not the point. Over the previous few decades, it had advanced, one step at a time, so that by the turn of the millennium it had reached a level of power that made the dreams of Steve Jobs viable.

Another parallel with 3D printing and the computer industry in particular is 2D printing. There was a time when a decent laser printer was too expensive for mass home usage. Desktop publishers working from home often used a local printing company to print out their work. However, as the cost of printers fell, this changed. The advances in the 2D printing industry may not have removed the need for mass scale printing companies, but they have changed the way in which individuals and companies print documents, presentations, and newsletters with low print runs. In an attempt to suggest 3D printing is over-hyped, by drawing similarities with 2D printing and its limitations, the sceptics shoot themselves in the foot. The fact is that the paper printing industry has been transformed by technology, and the desktop printing market revolutionised the way in which companies presented themselves – at least they did until the internet developed even more compelling presentation tools.

It will be like that with 3D printing too.

Powering the new industrial revolutions

Rubbish and nonsense —these are the two words that seem to be applied most often when the topic of energy comes up. Those who dismiss the idea of a new industrial revolution make a simple, but eloquent point. The innovations associated with steam powered the first industrial revolution. The use of electricity, oil and gas made the industrial strides of the 20th Century possible. In short, fossil fuels were the means by which we emerged from the mass poverty of an earlier era into the modern age. But, thanks in part to manmade or anthropogenic climate change, and also to a kind of Malthusian logic, which says the growth in the world's population is exceeding planet Earth's capacity to meet this population's energy requirements, we are heading for a lurch backwards; back to poverty and an era of de-industrialisation. Those holding the more extreme sceptical views, say that we are heading back to the Stone Age.

The harsh reality, continues this argument, is that we will have to become used to a world without growth; sustainable economics means that each generation must accept they will be no better off than the previous generation. As for the idea of a new industrial revolution, the logic asks how it will be possible to charge the billions of devices and processing power required to enable an internet of things. From where will the robotic devices draw their energy, and how can 3D printing, which is more power intensive than traditional manufacturing, be viable without a cheap source of energy? A new industrial revolution? Rubbish and nonsense!

A subset of this argument presents us with the idea of peak oil. Peak oil is supposed to apply to that date when the world's supply of oil goes into decline. The combination of peak oil at a time when China's thirst for oil seems virtually unquenchable; at a time when the demand from a rapidly growing emerging world includes highly populous countries such as India, Indonesia, Brazil, Mexico, the Philippines, and Vietnam, means that the price of oil and with all other sources of energy will inevitably head north faster than a polar bear retreating from melting ice caps.

But economic theory may present us with one flaw in that logic, and the story of convergence and humanity's incredible ability to innovate may provide additional flaws.

In fact, just as the industrial revolutions of the 18th, 19th and 20th centuries were powered by ever cheaper fuel, so will the industrial revolutions of the 21st century.

First, consider the economics. When demand rises faster than supply, price goes up, but so too does investment. When supply rises faster than demand, prices fall and so does investment. The economic cycle is charged, at least in part, by the time lags that occur as the markets try to align the forces of demand and supply.

So take oil. In the late 1990s and early 2000s the price of oil was cheap, very cheap In December 1998, the price of crude oil per barrel was just $8.64. In June 2008, it was $126. In December 2013, it was $86.[79] In other words, between the end of 1998 and the eve of the banking crisis of 2008, the price of oil rose 15 fold. Most said the rise in the price of oil was down to the increase in demand for so called black gold from China. This explanation is too simplistic and misses a key point.

---

[79] http://www.ioga.com/Special/crudeoil_Hist.htm

When oil was going for just $8.64, investment into exploration and into new techniques for drilling for the valuable resource was inevitably much lower than it would have been had price been higher. This lack of investment led to restrictions in supply, meaning that as demand rose, supply struggled to keep pace, and prices rocketed. Under different circumstances, when price rises, investment increases, new oil finds follow and advances in techniques for drilling for oil advance at a rapid pace.

This is the pattern of the oil industry. The price of oil fluctuates over time. For example, in the early 1980s the price approached $40 a barrel. After adjusting for inflation, oil was at a similar price level in the late 1970s and early 1980s as it was in 2008. As a result, investment rose, and the emphasis shifted to energy efficiency – in 1973, President Nixon proposed a national speed limit in the US of just 50 miles per hour, for example. [80]

In 2008 things were different. The credit crunch followed by the banking crisis of 2008 meant that there was a lack of funding for investment, and a high level of uncertainty. Indeed, in the wake of the crisis, the price of oil fell sharply. As a result, the normal surge in investment that accompanies high oil prices of did not occur – not immediately – and the price of oil remained high (relative to the late 1990s) for a much longer period than is normal for the oil cycle. This fuelled support for the idea of peak oil.

But the oil cycle didn't die, it was merely pining. In the US, the fracking and shale gas revolution has led to sharp falls in energy prices, which are now underpinning economic recovery. Beyond shale gas there is tight oil, the tar sands of Alberta, and innovations in our ability to extract oil from the

---

[80] http://en.wikipedia.org/wiki/National_Maximum_Speed_Law

previously inaccessible places of the Earth, such as beneath the ocean bed, or in the Arctic regions.

The effect of these new sources of oil on the price of energy is not easy to predict; the timings are imprecise. But the idea of peak oil, or at least of us reaching peak oil any time soon, is beginning to look outmoded.

The above dialogue is not meant to suggest that the recent advances in the oil industry are necessarily a good thing – not if you believe in anthropogenic climate change that is – but merely to point out the flaw in at least some of the logic that dismisses the idea of a new industrial revolution.

But oil has a rival; a utopian dream is emerging, one that not only provides us with the energy to charge the new industrial revolution, but can do so with no carbon emissions (discounting the manufacture of the devices). This energy source can be used without significantly draining the earth of its natural resources, and its price may steadily fall, ultimately providing the world with near free energy.

There are no shortages of cynics who dismiss this, but they forget about convergence.

According to *Scientific American*, in 88 minutes the energy beamed down upon the earth from the sun provides as much energy as humanity consumes in one year. In 112 hours, it provides 35 zettajoules of energy – as much energy as is contained in all proven reserves of oil, coal and natural gas. The publication states: "If humanity could capture one tenth of one percent of the solar energy striking the earth...we would have access to six times as much energy as we consume in all forms today." [81]

---

[81] http://blogs.scientificamerican.com/guest-blog/2011/03/16/smaller-cheaper-faster-does-moores-law-apply-to-solar-cells/

As we said in chapter five, the cost of energy generated by photovoltaic cells per watt has in fact fallen from $76.67 in 1977 to $0.74 in 2013. According to GTM research: "The US installed 4,751 megawatts of solar PV in 2013, up 41 percent over 2012 and nearly fifteen times the amount installed in 2008. The cost to install solar fell throughout the year [2013], ending the year 15 per cent below the mark set at the end of 2012."[82]

Take this quote from a report by Citi, entitled *Energy Darwinism*: [83] "The rate at which the price of solar panels has reduced has exceeded all expectations, resulting in cost parity being achieved in certain areas much more quickly." It carries on to argue that there is no sign of the era of these rapidly falling prices coming to an end, while conventional fossil fuels are likely to become more expensive.

To reiterate, the cost of a unit of energy generated from solar panels in 2013 was roughly 1 per cent of the cost in 1977.

So, why has the cost of solar fallen so fast and will the fall continue?

The Citi report came up with its own theory. It says solar panels have more in common "with a semiconductor wafer (indeed they are basically the same thing) and the technology sector than they do with mechanical electricity generation equipment." In other words, the very same factors that have enabled computers to develop so rapidly apply to solar too – solar power is falling in price rapidly because it employs similar technology to computers, and just as they benefit from Moore's Law, so can solar energy

---

[82] http://www.greentechmedia.com/articles/read/u.s.-solar-market-grows-41-has-record-year-in-2013
[83] https://ir.citi.com/Jb89SJMmf%2BsAVK2AKa3QE5EJwb4fvI5UUpIDOICiGOOk0NV2CqNI%2FPDLJqxidz2VAXXAXFB6fOY%3D

benefit from something very similar – or so goes the inference.

Yet such a view is controversial. In 2011, Nobel Laureate Paul Krugman [84]penned a piece for the *New York Times* in which he said: "We are, or at least we should be, on the cusp of an energy transformation, driven by the rapidly falling cost of solar power. That's right, solar power." Although Mr Krugman did not explicitly say solar has its own version of Moore's Law, he implied it. His article created a storm of protest.

One article by William Tucker that did the rounds of the internet stated: "The average amount of solar energy falling on a square meter of earth is 400 watts. It will never be any different." He said that at the moment we can covert around a quarter of this energy into electricity, and "if we could raise this conversion to a 35 per cent – 40 per cent increase – it would be a technological marvel. That's a lot different than doubling every two years." [85]

It is indeed the case that solar can never literally benefit from Moore's Law. But earlier in this book it was suggested that if we use Moore's Law as a metaphor to describe any rate of rapid technological evolution, then such a phrase is apt.

Using an engineer 's definition of Moore's Law, even adapting it as a metaphor to apply to areas other than integrated circuits, it may be true to say that solar energy can never have its own version of Moore's Law, but if we use an economist's definition the story changes.

Solar power generated by photovoltaic panels may be restricted by the energy falling on any given space, and can

---

[84] http://www.nytimes.com/2011/11/07/opinion/krugman-here-comes-solar-energy.html?_r=0

[85] http://spectator.org/articles/36579/paul-krugman-flunks-moores-law

never enjoy more than 100 per cent efficiency, but the potential for it to fall in price is considerable, and as far as an economist is concerned, that is what efficiency is.

There are as many theories as there are days in the year as to how long it will be before solar reaches grid parity relative to conventional fuels, and indeed how much its cost will fall from there. What we can say is that grid parity already exists in some parts of the world, and there is no sign of the period of falling cost coming to an end.

However, this is just the beginning of the story. New technologies such as solar paint [86] provide the potential to have buildings covered in solar power generating devices that are virtually invisible. The prospect of windows that are completely transparent, and that can be used as a means of generating solar energy beckons. [87] Because paint and windows carry material cost anyway, it is possible that in time adding the ability to generate solar power, may add little, if anything, to the cost of providing certain essential materials. Looking beyond that, some researchers are investigating having solar panels in orbit, beaming the energy captured to stations on the earth via lasers. [88]

There is even technology under development for providing MEMS with the energy they need from solar, with tiny solar energy generating devices forming parts of the MEMS themselves, freeing them from the requirement to obtain power from external sources. [89]

---

[86] http://cleantechnica.com/2013/05/15/caution-wet-solar-power-new-affordable-solar-paint-research/
[87] http://www.newenergytechnologiesinc.com/technology/solarwindow
[88] http://www.wired.co.uk/news/archive/2013-10/02/japan-solar-energy and http://energy.gov/articles/space-based-solar-power
[89]
http://robotics.eecs.berkeley.edu/~pister/publications/dissertations/Belle wColby.pdf

But while solar power is exciting, and offers great potential, at the moment wind power is cheaper, and is already at grid parity in far more locations than solar power. Although it does not benefit from the same learning rate as solar,[90] there are reasons to anticipate further advances in the efficiency of wind power. For one thing, advances in composite materials, such as carbon fibre, should boost the wind industry.

This is a classic example of convergence. According to GBI Research, global carbon fibre demand will hit 153,700 tons in 2020, climbing from 52,500 tons in 2012 – a massive increase of 193 per cent in just eight years. [91] The airline industry initially fuelled the increase in demand for carbon fibre, particularly the Boeing 787 Dreamliner and the Airbus A380.[92] When it comes to certain technologies – such as integrated circuits, 3D printing, solar power, and composite materials – the laws of economics are turned on their head. Economic theory tells us that as demand rises so does price. We now know that as demand rises for certain technologies, so does R&D, as do technological advances, and as a result price falls. Carbon fibre is set to benefit in such a way, with a knock-on effect on the materials used to make the blades for wind turbines – gradually replacing glass fibre reinforced polymer will confer greater rigidity, lower weight, and reduced cost. Beyond that, the future of wind power may be above the clouds, as companies look to develop wind turbines that float high in the sky, like kites or glider aircraft. Last year, for example, Google bought Makani Wind Power, [93] which produces the Makani Airborne Wind Turbine. In its

[90] A learning rate applies to the cost of generating energy as the user base, say of wind turbines, doubles
[91]

http://www.windpowerengineering.com/design/mechanical/blades/wind-energy-blowing-life-into-global-carbon-fiber-industry/
[92] http://composite.about.com/od/applications/a/What-Is-The-787-Dreamliner.htm
[93] http://www.businessinsider.com/google-buys-makani-power-2013-5

words, this is "a tethered wing that generates power by flying in large circles where the wind is stronger and more consistent." Makani says its product "eliminates 90 per cent of the material used in conventional wind turbines, and can access winds both at higher altitudes and above deep waters offshore." It continues: "Our goal is the utility-scale deployment of airborne turbines in offshore wind farms."

In addition, research is being carried out into vertical axis wind turbines to make energy capture more efficient and to ensure that fewer non-renewable resources go into their manufacture.[94]

Yet, despite the advances that are occurring in renewables, a mood of scepticism permeates much of the media and the general public, which in turn is reflected back by politicians kowtowing to erroneous perceptions instead of taking a measured and impartial stance.

Many politicians seem to have picked up some kind of speech impediment, in which they find it impossible to utter the words 'wind farm' without prefixing them with the word 'awful'. In August 2013, the shocking revelation that wind farms are not very effective when it is not windy made headline news. The media proclaimed that on some occasions wind farms around the UK could not even generate enough power to make a cup of tea. The Twittersphere was away with the story for a couple of days – yet curiously no mention was made of the fact that gas powered generation stations were not very effective when they shut down for repair work, yet such an occurrence (which is quite common) is analogous to the idea that wind farms aren't effective when it is not windy. On the same day Maf Smith — a spokesperson for RenewableUK — said: "Government figures show that in 2012 , more than 11 per cent of the UK's electricity came from renewable sources,

[94] http://www.carbonbrainprint.org.uk/pdf/CBrainprint-CS02-NOVA.pdf

with wind providing the lion's share."[95] Curiously, his statement garnered far fewer headlines.

But the greatest untruth told about renewables relates to the idea that that they are doomed technologies because they are not reliable – that's the idea that because wind power doesn't work when it isn't windy and solar doesn't work when it's dark, they are destined for the graveyard.

This argument is flawed, and it is flawed for two reasons:

Firstly, the more widespread wind and solar become, the more reliable they are. Critics focus on Denmark, and say that wind power has proven too expensive because of the cost of providing back-up power in case the wind stops blowing. They forget that Denmark is a tiny country. When wind power is situated over a larger geographic area, it becomes less likely to shut down en masse because of a sudden becalming of the winds. They forget that even conventional sources of power are not reliable and shut down on occasions with no notice. "The IEA estimates that the total integration costs of increasing the supply of intermittent renewable energy sources to be $5-$25/MWh."[96] These costs are not prohibitive.

The issue of renewable energy being ineffective at certain times goes away once we crack the problem of efficient energy storage.

Earlier in this book we wrote about how certain technologies designed to offer grid level energy storage are

[95] http://www.investmentandbusinessnews.co.uk/economic-news/the-wind-farm-bias/5131

[96] https://ir.citi.com/Jb89SJMmf%2BsAVK2AKa3QE5EJwb4fvI5UUplD0ICiGO Ok0NV2CqNI%2FPDLJqxidz2VAXXAXFB6fOY%3D

looking very interesting: namely Lightsail, Professor Don Sadowaym's progress in liquid metal batteries, and a rechargeable battery that uses a combination of fresh and salt water.

The point that needs to be borne in mind is that grid level energy storage has not been a priority until recently. As long as we obtained our energy from fossil fuels, batteries were not important – indeed what is oil or coal, other than an efficient form of energy storage?
But things are changing.

First, consider a facility in Spain called Gemasolar, which generates power via a process called concentrating solar power – which essentially involves focusing solar rays on a certain area to create steam to drive a turbine. Surplus heat generated is stored in a molten salt tank, providing a source of energy that can be tapped into for up to 15 hours. In short, the Gemasolar plant is the world's first solar power facility that can provide energy 24 hours a day.[97] While the cost of energy generated in this way may still be on the pricy side, the point is that this is new technology, and the cost is likely to fall, and probably fall rapidly.

Even more compelling is the story of Elon Musk and his plans to invest $5.1 billion in a lithium ion battery factory called Gigafactory.[98] Elon Musk is the co-founder of PayPal, and amongst others is the force behind Tesla cars, the company which makes electric cars, and whose stock has been soaring at the time of writing. Musk has said that he

[97] http://www.forbes.com/sites/tonyseba/2011/06/21/the-worlds-first-baseload-247-solar-power-plant/

[98] Musk's $5 Billion Tesla Gigafactory May Start Bidding War http://www.bloomberg.com/news/2014-02-27/musk-s-5-billion-tesla-gigafactory-may-start-bidding-war.html.
And Planned 2020 Gigafactory Production Exceeds 2013 Global Production, http://www.teslamotors.com/sites/default/files/blog_attachments/gigafactory.pdf

aims to cut the cost of Tesla cars by half within three to four years, but he needs to cut battery costs to do this, hence his investment into a massive new battery factory.

Meanwhile, a company called Solar City has announced a project to build lithium-ion batteries designed to work alongside photovoltaic panels made by Tesla.[99] In short, batteries designed for one purpose – electric cars – are being applied to another purpose – energy storage to accompany solar panels – ensuring homes can access energy generated by solar panels, for example attached to their roofs, at night time. Tesla says: "By the end of the first year of volume production of our mass market vehicle, we expect the Gigafactory will have driven down the per kWh cost of our battery pack by more than 30 per cent."[100]

The story of Tesla and Solar City is a classic example of convergence. The development of energy storage in this way has potential innovator's dilemma written all over it. But then again, the story of lithium ion has been like that from the start. Innovator's dilemma tells us technology developed for one purpose, can become more efficient, and in time disrupt other industries, or sectors within an industry. For example as companies making 12 inch disk drives for mainframe computers were outcompeted by companies which made nine disc drives for mini-computers and then the cycle repeated as we moved to 5¼ inch disc drives for desk top PCs. Demand for lithium ion batteries began to rise with the growing popularity of laptop PCs and mobile phones. It accelerated further with the emergence of smart phones and tablets. The technology has become more efficient and now its relevance to electric cars and running alongside solar panels has emerged.

[99] http://www.solarcity.com/residential/energy-storage.aspx
[100] http://www.teslamotors.com/blog/gigafactory

In July 2012, McKinsey wrote: "Our analysis indicates that the price of a complete automotive lithium-ion battery pack could fall from $500 to $600 per kilowatt hour (kWh) today to about $200 per kWh by 2020 and to about $160 per kWh by 2025." [101]

The industrial revolution after next

What about the one after?

Singularity assumes that things will accelerate, and that if you track the course of technology evolution on a graph, then the shape of the resulting curve is exponential. So if that is right, expect industrial revolutions to occur with ever more frequency.

This may be right, or alternatively, we may hit a kind of plateau; a point where the curve flattens.

Technology sceptics might say we are already at the flat part of the curve. At the other extreme, you have those who warn that singularity will descend upon us faster than even science fiction predicts.

---

[101]

http://www.mckinsey.com/insights/energy_resources_materials/battery_technology_charges_ahead

They may say that if the curve ever goes flat, it will do so in some future era when the likes of you and me have gone the way of dodos and the Tyrannosaurus Rex. A third interpretation might say that we are not at the flat bit yet, but we may be close.

Whatever the reality, this book would like to make a prediction. The industrial revolution empowered by the technologies described previously won't be the last one; it won't even be the last one in the next two or three decades.

Another industrial revolution will occur, and its impact will be even more dramatic than the one talked about above.

But timing is not precise. For that matter, the timing of the next industrial revolution led by the internet of things, big data, robotics and 3D printing and powered by advances in energy technology, is not precise.

The two revolutions may merge; the ending of one may overlap with the beginning of the next.

Alternatively, some of the technologies described above may take longer to gain full mass market commerciality than is widely assumed, and some of the next generation technologies that we will describe shortly may occur quicker than expected.

To reiterate, it is often said that we overestimate how quickly new technology will be developed, but underestimate the impact it will have when it does finally emerge.

Two types of technologies, which overlap with each other, combined with the advances described previously, will change things in a quite profound way.
These two technologies are artificial intelligence and nanotechnology.

You cannot fully separate them. Graphene is an example of nanotechnology, but when, or if, it is manufactured in mass quantities and researchers work out how to apply it in the areas where it has promise, computers may immediately become faster and more powerful, perhaps to the tune of a one thousand fold increase in processing power. Energy storage will be revolutionised; solar power transformed.

Some nanomaterials will make solar panels longer lasting, thinner, and more flexible.

Within the sphere of 3D printing, nanotechnology offers the promise of applying additive manufacturing at the atomic scale.

Take this quote from MEMSnet: "Some experts believe that nanotechnology promises to allow us to put...every atom or molecule in the place and position desired – that is, exact positional control for assembly." It suggests that in this way we make almost any structure or material consistent with the laws of physics." [102]

Alternatively, take this abstract published by the University of Texas: "The narrow choice of materials used in Additive Manufacturing (AM) remains a key limitation to more

---

[102] http://www.memsnet.org/mems/what_is.html

advanced systems. Nanomaterials offer the potential to advance AM materials through modification of their fundamental material properties." [103]

The point about converging 3D printing and nanomaterials is that it provides the potential to apply additive manufacturing at the atomic level to create just about anything.

If this dream was realised, it would not just be a game changer; it would be far more dramatic than that.

Back in 2004, at a conference entitled 'Advanced Technology and the Future of American Technology' it was said that: "Highly miniaturized, functional, and efficient electronics devices, and precise and selective biomolecular materials are part of...[the future]." But it suggested convergence was the key, as scientific and engineering disciplines, business managers, policy makers, and educators came together. The quote continued: "**Advancing these developments depends on the ability to foster multidisciplinary interconnections.**"[104]

It is the last sentence that demands particular attention because it supports a key premise of this book. Technological advances are occurring from convergence; from different technologies and disciplines coming together, and in their mix creating something new, and indeed something wonderful.

103

http://utwired.engr.utexas.edu/lff/symposium/proceedingsArchive/pubs/Manuscripts/2011/2011-56-Ivanova.pdf

[104] http://scitechstory.com/2010/06/01/a-coming-marriage-additive-manufacturing-and-nanotechnology/

No medium in history can match the internet for its ability to support convergence. This is the point that technology sceptics miss. You may not be able to eat the internet. You may not be able to wear it, neither can you use it to travel real distances, but it does provide us with a feast of information; it can enable scientists to dress up their ideas to appeal to a broader audience, and it can transport our minds into collaborative ventures spread across the world.

That is why we are having a new industrial revolution. The internet, by spreading ideas, has made this revolution possible.

The internet is set to expand our ability to converge in a unique way and which has no precedent. If you combine the internet with artificial intelligence, you suddenly have an enhanced, more sophisticated way of searching for information and ideas. Thanks to AI, we can provide our mind with a new set of tools, as important in shaping our ability to conjure up complex thoughts as writing once was.

We all know that if you are working on something tricky, it often helps to write it down, freeing up the mind for reasoning. Writing down our thoughts can help put all the information we require to make complex decisions in some kind of logical order. A phrase that has crept into popular usage to describe how paper and pen can help us with our reasoning is mind mapping. It is not unreasonable to assume that once most of us learned how to write, our ability to reason in more complex ways was enhanced.

However, the greatest tool for augmenting our cognitive ability since the invention of writing is evolving, and they call it AI.

We cannot rule out the more terrifying predictions about AI by science fiction writers, and we must be alert to the dangers of their reality occurring faster than we anticipate, but AI, by helping us tap into the power of the crowd and by enhancing our mental abilities, can give us the ability to develop strategies to ensure it is a force for good; for progress leading to a utopian dream, rather than one in which the only dreaming is done by androids, and involves counting of electric sheep.

You can't fully separate artificial intelligence from nanotechnologies, because it is the advances in nanotechnologies that may well create the extra computing power to realise the aspirations of those working in artificial intelligence.

In early 2014, Google bought the UK AI company DeepMind. Researching into what DeepMind does is a revelation in itself; a revelation in tease that is. At the time of the Google acquisition, the DeepMind web site had less information on it than some business cards.

At the time of the purchase, various media reports cited the words of Carnegie Mellon Professor Larry Wasserman, who had previously met up with DeepMind's founder Demis Hassabis, and he said that the company was trying "to build a system that thinks."[105]

There may be a more prosaic explanation for what DeepMind is up to, and why Google bought it.

In an interview at a gathering of TED in March 2014, Google co-founder and CEO Larry Page placed his emphasis on one word: search. "Computing is kind of a mess," he said. "Your computer doesn't know where you are. It doesn't know

[105] The Future of Machine Learning (and the End of the World?)
http://normaldeviate.wordpress.com/2012/10/30/the-future-of-machine-learning-and-the-end-of-the-world/

what you're doing. It doesn't know what you know." He said: "To change that, we need better search."

Alternatively, we can examine patents filed by DeepMind. In January 2014, the company filed two patents: one for 'reverse image search', the other relating to improving image search further still by homing in on a small area of an image.

The truth is that humans can do things that computers find almost impossible. We can recognise faces for one thing.

Take the example of Jewish Russian journalist Solomon V Shereshevskii. If you think you have a good memory, prepare to acknowledge a person who the media have christened as 'the man who could not forget.' The story of Mr Shereshevskii begins with a talk given by the neuropsychologist Alexander Luria. The frantic scribbling of journalists, the smell of ink on paper, dominated the room as the great Luria enunciated his theories. But at the back of the room, one hack sat listening, no pen in hand, no notes. After the talk, Luria cornered the journalist, and upon questioning, to his astonishment found that the fellow, who you may have guessed was none other than Shereshevskii, could recite Luria's talk, word for word; he didn't need to take notes because of his extraordinary memory. Remarkably, Shereshevskii didn't even realise that his gift for memory was unique, or indeed unusual.

It was too good an opportunity for Luria, and Shereshevskii became the subject of much of the neuropsychologist's work.

It turned out that Shereshevskii's memory was born out of his imagination. Objects, ideas, and names took on a distinct shape and texture in Shereshevskii's mind. Shereshevskii described a musical tone sung by Luria as "looking like pinkish fireworks with a rough texture and an ugly taste of briny pickles". He remembered because he had unwittingly developed a sophisticated system of mnemonics.

"One time," said Shereshevskii, "I went to buy some ice cream... I walked over to the vendor and asked her what kind of ice cream she had. 'Fruit ice cream,' she said. But she answered in such a tone that a whole pile of coals, of black cinders, came bursting out of her mouth, and I couldn't bring myself to buy any ice cream after she had answered in that way." [106]

Of course, computers can have even better memories than Shereshevskii. But there is one thing they have in common with the late Russian journalist. They are, or in the case of Shereshevskii were, both lousy with faces.

It is said that if someone coughed while Shereshevskii was looking at their face, then his memory of that face would always be linked with the sight of them coughing. Alas, he was unable to recognise this person, unless they were coughing – or so it is said. This became his problem. We never look exactly the same twice. It appears Shereshevskii's memory was too good. He remembered fine detail, but when the details on a face changed, he struggled with recognising that face.[107]

We do have a problem here. Shereshevskii died in 1958. The studies of his memory and his shortcomings were not rigorous, and much of the information we have is anecdotal.

[106] http://realdoctorstu.com/2010/10/24/the-man-who-could-never-forget/

[107] http://incorrectpleasures.blogspot.co.uk/2011/09/lurias-s-synaesthete-wasnt-face-blind.html

and the Ape that spoke, by John McCrone Picador, 1990

The story of Shereshevskii serves as a good metaphor for explaining the limitation of computers.

As humans, when we see faces, play sport, or listen to music our brain takes shortcuts. Without those shortcuts, our memories would be a tangle of detail, and the processing power required to sort through that detail would be too great.

This is why we have CAPTCHA, that annoying system of oddly shaped letters we have to translate before we can log into certain web sites. Now researchers into AI at a company called Vicarious claim to have cracked the problem of how a computer can read the characters in CAPTCHA. "It is easy to create an illusion of intelligence by using large datasets," says D Scott Phoenix at Vicarious, A child can easily identify the general shapes of letters, even in the form of CAPTCHA. The human brain is good at generalising. In fact, Phoenix calls this ability to generalise from limited information "the hallmark of intelligence." And Vicarious claims to have developed an algorithm that can recognise patterns.

Phoenix says that most AI systems, such as IBM's famous Watson, rely on brute force, analysing and connecting a massive amount of data. But he says: "The Vicarious algorithms achieve a level of effectiveness and efficiency much closer to actual human brains." [108]

The key to AI appears to lies partly in processing power but also in clever algorithms. How do you find programmers who are adept at writing clever algorithms? The answer may surprise you, because much of the talent that can advance AI algorithms, currently work in the field of video games. It is no coincidence that Demis Hassabis, the brains behind DeepMind, has a background in video and computer games.

---

[108] http://news.vicarious.com/post/65316134613/vicarious-ai-passes-first-turing-test-captcha

And that is why we are set to have another industrial revolution, one powered by nanotechnology and AI, which enhances our acquisition of knowledge and new discoveries.

The only question mark relates to timing. How soon will it happen? Will we see a convenient order, or will the advances of the internet of things, robotics, 3D printing, nanotechnology and AI all blend together, creating a kind of souped-up revolution, a big bang of technology evolution? It may not happen this decade. It may well happen in the next decade, but it will happen within 30 years.

Chapter six: The dawn of the great disruption, a sharing economy

"You say you want a revolution," sung John Lennon. "We are the young generation, and we've got something to say," sung the Monkeys. They were both right, it is just that they were 30 years too soon. The difference, at least in part, is the internet.

Lennon and the individuals who made up the Monkeys were baby boomers. This generation didn't change the world, but their kids might.

They call them the Millennials or Generation Y. They were born between 1976 (some say 1980) and 2001.

John Lennon also said: "We all want to change the world, but when you talk about destruction, don't you know that you can count me out." The millennial generation may not cause destruction, but they will be at the heart of the greatest wave of disruption in human history.

Guy Rigby is the head of entrepreneurs at Smith Williamson. He is also known as something of a guru among technology entrepreneurs in the UK. He said: "They say, if it isn't broken, don't fix it. I say if it isn't broken, break it."

In an interview on Ted in March 2014, Google CEO Larry Page said: "Companies are doing the same incremental thing that they did 50 years ago, 20 years ago. That's not really what we need. Especially in technology, we need revolutionary change, not incremental change."

Rigby says: "We need less evolution, more revolution or something in-between. There are individuals in larger organisations shouting from the roof tops that we need to change, but they are typically not in senior management positions yet."

So how will this change happen? The answer, of course, is in part technology, but the great wave of disruption also has a change in attitude at its heart. The combination of this shift in attitude with modern technology is going to change the world. As we shall see in a future chapter, banks, and the world's great car manufacturers will be rocked to their very foundations; many will go out of business. Indestructible companies, which rise above the business terrain like Californian redwoods, will crumble into dust within a few years.

The baby boomer generation and the following generation like the command and control management approach.[109] The people of this generation usually draw boundaries. The Millennial generation is different; there has been a switch from command and control to collaboration.
There is more than one reason for this, and lots of theories abound. Some put it down to the number of Millennials living with one parent, or same-sex parent families. Such theories look too far, trying to find an explanation when the reason is staring us in the face —or maybe it would be more accurate to say staring us in the Facebook.

The internet, online video games involving participation with users spread all over the world, and social media tools have fostered a new way of looking at things.

This is creating a clash between the Millennial generation and their managers, typically from older generations. 30 per cent of Millennials think it is important that their work is meaningful, whereas only 12 per cent of managers think the

[109] Gartner Research in Lynch, 2008, cited in http://www.kenan-flagler.unc.edu/executive-development/custom-programs/~/media/DF1C11C056874DDA8097271A1ED48662.ashx

same way. 25 per cent of Millennials emphasise a sense of accomplishment, while only 12 per cent of managers feel the same. Only 5 per cent of Millennials say responsibility is important, but 12 per cent of managers feel that way.

Most important of all, while only 28 per cent of Millennials rate high pay as important, 50 per cent of managers said high pay was important.[110]

According to research from Pew: "The typical internet user is more than twice as likely as others to feel that people can be trusted." It also found that users of Facebook "are even more likely to be trusting." It found that a regular Facebook user, that is to say someone who uses the social media tool several times a day, "is 43 per cent more likely than other internet users and more than three times as likely as non-internet users to feel that most people can be trusted."[111]

Guy Rigby says: "There is no doubt the business has become more social. Modern businesses don't understand the thought process of the 'y gens'. It will change," he says, "when the 'y generation' finally climb into positions of authority."

But when that does happen things will change. "They tell me it is evolution," said Lennon. And if that is right, it will be like one of the sudden moments in the story of evolution, such as when the meteorite wiped out the dinosaurs, or an ape stepped from the trees and learnt how to walk, or the Cambrian explosion before that (when within a few million years, or in the blink of an eye from an evolutionary perspective, life on earth was transformed).

---

[110] Rikleen, L. (n.d.). Creating tomorrow's leaders: the expanding roles of Millennials in the workplace. Boston College Center for Work & Family. Chestnut Hill: MA
[111] http://www.pewinternet.org/2011/06/16/social-networking-sites-and-our-lives/

Collaboration

Wind the clock back 30 years and who would have believed Wikipedia would exist? For that matter, who would have believed in the existence of Encarta?

The story from Encyclopaedia Britannica to Encarta to Wikipedia is one of innovator's dilemma   combined with collaboration. When you look at this story, it seems to be quite different, depending on when you look.

Take the year 1996 for example; Encyclopaedia Britannica went bust. Alternatively, look further back to the year 1985; Bill Gates told executives at Microsoft to focus on finding a business partner to develop a CD ROM. The first port of call was Encyclopaedia Britannica. Microsoft was rebuffed. Later that year Larry Grinnell, director of public relations at Britannica, said: "Encyclopaedia Britannica has no plans to be on a home computer. And since the market is so small, only 4 of 5 per cent of households have computers, we would not want to hurt our traditional way of selling."

Encyclopaedia Britannica, as you may know, had kudos. The middle classes wanted to own a set; it said something. It said something about their intellectualism, about how they supported their children. It said they were a family who appreciated education, who wanted the best for their children. It also said they could afford the $2,000 or so it cost to obtain a full set. There is a question mark about how genuine this thirst for knowledge was, however. Encyclopaedia Britannica's own research found that once the initial euphoria of owning a complete set of this prestigious set of books had diminished, people only tended to open a typical encyclopaedia once year. Still they were in good company. "George Washington, Thomas Jefferson, and

Alexander Hamilton all were said to have owned an Encyclopædia Britannica."[112]

The very idea of putting Encyclopaedia Britannica on a CD ROM, or licensing it to an upstart like Microsoft – when Encyclopaedia Britannica could trace its history back to 1768 – seemed like anathema to its publishers. More than one factor stood in the way of the two companies working together. For one thing, CD ROMS were viewed as little more than toys – a form of video game. Note the similarities with the disc drive industry, as incumbent players dismissed new technology. Note also comments made by Adrian Bowyer of REP RAP when he was interviewed for this book: "Many companies in the 3D printing business dismissed REP RAP as little more than a toy."

Other factors stood in the way of Encyclopaedia Britannica and Microsoft coming together. The older company relied on a business model in which salesmen drove the business. "Britannica executives and key decision makers had sold the Encyclopaedia door to door themselves and moved up through the ranks from there."[113] "As one executive said 'anyone who messed with the goose that laid the golden egg would have been shot.'" [114]

This is of course classic innovator's dilemma. It seemed impossible for Encyclopaedia Britannica to embrace computers and CD ROMS. For one thing, the opposition was not really seen as a threat and for another thing the feedback from those in the know, salesmen going door to door, said such a switch was seen as neither necessary nor sensible. Also, to make such a switch, the company's

[112] http://www.slideshare.net/renerojas/case-study-encyclopedia-britannica

[114] http://www.slideshare.net/renerojas/case-study-encyclopedia-britannica

business model would have needed comprehensive upheaval.

Whatever the reasons, the fact is that in 1990 the company had $650 million in revenue. In 1996, it was being sold off for $135 million. [115] The obvious explanation is that Encarta destroyed Encyclopaedia Britannica. A more subtle argument is that the PC was the murderer. PCs, and not encyclopaedias were seen as the route to educating children; it was the new way of learning.

It was a salutary tale. Yet, just a few years later, Encarta, the very product released by Microsoft after Encyclopaedia Britannica turned its corporate nose up at the maker of 'home computers', was in ruins.

In 2007, Microsoft shut Encarta down. Its web site said that encyclopaedias had changed, "People today seek and consume information in considerably different ways than in years past. As part of Microsoft's goal to deliver the most effective and engaging resources for today's consumer, it has made the decision to exit the Encarta business."

Microsoft didn't utter the precise reason, but we all know what the problem was. It failed because of Wikipedia.

Microsoft threw money at its product. It paid academics to write entries, but it could not compete. How could it compete with a product created by an army of volunteers? If Bill Gates had invested his entire fortune in trying to match Wikipedia, with its 4,481,854 entries, [116] he would have been left as a pauper. The issue here is not so much the cost of writing a single article, it is in updating it with regularity.

---

[115] http://www.wired.com/business/2012/03/wikipedia-didnt-kill-brittanica-windows-did/
[116] AS at 29 March 2014)

The real shock delivered by Wikipedia, however, was the way in which it was produced. Its production should have thrown economic theory on its head. Still, as Ronald Reagan said: "An economist is someone who sees something happen in practice and wonders if it would work in theory." [117] The truth is that while Wikipedia is a real world phenomenon, it does not exist in theory. How can it? Economic theory takes no account of the idea of collaboration.

It is odd because evolutionary theory does. How else do you explain us? We are, after all, made up of billions of cells and bacteria. This is the idea behind Richard Dawkins seminal book "The Selfish Gene". [118] As Dawkins said: "Single individual organisms, such as ourselves, are the ultimate embodiment of many mergers." Evolution teaches us that the individual organisms that we are made from are an example of collaboration promoting the interests of each and every one of us. It is a subtle, but important point. In an earlier version of the *Origin of Species*, Charles Darwin did not even refer to the phrase 'survival of the fittest'. In fact, it was Herbert Spencer who first used this description when describing Darwin's work. Wallace, co-discoverer of Darwinian evolution, proposed that "survival of the fittest" may be an apt description. Darwin himself tended to put more emphasis on cooperation. He said: "Tribes of moral men have an immense advantage over fractious bands of pirates." [119]

Dawkins also said: "An animal's behaviour tends to maximise the survival of the genes 'for' that behaviour,

---

[117] The Other-worldly Philosophers, Economist, July 18, 2009, 65–67.
[118] Richard Dawkins; The Selfish Gene
[119] Buller, David J.; 'Evolution of the Mind: 4 fallacies of evolution', Scientific American December 2008

whether or not those genes happen to be in the body of the particular animal performing it."

Just as the human body works via billions of tiny cells forming something quite wonderful, Wikipedia has no less than 21 million editors.[120] Many of these individuals contribute a small amount of time. They are told not to worry about the possibility there may be typos in their contributions, because someone else will edit it.

This all begs the question: why do individuals contribute to Wikipedia? The product itself cites [121]research by Oded,[122] who defines six motivations.

To quote from Wikipedia these motivations are:
- Values – expressing values to do with altruism and helping others.
- Social – engaging with friends, taking part in activities viewed favourably by others.
- Understanding – expanding knowledge through activities.
- Career – gaining work experience and skills.
- Protective – eg reducing guilt over personal privilege.
- Enhancement – demonstrating knowledge to others.

To these six motivations he also added:
- Ideology – expressing support for what is perceived to be the underlying ideology of the activity (eg the belief that knowledge should be free).
- Fun – enjoying the activity.

[120] http://en.wikipedia.org/wiki/Wikipedia:Wikipedians
[121] http://en.wikipedia.org/wiki/Wikipedia_community
[122] Nov, Oded (2007). What Motivates Wikipedians?. Communications of the ACM 50 (11): 60–64. doi:10.1145/1297797.1297798. Retrieved 11 August 2011.

Research by Heng-Li Yang and Cheng-Yu Lai found that "the most likely motivation for continuing to participate is self-concept based motivations such as 'I like to share knowledge which gives me a sense of personal achievement'." [123]

You don't have to be born into generation 'y' to appreciate these motivations, but it is not unreasonable to suggest that on average, a generation 'y' member is more likely to appreciate them.

And so it was that, a product based on collaboration, on zero financial reward, a product that economic theory says shouldn't even exist, wiped out Encarta.

There is some irony in this story. Encyclopaedia Britannica still exists. Since it was purchased in 1996, it has filled a niche for itself as a high quality, detailed source of reference, to which you have to subscribe to fully enjoy. The world of academia frowns on students using Wikipedia as source material (there is an element of elitism in such attitudes by the way, of noses still being turned up, when in fact Wikipedia is a superb product, with an extraordinary variety of entries), and Encyclopaedia Britannica is preferred as a source. All book authors will know the frustration. You find something out on Wikipedia in no time, then you have to find other independent sources to corroborate your findings, and that can take an age.

Shane Greenstein and Michelle Devereux, in their paper *The crisis at Encyclopaedia Britannica* quoted Suzy Deline, a former employee, who said the company "hired the best brains out there and were paying them a pittance to

[123] Yang, Heng-Li; Lai, Cheng-Yu (November 2010). Motivations of Wikipedia content contributors. Computers in Human Behavior 26 (6): 1377–1383. doi:10.1016/j.chb.2010.04.011. Retrieved 2 August 2011. cited at http://en.wikipedia.org/wiki/Wikipedia_community

contribute. These people wanted Britannica on their resume so they didn't care."[124]

In a way then, the remuneration model applied by Encyclopaedia Britannica was similar to the one applied by Wikipedia. In the case of Encyclopaedia Britannica, the reward was modest financially but also entailed kudos; for Wikipedia the reward was zero and partially kudos. Admittedly, a modest financial reward is infinitely more than a zero award, but both applied a very different model for securing content than the one applied by Microsoft for Encarta, which was altogether more commercial. It may be telling that the only one of this threesome that is no longer with us is Encarta.

This is the collaborative model. As well as Wikipedia, collaboration has created Linux. Although Amazon and Trip Advisor are commercial, both rely heavily on user generated content, which is offered for no financial reward, and indeed, little obvious reward at all.

Emergence

Another example of collaboration is crowd sourced funding. And this takes us to an important point. The collaboration does not have to be deliberate.

There is a theory to explain all this. It is called emergence. Let's get the definition out of the way straight away: "Emergence is the way complex systems and patterns arise out of a multiplicity of relatively simple interactions." [125]

[124] http://www.slideshare.net/renerojas/case-study-encyclopedia-britannica

[125] http://en.wikipedia.org/wiki/Emergence

And apologies to the purists, but the best and most simple definition of emergence comes courtesy of Wikipedia.

Examples of emergence include the way in which ants in an ant's nest work together to achieve common aims; the way in which the neurons in the brain interact with each other to create consciousness; or the way in which individuals work together to create an economy. In each case, there is no system of command and control. Hollywood, and in particular Disney, may preach the idea of the queen ant in her robes, holding a sceptre and giving out orders. In truth, the order of a colony is created by each ant interacting with other ants in a very simple way. Simple messages conveying such meanings as "There's food over there," or "Run away", are communicated between foraging ants. They also carry a system for processing simple probability. If an ant receives a certain message from many ants coming from a certain direction communicating the existence of food, it will travel in that direction, whereas it may ignore a small number of messages from ants suggesting there is food in another direction. From this apparent chaos, we get the order of the ant colony.

This is the point about emergence. Order is created without recourse to central control.

The idea that a business should be run in such a way may seem quite appalling to a typical baby boomer, but the modern way of business thinking tends to place emphasis on creating the right corporate culture. Of course, senior managers need to set the right strategy, and make the right big decisions, but micro management is seen as the old way, while modern practises such as Google's famous 20 per cent time, where employees are free to work on their own projects, are seen as being more appropriate. Although recent media reports have suggested that Google has dropped this policy, the truth is slightly different. Work pressures have made the idea of individuals devoting 20 per cent of their working time to work on their own project unfeasible. Instead, we see workers increasing the length of their working week, as it were, to work 20 per cent longer hours, and to devote these additional hours to working on their own projects.[126]

But the theory behind emergence shows us how order can be created without command and control. The Millennial way may seem absurd; a recipe for disaster to the way of thinking of those brought up in older ways, but there is plenty of science to suggest such an approach is not only viable, but also highly effective.

Crowd sourced funding is a form of collaboration. It may not be deliberate, but it is proving to be highly popular, and may yet transform the way in which businesses are funded.

Why the change?

So, why the change?

Guy Rigby says: "Technology is an enabler not a cause." Then he qualifies that statement: "It was originally an enabler," he says, "but the world has changed because of technology; it has engendered a fundamental mindset to this collaboration and needing a cause to work with."

He says: "There are no secrets on how business works, but there are plenty of books on the subject." And this availability of knowledge has removed an edge that was once the exclusive property of a few, who had access to a top education. Now the secrets to good businesses are in the public domain. This has helped to foster this switch in attitudes.

---

[126] http://qz.com/116196/google-engineers-insist-20-time-is-not-dead-its-just-turned-into-120-time/

Mark Zuckerberg says "privacy is history", or so quotes Thomas Power, the man who co-founded eAcademy and a great advocate of the collaborative economy, in a talk he gave at TED. [127] He talks about a "digital mindset."

He says that to take on a digital mindset, you need to be "open, random, and supportive." But he says most companies, governments, and educational institutions, operate a closed, selective and controlling mechanism. He called it CSC.

And so to a baby boomer who has not understood this, or indeed to generation Y or X, he recommends being open to everything and being supportive of people around you. He said this is the concept of Twitter, which he argued is a bigger idea than both Facebook and Google.

Companies, says Power, claim they have to operate with their CSC system because of regulation and government controls, and are scared to change.

It is certainly the case that authorities seem to be on the side of the old way of doing things. In March 2014, for example, the FCA, the UK's regulator of financial services, changed the rules on peer to peer lending and crowd sourced funding. They have introduced a rule which means that individuals are not allowed to invest more than ten per cent of their non-property based investment portfolio into crowd sourced funding projects, unless they can show themselves to be sophisticated investors or of high net worth. In other words, it inserted a barrier into the process of crowd sourced funding, and in so doing has shown itself to be guilty of applying 20th century logic to 21st century problems.

---

[127] https://www.youtube.com/watch?v=fVs6Zogzg4g

The scandals relating to Wikileaks and Edward Snowdon also illustrate a clash between command and control type systems and those based on transparency and collaboration.

Wisdom of crowds

The idea behind crowd sourced projects also has its roots in scientific research; in particular in the concept of the wisdom of crowds, made famous by Francis Galton. It was 1906, and Galton attended a livestock fair, where villagers were asked to guess the weight of an ox on display. Galton, who was something of a numbers man, closely associated with a handful of theories in the field of statistics, noticed that not a single guess was right. Yet, when he took the mean of all attempts, it was remarkably close. [128]

According to JC Glick and K Staley, a small group of doctors working together as a team are more likely to make an accurate diagnosis than if they were working alone; college students sitting examinations perform better when students work together than when working individually. [129] So compelling is the evidence to support the idea that students perform better when they work in groups that a number of universities have started implementing what has become known as "collaborative learning techniques."

If you combine the ideas of the wisdom of crowds with emergence, you can see why collaboration can be such a powerful force.

---

[128] James Surowiecki in The Wisdom of Crowds: Why the Many Are Smarter Than the Few and How Collective Wisdom Shapes Business, Economies, Societies and Nations.
[129] Forsyth, Donelson R. "Group Dynamics", Wadsworth, Cengage Learning, 2009
http://www.cengagebrain.com/shop/content/forsyth99522_0495599522_01.01_toc.pdf, May 27 2011

Sharing economy

Combine the ideas of collaboration with technology, and the internet in particular, and the internet of things, and the processing power of modern computers, and the possibility of a sharing economy emerges.

According to Rachel Botsma, a Millennial generation thinker known for her ideas on collaboration, "80 per cent of all car rides in the US are single occupancy rides, therefore the system runs at 20 per cent efficiency...The average utilisation of a commercial office is 35 per cent ... there is a massive amount of value and liquidity locked up in that under-utilised space."

She cites the case of hotel chain Marriott, which is now offering workspace when demanded as part of its conference offering. She said: "Marriott is no longer just a place to stay, it becomes a place to meet people, to work – it brings other customers through their doors."[130]

But you can drill down from there. Airbnb enables individuals with a spare room - from people living in castles to igloos, and from boats to tree houses - to rent out their spare space. To date no less than 11 million travellers who wanted to experience cities, not as tourists but as locals, have used Airbnb. [131]

Or take carpooling.com, which is a system for enabling people to share a ride. Carpooling.com[132] claims to connect people in over 40 countries so they can travel together. Or

---

[130] http://www.edie.net/news/5/Brands-look-for-greater-ownership-stake-in-sharing-economy-/?utm_source=weeklynewsletter&utm_medium=email&utm_content=news&utm_campaign=weeklynewsletter

[131] https://www.airbnb.com/economic-impact

[132] http://www.carpooling.co.uk/

there is Taskrabbit, a system for enabling people who need certain tasks, chores perhaps, or that most frustrating of activities assembling Ikea furniture, to find local people who are able to perform those tasks. You can find a cleaner or a handyman, for example, or a personal assistant, or someone to run errands.[133] There is also stack overflow, which is a questions and answers web site for professional and enthusiast programmers. The crowd, in this case a crowd of programmers, will answer your questions.

Rachel Botsma says we are entering an era of collaborative consumption. She says, in this era: 'instead of consuming to keep up with the Jones's we are consuming to get to know the Jones's." [134]

A key currency of this new collaborative culture will be trust. Ms Botsma says: "Reputation will be more powerful than our credit history in the 21st century." She continues: "In the 20th Century the invention of traditional credit transformed our consumer system, and in many ways controlled who had access to what. In the 21st century new trust networks and the reputation capital they generate will re-invent the way we think about wealth, market power, and personal identity in ways we can't even imagine." Mark Pagel, wrote in *Wired For Culture:* "A good reputation can be used to buy cooperation from others, even people we have never met."

Rachel Botsma says: "We are at the start of a collaborative revolution that will be as significant as the industrial revolution."

The baby boomers, might cite John Lennon, and say: "Nobody told me there would be days like these." The

Monkeys said: "We're just trying to be friendly." However, Lennon also said: "Strange days indeed."

Chapter seven: Healthcare

Henry VIII of England may have been a very wealthy man, but he still died aged 56. We are not sure what killed him; it may have been syphilis. It seems probable that if someone today - even someone relatively poor by western standards - suffered from the same condition that killed one of the most powerful men in the world 500 or so years ago, that person could now be cured. Technology has revolutionized healthcare and medicine, perhaps more than any other area, and it is about to do so to an even greater extent. There are those who fear that technology will result in only the very rich being able to afford modern healthcare, and they may be right, but such fears are not borne out by the lesson of history; they forget about Henry VIII.

Just as importantly, those who say technological progress has somehow peaked, that all the great advances in the story of our species are behind us, overlook a crucial point. Technology is set to change us, to transform the treatment of diseases, indeed to cure diseases once thought incurable, and enable people who in a different era were destined to never walk or see again, to not only walk, but run, ski and jump; not only to see again, but to enjoy enhanced vision.

We are set to see a truly radical change. Healthcare will focus on prevention. Up to now, healthcare has always concentrated on diseases. We only tend to receive medical attention if we are ill. Technology will be used to prevent us from becoming sick. It will also help sportspeople to avoid injuries, and enhance us all in ways that were once thought to be the exclusive domain of science fiction.

Technologies that will create the transformation include wearable technology, 3D printing, nanotechnology, regenerative medicine, genome sequencing, the collection, mining and analysis of big data, bionic technologies, and exoskeleton technology.

These days, diseases that kill us are rarely epidemics; instead, they are diseases of lifestyle. If we could only make better decisions about our lifestyle, we could eliminate more than half the deaths from modern conditions.

Technology is set to enable us to make these decisions. It will also enable us to enjoy better, more customized care and live longer in the future.

Let's start with the story of data.

Big and little data

Thomas Goetz, author of *The Decision Tree: Taking control of your health in the new era of personalized medicine*, once said: "Healthcare isn't a science problem, it's an information problem." He is right, data matter and they are being made accessible like never before in the history of humanity.

Firstly, it can be small data, specific to an individual and used solely to help us manage our own health, or help our doctor, nurse or carer to support us directly. Wearable technology and advances in genome sequencing are creating information that can ensure that we apply healthcare technology in the most effective way for each of us.

Alternatively, it can be big data – used by doctors, health insurers, hospitals, and governments in the planning of healthcare. We can use these data to diagnose diseases more effectively; to implement superior preventative healthcare, and to allocate resources more efficiently. Advances in computer technology have created possibilities in the field of big data; possibilities that technology sceptics are failing to appreciate. [135]

Little Data – Wearable technologies[136]

The first generation of wearables come with just one sensor built into them, and they are already making a difference. Wearable devices such as Fitbit or Jawbone UP can, for example, tell us how far we walk in a day, or a week or a month. They can also tell us about the quality of our sleep. More to the point, such products encourage us to improve our habits through something called gamefication. This can involve incentivising and rewarding people to meet pre-set goals using techniques often used in games, for example rewards, or a progress bar, and peer pressure via social media.

---

[135] Take as an example the four Vs of big data:
*   Variety: the types and sources of data now available.
*   Veracity: the quality and trust in the data now available.
*   Velocity: the speed at which health related data is now available.
*   Volume: the exponential growth of the volume of health related data – growing at 40 times the global population growth.
[136] The combination of wearable technology, trackers and sensors, will:
* Create a wealth of data at individual level in real time.
* Measure physiological parameters easily.
* Relate trends, behaviour and environment to health and wellness.
* Analyze trends to understand the health ecosystem at individual and community levels.

Next generation wearables will contain many more sensors. They will measure different types of activity, such as heart rate. This means we will be better informed and we will be guided in taking appropriate decisions about our own health.

Don't limit your imagination to the various bracelets we have seen so far. Next generation technologies will be embedded in our clothes and cars, and places that until recently only writers of science fiction had considered.

Little data – wearable technologies, the real world and the end of the stethoscope

Thanks to advances in the computing power of handheld devices, combined with an increasing number of sensors built into them, it is becoming practical and realistic for patients to manage their own healthcare in a way that was never possible before. For example, asthma patients are able to use their smartphones to collect data and organize feedback to help them better manage their chronic disease. Other chronic diseases, such as diabetes, can also be better self-managed with apps that help to measure carb intake, calculate administering insulin quantity and receive tips on diet and lifestyle modifications essential for slowing down the progress of the disease.

A very similar revolution is taking place in the medical environment. Take for example AliveCor. This is a peripheral that, attached to a smart phone, enables users to record and share their own electro-cardiograms. Amongst other things, this device will probably spell the demise of the stethoscope. *Doctors could prescribe the device for at-home use* so that they can monitor patients remotely. Today, if patients don't have the symptoms of heart disease it is assumed they don't have the disease. Home use would enable a doctor to track whether a patient's asleep heart rate is rising over a period of time and therefore tackle potential heart disease early. In this way, patients can also determine whether therapy they have been prescribed is effective.[137]

Imagine slapping a sticker on your arm that could measure a wide array of medical indicators—heart rate, body temperature and more —and transmitting that data wirelessly to your smartphone. MC10 is developing products that can be used both on and inside the body, that monitor head impact, heart rate, brain activity, muscle function, body temperature and hydration. It is also developing an entirely new class of intelligent medical device with embedded sensors for enhanced sensing and therapeutic

---

[137] The treatment of chronic diseases such as asthma, diabetes, and epilepsy is enhanced if patients keep track of their symptoms, triggers and use of medications. This is of course easier said than done – we all forget; we are, after all, only human. The combination of sensors and mobile devices enables chronic disease sufferers to keep track of their medication. For example, asthma sufferers can attach a small sensor to the top of their existing inhaler, which can be used for tracking symptoms and adherence respectively. The resulting data will help patient and physician alike to better understand and manage the disease.

capabilities. Combine this with advances in nanotechnology (read on), and the same sticker will also be able to release drugs stored inside nanoparticles when data from the sensors suggest it is required. This technology will fundamentally change the way in which medicine is administered and how chronic diseases such as Parkinson's are managed.

You won't need to be as rich as Henry VIII to avail yourself of such technologies. They will create more efficient use of doctors' time, and as such this will be technology for the many, and not just the few.

Little data– Genomics and supercharged data: a map of you, and a map of me

Human genome sequencing provides scientists with a roadmap of the human body.

When we look at GoogleMaps, so much more information is available than when we use a conventional map. We can gain information about the types of roads, where the petrol stations, speed cameras, good restaurants, or traffic accidents are. Each piece of useful information is a layer, a category of information, which makes our decisions more informed and smarter.

Now imagine the same type of information, but this time about you, your body and your health. It will be available to the physician during a check-up. The doctor will be able to make a much more accurate diagnosis and provide treatment customized to you.

Genome sequencing enables each one of us to have our own human body roadmap. When combined with the other layers of information, this map will provide us and our doctors with a holistic and very precise profile of our health and contributory factors.[138]

Big data in health care
The benefits

Just as the internet of things will provide data to transform the production process, and just as big data will revolutionize the world of marketing, it is providing us with the information we require to radically enhance healthcare.

It will provide doctors with the tools for predictive analysis.[139] Natural language processing will also turn the data into insights about compliance and behaviour; and doctors will take data from individual departmental or hospital silos and use it to gain a much deeper insight into

---

[138] Genome sequencing, when combined with the other layers of information, will provide us and our doctors with a holistic and very precise profile of our health and contributory factors as follows:

1. Exposure, which encompasses the totality of human environmental (i.e. non-genetic) exposures from conception onwards.
2. Signs & symptoms of the disease / ailment.
3. Genome, which is the genetic roadmap.
4. Epigenetics, which is the study of heritable changes in gene activity that are not caused by changes in the DNA sequence.
5. Microbiome describe either the collective genomes of the micro-organisms that reside in an environmental niche or the micro-organisms themselves.
6. Patient data as collated by the doctor and then recorded in the electronic health records.
7. Patient himself/herself.

[139] The aggregation of population health data; for example, big data will also lead to greater public awareness of health issues, leading to better planning and prevention. New software based analytical tools are now able to scan social media to forecast and track outbreaks of disease. Google Flu Trends (GFT), SickWeather and, more recently, MIT focusing on Wikipedia have been used to forecast 'flu trends based on internet user searches and/or their tweets.

the incidence of a particular disease.[140] Thanks to this data, governments will be able to plan better and allocate resources according to need and demand: the result will be significant. Health insurance companies will be able to define better policies and premiums according to individual risk profile. [141]

Big data– The technology

Big data is being made possible in part by Moore's Law, as computers are able to process more and more information. The cloud is emerging as a massive depository of medical data, which can be accessed by doctors and other medical professionals. Supercomputers, such as IBM's Watson, are now enabling deep analysis and evidence-based reasoning for more precise diagnosis and clinical decision-making. IBM's Watson is able to read 200 million papers in three seconds, which will enable it to process patients' electronic health records, genomics, clinical data and health care professionals' peer-reviewed publications. It is also able to monitor real time data and new articles as they are published.

Big data and its analysis in the real world

By taking advantage of these technologies, medical scientists are improving leukaemia treatment through data mining medical literature. Health insurers are using Watson to speed pre-approval processes for patients. Teaching hospitals began working with IBM Watson to improve

---

[140] This will allow us to define more effective methods of treatment, and to run demographic studies or undertake population health analysis. So, for instance, we could see precisely how many people from a particular city or region are likely to contract a disease or respond well to a new drug.
[141] A smoker who takes little care of his/her diet and has a sedentary lifestyle will be paying more for their health care than a non-smoker who leads a healthy lifestyle.

medical school training, where they are collaborating to offer doctors real-time analysis of patient records to improve care.

Apps that allow doctors and medical practitioners to look up databases containing information on thousands of diseases, including signs, symptoms and lab findings, are now a reality. The physician is often guessing at what is wrong with you based on your answers to his questions, and his knowledge. This cannot be infinite so he will need additional data points. These are usually lab tests and/or second opinions from a peer or a referral. In the future, the access to a wealth of data, AI analysis, as well as peer to peer (P2P) will enable more accurate diagnosis. For example, uploading a photo of a skin rash will generate a more accurate diagnosis through comparison with other patient cases and research databases.

Big and little data working together

It won't be long before we start seeing Google Glass, or a variant, appear in doctors' surgeries and in operating rooms. Augmedix has developed an application, which, in combination with Google Glass, enables doctors to spend less time behind their computer, inputting or retrieving data from electronic health records, which allows more time with their patients. Combine this with apps that support a doctor's diagnosis by smartly and quickly analyzing data from the big data cloud and the patient's own sensors and trackers, and the relevance and accuracy of diagnosis will improve.

New technologies to enhance treatment

Data gives us information. Information is vital in the war against disease and in creating a more healthy society. But we need technologies to implement the findings of data.

Treatments, including the probability of an imminent cure for cancer, are being developed.

Take nanotechnology providing the possibility of delivering drugs to specific cells using nanoparticles as an example. The overall drug consumption and side-effects may be lowered significantly by depositing the active agent only in the affected area and in no higher dose than needed. This highly selective approach would reduce costs and human suffering. [142]

Advances in sequencing the genome mean that in five to ten years cancer will be downgraded to a curable disease. It sounds like an outrageous piece of futurism, but in fact healthcare scientists agree that the genomic break-through in cancer treatments are already underway and it really is transforming treatment of the disease.

"Chemotherapy is just medieval," says Eric Topol, a leading American cardiologist, geneticist, and researcher. "It's such a blunt instrument. We're going to look back on it like we do the dark ages. Tumours can now be sequenced and drugs tailored to the individual. It's the dawn of personalised medicine."

---

[142] Researchers in the US reported using nanoparticle chains to deliver doxorubicin to breast cancer cells in a mice study. Three magnetic, iron oxide nanospheres were chemically linked to one doxorubicin-loaded liposome and formed a 100 nm long nanoparticle chain. After the nanochains penetrated the cancer tumour, a radiofrequency field was generated that caused the magnetic nanoparticles to vibrate and rupture the liposome, dispersing the drug in its free form throughout the tumour. The result showed that the nano treatment was more effective in halting the tumour's growth than the standard treatment with doxorubicin. It is also less harmful to healthy cells since only 5 to 10 per cent of the standard dose of doxorubicin was used.

Regenerative medicine and the creation of organs and bones for transplant

3D printing technology has mutated to give us bioprinters, which use a "bio-ink" made of living cell mixtures to form human tissue. The bio-ink is used to build a 3D structure of cells, layer by layer, to form tissue. Eventually, medical researchers hope to be able to use the printed tissue to make organs for organ replacement. Bioengineers at Cornell University have printed experimental knee cartilage, heart valves and bone implants.

Then there is the field of regenerative medicine. When injured or invaded by disease, our bodies have the innate response to heal and defend. What if it was possible to harness the power of the body to heal, and then accelerate it in a clinically relevant way? What if we could help the body to heal itself more effectively?[143]

Regenerative medicine includes the possibility of growing tissues and organs in the laboratory and safely implanting them when the body cannot heal itself. This can potentially solve the problem of the shortage of organs available for donation. If the organ's cells are derived from the patient's own tissue or cells, the problem of organ transplant rejection can be overcome. Researchers in regenerative medicine are developing a 3D skin printer that deposits cells directly on a wound to help it heal quicker.

Although still very much in its infancy, regenerative medicine is likely to transform three key areas of medicine:

---

[143] Regenerative medicine is the "process of replacing or regenerating human cells, tissues or organs to restore or establish normal function". This field holds the promise of regenerating damaged tissues and organs in the body by replacing damaged tissue and/or by stimulating the body's own repair mechanisms to heal previously irreparable tissues or organs.

medical devices and artificial organs,[144] tissue engineering and biomaterials (regenerative medicine has already successfully grown heart valves from human cells),[145] and cellular therapies (think of a bank of your own cells, that can be used to regenerate your system back to normal).[146] It is now possible to turn an adult cell in an embryonic stem cell through the use of cloning techniques similar to those used to create Dolly the Sheep. The use of this

---

[144] Imagine if you were unable to control your bladder. Yes, your bladder. People all over the world are unable to do this due to a birth defect called spina bifida. Some patients must manually empty their bladder but the complications don't end there. The inability to urinate at will, or even to regulate the build-up of urine, could cause back up into the kidneys, creating life-threatening damage. But wait, a revolutionary event has occurred! A series of child and teenage patients have received urinary bladders grown from their own cells!

[145] The goal of regenerative medicine is to one day be capable of maintaining the body in such a way there will be no need to replace whole organs. Some diseases are so destructive that traditional medicine can only cure them by giving patients entirely new organs. Heart disease affects many of us and the only current solution requires a heart transplant. Even if a patient is able to survive long enough to receive a heart, there is no promise that the body will not reject the foreign organ. Heart disease affects the valves of the heart causing them to fail. The two conventional ways to replace heart valves include implanting a mechanical device or a pig aortic valve. However, complications are very common. Blood clots can easily form around the mechanical devices, forcing patients to take blood thinners. Also, in an effort to stop the body from rejecting the pig aortic valve, it is chemically treated. Inadvertently, this chemical changes the biological make-up of the cells rendering them unable to regenerate when common minor tears form. Regenerative medicine has already successfully grown heart valves from human cells. With the use of biomaterials to create a mould, scientists engineer the cells to grow in the form of a heart valve. Once mastered in clinical trials, any transplant patient will be able to receive a heart valve that is essentially their own, making rejection a non-issue. Regenerative medicine hopes one day to be able to repair these valves without even having to perform surgery.

[146] Our body uses stem cells as one way of repairing itself. What if you could choose to collect and store those stem cells There could be a possibility that those cells might be used in the future to help your body to stay healthy. For example, the dream of developing a cure for diseases such as diabetes is one step closer thanks to stem cells.

232

technique eliminates the need to manipulate the cell's genes, a process that can trigger cancer.

In the field of nanotechnology, nanomedical research has developed a "flesh welder", which is used to fuse two pieces of chicken meat into a single piece. The two pieces of chicken are placed together, touching. A greenish liquid containing gold-coated nanoshells is dribbled along the seam. An infrared laser is traced along the seam causing the two sides to weld together. This could solve the difficulties and blood leaks caused when a surgeon tries to re-stitch the arteries that have been cut during a kidney or heart transplant. The flesh welder could weld the artery perfectly.

Nanotechnology may be able to help to reproduce or repair damaged tissue. "Tissue engineering" makes use of artificially stimulated cell proliferation by using suitable nanomaterial-based scaffolds and growth factors. For example, bones could be re-grown on carbon nanotube scaffolds. Tissue engineering might replace today's conventional treatments, such as organ transplants or artificial implants.

A factory for making body parts! How we can re-build him, or her

The famous TV series from the 1970s, *The Six Million Dollar Man* began with the words: "Gentleman we can re-build him." The hero of the show, Steve Austin – the bionic man – was given super powers after suffering from a near fatal accident. Technology cynic and economist Robert Gordon asks us to consider what life was like 30 years ago, and then 30 years before that and so on. He suggests that the 30 year intervals in the late 19th and early 20th century saw much greater change than what we are seeing today in 30 year intervals. Yet, when the bionic man hit the TV screens just 40 years ago, it seemed like the stuff of dreams; of a future that belonged to kids' comics. The series was more comedy than serious, so improbable was the future it asked us to imagine. Another truly absurd idea related to the fictitious Iron Man, a character from kids' comics, because we all knew that could never happen.

Gentlemen (and ladies) we now have the technology. Thanks to advances in 3D printing, prosthetics and in the construction of human exoskeletons, the creation of real life bionic men and women, and even of iron men, is looking realistic. At first, the beneficiaries of such technology will be people who, like Steve Austin, suffered from nasty accidents or injuries, or people who have been either rendered disabled in some way by disease or were born that way. In time, the technologies that enhance our physical abilities will be available to all.

Back in the 1970s, six million dollars seemed like a lot of money, yet compare that sum with the amount NASA spent on computer technology during the moon landings, and it would appear that the fictitious agency that created Steve Austin got a relative bargain. Today, our smart phones costing just a few hundred pounds have more processing power than that possessed by NASA during the space programme of the late 1960s. Likewise, the technology to give us the powers of a bionic man will cost an order of magnitude less than $6 million.

3D printing and real life bionic men and women

The dream of 3D printing being employed so that there is a factory on every desk in every home may be possible or it may be a pipe dream, but it is clear that 3D printing is set to have a radical impact on healthcare.

Printing off a kidney or another human organ may sound like something out of a science fiction novel, but with the advancements in 3D printing technology, the idea may not be so far-fetched. While 3D printing has been successfully used in the healthcare sector to make prosthetic limbs, custom-made hearing aids and dental fixtures, the technology is now being used to create more complex structures — particularly human tissue.[147]

Prosthetics and real life bionic men and women

Prosthetics are artificial devices that replace a missing body part, which may be lost through trauma, disease, or congenital conditions. Prosthetics have been mentioned throughout history and have become more sophisticated over the past few decades with advances in engineering and greater research funding. The 2012 London Olympics made these advances very public thanks to the disabled South African runner Oscar Pistorius competing with able-bodied athletes.

Advances in prosthetics driven by the power and miniaturization of computers have combined with lighter and stronger materials and 3D printing. These technologies have enabled the field of prosthetics to make significant

---

[147] Only a few months ago, a 22-year-old woman from the Netherlands who suffers from a chronic bone disorder - which has increased the thickness of her skull from 1.5cm to 5cm, causing reduced eyesight and severe headaches - has had the top section of her skull removed and replaced with a 3D printed implant. A team of neurosurgeons at the University Medical Centre Utrecht performed the operation and the university claims this is this first instance of a successful 3D printed cranium that has not been rejected by the patient. The patient's skull was so thick that, had the operation not been performed, serious brain damage or death may have occurred in the near future. The skull was made specifically for the patient using an unspecified durable plastic. Since the operation, the patient has gained her sight back entirely, is symptom-free and back to work. It is not known whether the plastic will require replacing at a later date or if it will last a lifetime. This technology, once perfected, is likely to be used for patients with other bone disorders or to repair severely damaged skulls after an accident or tumour.

progress in moving inert or semi-inert prosthetics into Bionics. In this way, the replacement bionic limb is able to produce bionic propulsion technology to replace lost muscles and tendons. Using battery-powered "bionic propulsion," two micro-processors and six environmental sensors adjust ankle stiffness, power, and position thousands of times per second.[148]

These technology advances enabled Adrianne Haslet-Davis – a professional dancer whose leg was partially amputated after the 2013 Boston Marathon bombings – to dance a rumba on stage in March 2014 using one of these "bionic" prostheses.

Looking forward, these prosthetic advances will not only help individuals with missing limbs, but will also improve the lives of those suffering from conditions such as osteoarthritis. As we age, the loss of fast muscle fibres and excessive force, cause the ankle and calf muscles to lose power, creating painful joint disorders such as knee osteoarthritis and lower back pain. [149]

Exoskeletons and real life bionic men and women

An exoskeleton is the external skeleton that supports and protects an animal's body, in contrast to the internal skeleton (endoskeleton) of, for example, a human. Some of the larger kinds of exoskeletons are known as "shells". Examples include insects, such as grasshoppers and cockroaches, and crustaceans, such as crabs and lobsters. For years, man has explored whether the addition of an exoskeletal device could make him or her "super strong".

---

[148] At heel strike, the system controls the ankle's stiffness to absorb shock and thrust the tibia forward. Then, algorithms generate fluctuating power, depending on terrain, to propel a wearer up and forward.

[149] Across the elderly population, osteoarthritis in joints is a leading cause of mobility impairment.

In March 2014, a company called 3D Systems announced a first on the healthcare front: the first 3D printed hybrid robotic exoskeleton suit, which it teamed with Ekso Bionics to produce. The suit was made for Amanda Boxtel, whose skiing accident in 1992 left her paralyzed from the waist down. She was able to stand and walk, assisted by crutches, during a public event in which she debuted the suit.

Enhancing the physical abilities of people who are already healthy

The technology behind prostheses could also lead to innovations in a closely related field: humanoid robotics. Imagine a future where we will have bionic feet, ankles, knees, and hips that are technologically optimal.

Ongoing research work in this field will help to revolutionize the idea of "personal bionics," blurring the lines between electro-mechanics and the human body; for instance, bionic limbs that can be controlled by the mind and attached to the body.

Researchers at MIT have developed a leg exoskeleton capable of carrying an 80-pound load without the use of motors. According to its developers, the prototype can support 80 per cent of this weight while using less than one-thousandth of a per cent of the power used by its motorized equivalents. The aim of developing leg exoskeletons is to make it easier for people to carry heavy loads. By designing mechanical structures that transfer much of the load directly to the ground, rather than via the walker's legs it should be possible to enable soldiers, firefighters or removal workers, to carry heavier loads while reducing the risk of injury and the amount of metabolic effort they expend in doing so.

A real life iron man as such may never be a reality, but the day when all of us can have our strength enhanced by exoskeletons and prosthetics or – thanks to prosthetics – run faster and over longer distances, may be a reality in the life-time of most readers of this book.

Convergence

Wearable technology is being incorporated into virtually every piece of equipment professional athletes use in order to monitor not only their performance but also their safety. This includes sensors in the helmets of NFL players so that concussion can be detected when it happens. Major League Baseball has been testing smart compression shirts that have been wired to measure arm movement and technique to determine a pitcher's effectiveness.

These hi-tech devices measure hundreds of data points from acceleration to biometrics. They are discreet and nearly weightless, commonly used under a waistband, for example. This enables the devices to be worn and collect data during training and games. This data can be mined to identify countless performance benchmarks, improve game strategy, "make teams smarter," and keep players on the court more. Wearable analytics will be a critical advantage in professional sports.

The Harlequins, a London based rugby team, is able to identify injury and ill health amongst the team before it manifests itself visually and therefore can rest a player early and limit the impact on the player and the team's performance.

Athletes are predisposed to injury when they become fatigued during practice and games. Fatigue also reduces skills necessary to compete at an elite level. Fatigue may be mechanical, physiological or neurological in nature. Trackers and sensors embedded in athletes' clothing enables micro-level recognition of motion and sub-optimal pattern discrimination to be used by coaches.

Similar technology and analysis is now also becoming available and affordable to you and I, which will further enhance the ownership of our own health.

Much like the automobile industry where Formula 1 technology developments eventually make their way into the cars we drive, the sporting world is contributing to the technological advancement of the wearables/trackers/sensors we will one day wear. The diagnosis and prevention of many trauma type injuries will evolve as a result.

We are also seeing convergence with video games. Techniques learned from game developers are being successfully used to help patients to improve medication compliance and build user-friendly disease awareness.

Even more dramatic technologies

We are beginning to hear claims about the possibility of using nano-robots in medicine, which would totally change the world of medicine once it is realized. Nano-robots could be introduced into the body, to repair or detect damage and infections. According to the Institute for Molecular Manufacturing, a typical blood borne medical nano-robot would be between 0.5–3 micrometres in size, because that is the maximum size possible due to blood vessel size limitations.

Nanodevices could be observed at work inside the body using MRI. Medical nanodevices would first be injected into a human body, and would then go to work in a specific organ or tissue mass. The doctor would monitor the progress, and make certain that the nano-robots have reached the correct target treatment region. The doctor would also be able to scan a section of the body, and actually see the nano-robots congregated neatly around their target (a tumour mass, etc.) so that he or she can be sure that the procedure was successful.

The art of the possible enabled by nanotechnology is mind blowing and is in fact a book in itself.

Far Future – Healthcare 2050

Predicting the distant future is the stuff of crystal balls, particularly when we are being asked to consider technologies and developments that go way beyond what has been described in this chapter. Ray Kurzweil, in his book *The Age of Spiritual Machines*, suggested that it is not too unlikely that the disease curing machine we saw in Matt Damon's movie *Elysium* will be available.

Last year, Google launched Calico, which it described as a new venture focusing on reversing and stopping the process of ageing and age-related diseases. One of the venture's major initiatives will be to expand human lifespan significantly. Nobody knows what to expect yet but *Time* magazine's headline was "Can Google solve Death? That would be crazy if it wasn't Google". The myriad of new technologies described in this healthcare focused chapter, which is not an exhaustive list, combined with all of Google's innovative and experimental capabilities makes the *Time* headline all the more believable.

It is an exciting and optimistic – if a little unsettling – view of the future of healthcare. We only hope to give our readers a glimpse of how medicine can and will be transformed in the next decade.

Part three: Disruption

Chapter eight: Business disruption: Great gales of creative disruption

The next three chapters look at disruption, or, if you prefer, what the economist Joseph Schumpeter calls creative destruction. Destruction is an emotive word and carries negative connotations. Creative destruction implies technologies that can destroy, such as bombs, weapons, and artificially manufactured diseases. Disruptive technology rather implies change; radical change for sure, even upheaval, but if we play it right, the end result is an improvement.

At least it is an improvement for some, and hopefully most of us. But make no bones about it, for some companies and sectors, the effect of new technology can be destructive, leaving once mighty companies in ruins.

Just as 29 of the world's largest companies in 1912 were bust by 1995, and 48 had disappeared,[150] many of what are currently the world's largest, apparently most invincible companies will be forced out of business by new technology. It is just that we won't have to wait until 2095 before many of the world's largest companies in 2012 are no longer with us. Here is a prediction; we will wait no more than 30 years, and probably a good deal less before the list of the world's largest companies is radically changed. If only 19 of the world's largest 100 companies in 1912 were still in the top 100 in 1995, then an analogous story would suggest that only 19 of the world's 100 largest companies in 2012 will be in that list in 2042, and an even tighter timeframe could probably be applied.

Over the next one, two and three decades, a substantial number of the world's largest companies will go bust, or

---

[150] See chapter three

have been reduced into a vague shadow of their former selves. A corporate takeover may save some from collapse but this is likely to be at a price, which is a fraction of the amount that the company was worth in 2000. Alternatively, a government may bail them out.

We saw a rehearsal in 2008. Banks were bailed out, so were the big three US car companies. And we all know that there are certain car companies in this world that are kept afloat by regular government bail-outs/subsidies that would have gone to meet their maker long ago if things had been left to the markets.
You may also recall that there was a hint of arrogance among the bosses of the US car makers at the time of their bail-out, flying in private jets to a meeting with US president Barack Obama to discuss how the US government could save them.

For some countries, having a car manufacturer they can call their own is like a mark of machismo, or at the very minimum of prestige. It is as if that country's credentials as a leading economy are in doubt if there is no famous car brand associated with it.

Yet the big three US companies really did totter in the first few years of this century. Part of the challenge they faced related to healthcare packages for workers, which just weren't viable. It is hard for companies of that size to change in any radical way, especially if such change affects the workforce and have implications regarding government subsidies.

But the big three in the US made another mistake, and this cuts right to the heart of this book. In the US, a country where the idea of anthropogenic climate change was largely ignored until recently, fuel efficiency just wasn't a priority. The big three US companies made huge monsters of the highway, guzzling liquid like a drunk on New Year's Eve. It wasn't until 2006 that US president George W Bush said that the US was addicted to oil.[151] By then it was too late. The US car industry had fallen victim to foreign invaders, the likes of Toyota, with their onus on fuel efficiency – the 'car in front'. The experience was analogous to innovator's dilemma.

The backlash came in part with a government bail-out, and then the regulators and patriotic US press sided with the US brands, as Toyota fell foul of a media and a regulatory witch hunt, in which every Toyota car fault, every recall, was put under the microscope of media analysis, while similar faults in US cars were virtually ignored.

That is what it is like within the car industry. Things are not rational. Car companies take on a level of importance within the psyche of a country that is not reflected by the markets. This makes large companies more vulnerable than ever to potential upheaval.

For banks it is different. Banks have long been easy targets. No one likes the person that has lent him or her money.

Banks and car manufacturers are among the world's great companies that will be rocked in the next few years. Add to that list energy companies, media and entertainment, travel and holidays, and retail. There are others, too of course. But here the focus is on these areas.

Let's start with banks.

---

[151] http://www.nytimes.com/2006/02/01/world/americas/01iht-state.html?pagewanted=all&_r=0

The problem with banks

When you step into a bank, you can feel small. A big, thick, imposing front door, high ceilings, solid walls and the knowledge that somewhere at the back there is a large safe, can help to confer a feeling of permanence, reliability and trust.

A bank's value, at least in part, is tied up within its network of branches, and the brand image they reflect.

It is hard to say for sure, when this image began to change, but it was surely before the banking crisis of 2008.

Over the last ten years or longer, the nature of banks has changed. They mutated from one represented by solid, trustworthy individuals, pillars of the local community, working in solid buildings, behind barriers of reinforced glass, to an image of openness, of friendly staff, who mingled with customers, who sat at desks, open on all sides, with signs saying "can I help you?"

The move was inevitable. Nearly everyone agreed that it was a good thing. But in changing their image in this way, banks may have made themselves more vulnerable to the forces of disruption. Now the barriers that lie between them and the new entrants to the market may be made from the flimsiest of materials.

There may be an analogy with the music industry and the short-sighted way in which it migrated customers from vinyl to CDs. Many would agree that CDs have been a disappointment. Their small shape feels somehow clinical and functional, and some magic seemed to seep out of the industry with their emergence; magic that vinyl with its large album covers, resplendent with beautiful artwork had created. Once the market had been persuaded to adopt a more soulless CD, the barriers put up against digital music were lessened. The internet may or may not have had a positive impact on the quality and variety of music produced today, but it clearly had a devastating effect on music retailers. Maybe if they had not been as quick to promote CDs, and persuade millions of music lovers to replace their much loved music collection on vinyl with those shiny little silver discs, there would have been greater resistance to MP3 players, and music retail would still be an important part of shopping centres. Equally, if music retailers had embraced the digital channel as an additional channel rather than suing start-ups, they might still have the upper hand.

Likewise, banks have made themselves vulnerable.

Take as an example a report from the UK British Bankers Association (BBA) published in March 2014.[152] The report found that no less than 12.4 million bank apps were downloaded in the UK in 2014. There were 18.6 million transactions a week from mobile phones, compared to 9.1 million in 2012. Customers of British banks made nearly 40 million mobile and internet transactions a week in the year, and 28.4 million debit and credit cards were fitted with contactless technology. Banks sent 457.7 million SMS balance alerts and other text messages in 2013.

The BBA's chief executive Anthony Browne said: "A revolution is underway in how people spend, move and manage their money." He went on to add: "Make no mistake, the branch will remain integral to banking services in the 21st century – especially for those big moments in life such as arranging a mortgage. But the day-to-day use of branches is falling and part of that is because there is a groundswell of people who now find that banking on the move is fast, easy and convenient."

---

[152] https://www.bba.org.uk/landingpage/waywebanknow/

Is what he said about the importance of bank branches right? If banks still had that image of trust, dependability, of permanence, he may well have been right.

But this image has slowly been ebbing away. Instead, banks are being seen as place where people sell to you.

The banking crisis, bail-out and then the controversy over bankers' bonuses; of them being rewarded with seven figure packages for running banks into the ground, have left their mark. Multi-million dollar bonuses may or may not be morally defensible, but it is clear that the public's perception is that they are not. This has had a knock-on effect on the brand image of all banks.

According to the Millennial Disruption Index, of the six biggest sectors – that's banking, personal computing, mobile, discount retail, household goods and online – banking is at the greatest risk of disruption as the Millennial generation ages.

71 per cent of Millennials would rather go to the dentist than listen to what their bank has to say. One in three said that they are open to switching bank accounts in the next three months. 68 per cent said that the way they access money will be totally different in five years' time, and 70 per cent said the way we pay for things will be totally different. A staggering 33 per cent say they don't need a bank at all.

The compilers of the Millennial Disruption Index said the change to banking will be seismic.
But here is the statistic that should have senior managers in banks – not to mention their shareholders – quaking in their boots: 50 per cent of Millennials are counting on tech start-ups to overhaul the way in which banks work. 73 per cent said they would be more excited about a new offering in

financial services from Google, Amazon, Apple, PayPal, or Square than from their own national bank.

The truth is that the image conveyed by the network of banks with its more 'salesy' type of approach, combined with the 2008 bail-out and the scandal of bankers' bonuses, have left the industry more vulnerable than at any time in modern history.

One gripe held against banks emanates from entrepreneurs. They accuse the bankers of failing them; of not lending. Such accusations may not be wholly justified. All entrepreneurs think their ideas are the greatest, and they can't understand why others don't share their excitement. Indeed, they don't know why banks are not beating a path to their door, begging to supply then with much needed capital. Not all this confidence is rational or appropriate. Even in Jeffery Archer's bestselling book *Kane and Abel*, a hardworking and brilliant Abel could not forgive the banker Kane for refusing to back his business – ultimately creating animosity between the two men.

Part of the problem may relate to a question mark over whether banks are the best institutions for supporting entrepreneurs. Too many entrepreneurial businesses fail, but a small number can succeed spectacularly. In such circumstances, funding is only really viable when the funder takes a share of profits, thus compensating him/her for the businesses that fail and don't repay debt. It is a point that even Jeffery Archer picked up on, with Kane secretly investing in Abel's business.

This antipathy from entrepreneurs towards banks may not be fully justified, but it is there all the same. When, in the aftermath of the banking crisis, banks bailed out by tax payers refused to lend money to businesses, this resentment grew into something more tangible.

Besides, there is evidence to suggest that banks had lost touch with one of their core purposes; to provide the lubrication for business by freeing up capital that was otherwise lying idle. As Nobel Laureate Edmund Phelps told *Spiegel* in November 2008, over the previous 20 years or so banks have focused on making money from residential and commercial mortgages. He suggested that in so doing they "appear to have lost their expertise to make business loans and investments." He said: "It seems likely that highly regulated banks are not the ideal sources of finance for business investment, particularly for innovative investments."[153]

So if a bank is not the ideal source of finance for innovative investments, what is? Venture Capital is an alternative, but in this digital era, we are also seeing the growing popularity of crowd sourced funding.

This is proving to be a valuable tool for both businesses looking for funding, and individuals looking to invest. The bank seems to be almost irrelevant in this process. And while regulators put up barriers, the power of crowd sourcing or collaboration is great. Ultimately, regulators standing in the way of such change is as futile as King Cnut trying to stop the tide.

Even the more obvious banking activities of lending money and paying interest on it is bypassing banks, thanks to peer-to-peer lending.

With interest rates at record lows across most of the developed world,[154] depositors are craving better returns on their money. Peer to peer lending may even make central banks redundant, as interest rates are set by the forces of

---

[153] http://www.spiegel.de/international/world/edmund-s-phelps-what-has-gone-wrong-up-until-now-a-590030.html
[154] As at March 2014

supply and demand rather than by the open market operations of central banks.

Another threat to banks lies with virtual currencies, the most famous of which is the bitcoin.

The bitcoin story

To tell the story of bitcoins you need to bear in mind three dates: 1494, 3 January 2009, and the year 2140.

The first of those dates relates to when Luca Pacioli, a Franciscan friar and collaborator with Leonardo Da Vinci no less, published a book entitled *Summa de arithmetica, geometria, proportioni et proportionalità*. It was the first written account of double entry book keeping, the invention of which transformed business. It created a system of accounting that enabled third parties to trust the financial records of companies, thereby making it easier for firms to secure investment from third parties, and in the process catapulting the profession called accountancy to the forefront of business.

The second of these dates is the occasion when Satoshi Namkomoto minted 50 bitcoins, in the process launching a new virtual currency onto the world.

The year 2140, relates to that point when the total supply of bitcoins will become fixed. At that point, assuming the currency is still in use, there will be 21 million bitcoins and never more than that number.

Many argue that the bitcoin is an example of a bubble, with comparisons often being drawn with the Dutch Tulip bubble of the 17th century*[155]. They say that investing in a bitcoin is

---

[155] In his book, Extraordinary Popular Delusions and the Madness of Crowds, published in 1841 Charles Mackay wrote: "An amateur botanist

akin to taking part in a Ponzi scheme. But the consideration of the bitcoin's relationship to Luca Pacioli and its ultimate limited supply do make the virtual currency rather interesting.

Some say the innovation of double entry book keeping was one of the most important in the history of business, but the bitcoin goes one step further. It is recorded on a triple entry public ledger, meaning that it is very hard (some say impossible) to cheat the bitcoin network.

Imagine you are playing Waddington's classic board game Monopoly, and imagine that each player in the game receives a record of how much money and how many properties each other player has. In such a scenario, it would be very hard to cheat.

---

happened to see a tulip-root lying in the conservatory of a wealthy Dutchman. Being ignorant of its quality, he took out his penknife, and peeled off its coats, with the view of making experiments upon it. When it was by this means reduced to half its original size, he cut it into two equal sections, making all the time many learned remarks on the singular appearances of the unknown bulb. Suddenly the owner pounced upon him, and, with fury in his eyes, asked him if he knew what he had been doing?

'Peeling a most extraordinary onion,' replied the philosopher.

'Hundert tausend duyvel!' said the Dutchman, 'It's an Admiral Van der Eyck.'

'Thank you,' replied the traveller, taking out his notebook to make a memorandum of the same. 'Are these admirals common in your country?'

'Death and the devil,' said the Dutchman, seizing the astonished man of science by the collar. 'Come before the syndic, and you shall see.'

In spite of his remonstrances, the traveller was led through the streets, followed by a mob of persons. When brought into the presence of the magistrate, he learned to his consternation that the root upon which he had been experimentalising was worth four thousand florins; and, notwithstanding all he could urge in extenuation, he was lodged in prison until he found securities for the payment of this sum."

It is a little like that with bitcoins, only on a huge scale. Each bitcoin transaction is recorded three times: the person who buys, the person who sells, and a third party who is responsible for confirming the transaction. The public ledger must tally with the accounts of each of these parties.

The process of clarifying the transaction eats up a considerable amount of computer processing power. The third party who provides the processing power is occasionally rewarded with additional bitcoins. These third parties are known as bitcoin miners.

The total computational power of the bitcoin global mining network is more than seven million gigahashes, which is 256 times greater than the combined processing power of the top 500 super computers in the world.[156]

To cheat the bitcoin network, one would need processing power greatly in excess of the cumulative processing power that was employed in creating the bitcoin ledger.

The system is developed in such a way that, over time, the process of mining bitcoins becomes more processor intensive, and the increase in supply reduces, until by 2140 no more coins are minted.

The combination of the fact that there is an ultimate limit to how many bitcoins can be minted with the triple entry book keeping system, which is apparently impossible to cheat, has made the bitcoin offering appear quite compelling to many investors.

Add to that the apparently anonymity of the bitcoin network – although considering the public ledger records every transaction ever made, this benefit may be

[156] http://p2pfoundation.net/bitcoin

exaggerated – and the bitcoin has taken on considerable popularity.

Any new currency faces a chicken and egg situation. It is only worth something if people think it is worth something. How do you get people to think it has value in the first place? The bitcoin has broken through this chicken egg situation. At the time of writing, a single bitcoin is worth $456 dollars[157]. On 30 December 2012, it was worth $13.25, by 13 October 2013 it reached $124, and it passed $1,000 on 24 November 2013 before halving after the MtGox fiasco.

This leaves us with four questions:

Why Bitcoin?

Is it the centre of a bubble?

Why might it be a threat to banks?

What is the future of virtual currencies and what is their threat to banks?

Why Bitcoins?
To answer the first question, we need to take a number of factors into account:

Firstly, the banking crisis of 2008 damaged confidence in the banking system.

Secondly, the perception that the underlying cause of the banking crisis was a bubble in debt, which some argued was made possible by the fiat banking system, in which banks

---

[157] 3 April 2014,
http://www.plus500.co.uk/Instruments/BTCUSD?gclid=CObmqbndxr0CFer nwgodDG4A9w

created money through lending and further undermined confidence in banks.

The large levels of government debt in Japan, the US, Europe and even China, led to the belief that governments could use inflation as their way out of debt via the creation of money.

This belief was exacerbated when central banks in Japan, the US and the UK, engaged in the policy of quantitative easing. Such fears may have been misguided, but they were there all the same.

The Cypriot banking debacle, in which some depositors in Cypriot banks had to take a loss on their money on deposit, further strengthened the belief that banks could not be trusted.

The popularity of bitcoins was also enhanced by the growing popularity of a libertarian philosophy, as advanced by the likes of Ron Paul in the US, which among other things suggested that the control of the money supply should be left to the markets. In his book *Anti Fragile*, Nassim Taleb makes the case for the libertarian point of view. He says: "Ask a US citizen if some semi-governmental agency with a great deal of independence (and no interference from Congress) should control the price of cars, morning newspapers and Malbec wine....He would jump in anger as it appears to violate every principle the country stands for, and call you a communist post-Soviet mole for even suggesting it. Then ask him if the same government agency should control foreign exchange, mainly the rate of the dollar against the euro and the Mongolian tugrit. Same reaction: "this is not France." Then very gently point out to him the Federal Reserve bank of the US is in the business of controlling and managing the price of another good, another price called the lending rate, the interest rate in the economy (and has proved to be good at it). The libertarian presidential candidate Ron Paul was called a crank for suggesting the abolition of the Federal Reserve or even restricting its role. But would he also have been called a crank for suggesting the creation of the agency to control other prices?"

Is it the centre of a bubble?
With the debacle of MtGox, a bitcoin exchange, which shut down, resulting in many holders of the currency losing their holdings of bitcoins, many said the currency was set to die. Yet, at the time of writing, several weeks after this event, the currency is still proving popular. Taleb might argue that the fact that the bitcoin exchange can fail is precisely the point. The markets might make individual exchanges vulnerable, but in so doing it enables the system to evolve. (Evolution needs failure for it to work.) Taleb argues that a system that can have individual failure is more than robust; rather it is like a muscle that gets stronger when subjected to pressure. To use Taleb's own phraseology, bitcoins are anti-fragile, which is the opposite of fragile, whereas the global banking system, propped up as it is by governments, is always vulnerable to collapse. It is fragile.

In part, that is why many suggest that bitcoins are not the stuff from which bubbles are made.

The ultimate limit in the supply of the bitcoin has led many to suggest that its price can only ever rise in the long-term. They may be right. There is another way of looking at this.

It is well-known that if there is a sudden injection of money into the economy, without a corresponding rise in production, inflation usually results. For example, when South America was first invaded by the conquistadors, gold was shipped back to Spain and Portugal in massive quantities. Since gold was the currency of that time, this led

255

to severe inflation in both countries, perhaps leading to their loss of pre-eminence. However, just as a rapidly growing currency can lead to inflation, one that is not growing fast enough can lead to falling prices, or deflation. If the global economy used bitcoins instead of dollars, yuans, yens and euros, then prices measured in bitcoins – thanks to the limited supply of the currency – would probably fall, and we would see permanent deflation.

Why might it be a threat to banks?

In answering why bitcoins may pose a threat to banks, a new, even more compelling, benefit of the currency is revealed.

As Marc Andreessen[158] argued in the *New York Times*, it is possible to buy and sell bitcoins at virtually no cost. You can for example exchange dollars for bitcoins and send them to someone else in another country, say China, who could then sell the bitcoins you sent to them in exchange for yuans. The whole transaction costs nothing.

You can use bitcoins to make tiny payments, for example to pay to read an article in a magazine, when bank charges may have made such a transaction prohibitively expensive. And companies that supply products with very low margins may find bank charges significantly eat into their profits. By using bitcoins to facilitate transactions, they can save enough money to make an otherwise unviable business profitable.

Companies that sell products at a very low margin could use bitcoins as the means of exchange, again removing bank charges that may have made such transactions un-economic.

---

[158] http://dealbook.nytimes.com/2014/01/21/why-bitcoin-matters/?_php=true&_type=blogs&_r=0

Using bitcoins, it may be possible to charge a tiny sum to send out emails, so that the cost would not be prohibitive to someone with a legitimate reason to send an email, but would represent a major barrier to mischievous distributors of spam.

And what is the future of virtual currencies?

Bitcoins are not perfect, and the system does suffer from major drawbacks. For one thing, of the nine million bitcoins in existence, only two million appear to be in use, suggesting that people are hoarding most of the supply of bitcoins. If they were released onto the market, the price may crash.

It has been suggested that most of the non-circulating bitcoins may be controlled by a small number of people, which means that control of the currency may be in the hands of a small body of very powerful people. This would nullify the very argument libertarians make to support bitcoins over, say, the dollar, which they say is controlled by the Fed, and a small number of banks that own the Fed.

As we shall read in the next chapter, the fact that the bitcoin may be a deflationary currency is probably undesirable from a macro-economic point of view.

However, the technology behind bitcoins may give rise to other currencies, perhaps backed by something more solid, such as kilojoules of energy, kilobits of bandwidth, or backed by the provision of certain goods and services – for example, meals in restaurants or tickets for the theatre. [159]

---

[159] To elaborate, you would be able to exchange your virtual currency for say a coffee in a certain coffee shop, or use it as a form of currency. The British pound is called a pound because it used to be worth one pound of silver. The terms of conditions that come with a virtual currency may say: "I promise to pay the bearer one kilojoule of energy, or six bananas, or a barrel of oil," but in practice it would be used as a means of exchange. As the supply of energy, or bananas or oil rises, so would the supply of the currency.

Because virtual currencies can remove banks from the transaction chain, they threaten to supplant one of their most important functions. For this reason, we may well see a regulatory threat to virtual currencies. However, it seems unlikely that in the long run regulators can impede the evolution of virtual currencies, and the internet may make their ultimate success inevitable.

The combination of virtual currencies, the emergence of peer-to-peer lending and crowd sourced funding, the collapse in a trust premium held by banks, and the attitudes of the Millennial generation, pose a major threat to retail banks; one that may have a devastating effect upon the industry.

However, it may be worth noting that investment banks, or casino banks as some call them, may be immune to such pressures.

You may also note that this section has not, until this point, referred to potential under-capitalisation of some banks. The risk of another banking crisis, similar to the one we saw in 2008, has not gone away. The threats to a businesses are often the ones that are not foreseen – or at least not by many. Banks and regulators are so busy fighting the last war – namely banking fragility caused in part by under-capitalisation – that they are surely missing the threat posed by technology. Not that this threat is necessarily a bad thing for the public.

Which car companies can survive to the end of the next decade?

The car industry faces threats on several fronts. No one threat on its own is likely to be enough to cause major disruption, but put them all together and the result may be more disruption to the global car industry in the next ten to 15 years than that seen over the past half a century.

Threat number one relates to something called peak car.[160]

There is more than one way of looking at this one; there is theory, and there are hard data.
The theory looks like this:[161]

---

[160] Peak Car' Where did the idea come from? And where is it going? Phil Goodwin
Emeritus Professor of Transport Policy
file:///C:/Users/User/Downloads/WC2012_goodwin_peak_car.pdf
and Peak Travel, Peak Car and the Future of Mobility Evidence, Unresolved Issues, Policy Implications, and a Research Agenda. Phil Goodwin. October 2012. OECD
[161]

http://www.transportxtra.com/magazines/local_transport_today/opinion/?id=23221

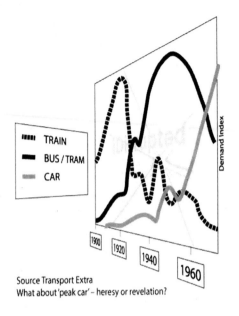

What about 'peak car' – heresy or revelation?

The graph above seems to tell a pretty clear story. In the history of transport over the last 100 years, starting with the train, then buses and trams and then the car, a pattern has emerged – at least it has emerged for the train, bus and tram. At first demand soared, but once it peaked, it went into steady decline. Why should the motor car be any different?

Or take this evidence:

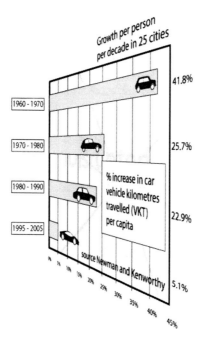

Growth per person per decade in 25 cities

1960 - 1970 — 41.8%

1970 - 1980 — 25.7%

1980 - 1990

1995 - 2005 — 22.9%

% increase in car vehicle kilometres travelled (VKT) per capita

source Newman and Kenworthy — 5.1%

It appears that car usage is showing signs of peaking. And from here on in, it is forecast it will go into decline.

Other data suggest that European petrol consumption today is no higher today than it was 25 years ago, although this may be a feature of the increasing efficiency of modern engines.

The trend is not specific to one country. In the US, over the last decade [162] driving by men declined in every age group except those who were 65 or older. The vehicle miles travelled by women who are 20 to 34 years of age has

---

[162] Measured to March 2014, http://www.volpe.dot.gov/news/has-growth-automobile-use-ended

dropped since the early 2000s, but women in their mid-30s to mid-60s are driving more, and seniors of both genders are also driving more.

Nick Butler visiting professor and chair of the Kings Policy Institute at Kings College London wrote in the *Financial Times*: that in the US "transport sector demand is falling." He said that this is not "a temporary phenomenon", and it is not just down to the economic shenanigans of recent years. He said it was "a structural shift reflecting changes in life style and work patterns as well as gains in fuel efficiency."[163] In January 2014, in a video interview on the *Financial Times* website,[164] he said: "People are just not driving as much as they used to. I think we are, in the US and Europe, at peak car." He forecast global peak car numbers between 2025 and 2030.

According to the *New York Times* back in 1998, 64.6 per cent of potential drivers had a driving licence; in 2008 that number was down to 46.3 per cent.[165]

Spiegel magazine cited figures from the Fraunhofer Institute, predicting that the number of automobiles in Germany are expected to fall by 50 per cent by the midpoint of this century. It said that by then: "The cities are green, pleasant places to live, pedestrian- and cyclist-

---

[163] http://blogs.ft.com/nick-butler/2013/12/15/peak-oil-the-trend-to-watch-is-peak-car/?ftcamp=published_links%2Frss%2Fcompanies_energy%2Ffeed%2F%2F product December 15, 2013 by Nick Butler Peak oil? The trend to watch is peak car. FT

[164] Peak Car, FT, 26 January 2014, https://www.youtube.com/watch?v=2caGrXOW4xo

[165] As Young Lose Interest in Cars, G.M. Turns to MTV for Help, By AMY CHOZICK New York Times Business Day, March 22, 2012

friendly; there are ample car-sharing parking spots and cycle stations at every larger transport hub."[166]

Why might this be?
There are many theories. One theory is that as we get richer, we substitute new superior forms of transport. And now air transport is replacing the car. It is an interesting theory, but it does rather contradict some of the ideas put forward above. It may be that car use is declining, or at least its growth rate is declining, because of costs; the costs of fuel and insurance for example. If that is so, it is hard to square this with the argument that car use is declining as wealth rises.

Maybe a factor at play here is that traffic congestion is turning drivers off. It is well -known that Mexico City and Jakarta in Indonesia are plagued with traffic so dense that you can hardly see the roads for cars. As we see a global trend of people migrating from the country to cities, and as many cities see improvements in public transport systems, cars may lose popularity.

Alternatively, there is the internet effect: online shopping and working from home. If video killed the radio star, might Skype kill the motor car?

Or maybe what we are seeing is a trend towards more pedestrianisation in cities and towns, coupled with traffic calming measures, such as the congestion charge in London, or even more bike lanes.

Another theory suggests that technology is becoming more important to us than cars. It is well known that some people love their cars, but is it the case that smart phones and tablets are taking over as the objects of their owner's love?

---

[166] http://www.spiegel.de/international/zeitgeist/car-sharing-increasingly-popular-in-german-cities a-913891.html

It is important to appreciate that the idea of peak car is controversial. In the UK, for example, the Department for Transport has rejected the idea of peak car. It predicts that road traffic in England will increase by 43 per cent by 2040.[167] One thing is for sure, if the peak car theorists are right, then current infrastructure spending in the UK will lead to a good deal of spare capacity. Others say the reason why car use has declined is down to the economic slowdown, which began in 2008. However, data do appear to show that this trend was self-evident before 2008.

What happens if we combine the idea of peak car with a change in attitude noticeable amongst the Millennial generation?

According to Zipcar's annual Millennial survey: [168] "Millennials are the only generation that believes losing their phone would have a greater negative impact on their life than losing their car. Nearly 40 per cent of Millennials chose their mobile phone over their car, TV, or computer/tablet compared to only 16 per cent of those in the 35+ age bracket... More than 50 per cent of Millennials say they would drive less if other transportation options, like public transit and car sharing, were available in their area. 35 percent reported that they are actively seeking substitutions for driving, both significantly higher adoption rates than older counterparts."

---

[167] Road Transport Forecasts 2013, The National Transport Model, Department for Transport
https://www.gov.uk/government/uploads/system/uploads/attachment_data/file/212474/road-transport-forecasts-2013.pdf 7 April 2014.
[168] zipcar's annual millennial survey shows the kids are all right
http://www.zipcar.com/press/releases/fourth-annual-millennial-survey

Self-driving cars

Around the year 2015, or maybe 2016, the town of Milton Keynes in Buckinghamshire, England is set to see self-driving cars roam its streets. The town, which is famous across the UK for its roundabouts and concrete cows, will be one of the first in the world to trial self-driving cars. It will be one of the first towns, but not one of the first locations; there are already driverless pods at Heathrow airport, for example.

But what is unusual about the Milton Keynes project is that these cars will not just travel in a straight line, as if they are on a bobsleigh track, they will turn right, or left, and stop, when appropriate. Their proximity to the public is what makes them especially interesting.

At first, taking the form of two-seater pods, the Milton Keynes self-driving cars will link just two locations: the town's shopping centre and railway station, a distance of roughly one mile. The plan is for there to be 100 such vehicles by 2017. They will come with a screen that gives passengers internet access, and will travel at the grand speed of 12 miles per hour. There are no plans for a man carrying a red flag to walk in front of the pods. However, judging by the reaction of the public it won't be a surprise if there is a public call to bring back the Red Flag Act, a piece of legislation which required all automobiles to be preceded by a man carrying a red flag and was repealed in the UK in 1896.

According to Enrico Motta, professor of knowledge technologies at the Open University, who has been involved in the Milton Keynes Smart City project, at first the pods will move up and down lanes, bordered by a soft barrier. The barrier won't be there to protect people from the pods says the professor, but to protect the pods from normal cars. He also said there is a psychological element, the pods may not pose a threat to the public, but the public will need to be reassured anyway.[169]

In time, however, the pods will move over a larger area, and as the public become more used to them, might mingle with pedestrians and bikes. Their particular application may apply to large pedestrian areas, but mixing with cars may be a little way off yet.

According to a study *Emerging Technologies: Autonomous Cars—Not If, But When* published in January 2014:[170] "Self-driving cars that include driver control are expected to hit highways around the globe before 2025 and 'self-driving only' cars are anticipated around 2030."

But the report predicts a massive hike between 2030 and 2035.

The breakdown looks like this:

Projected number of self-driving cars – IHS – Emerging Technologies: Autonomous Cars—Not If, But When.

2025	2030	2035	2050
Seven million	11.8 million	54 million	All cars either self-driving or self-driving commercial vehicles

As for costs, it forecasts the price premium for "self-driving cars electronics technology will add between $7,000 and $10,000 to a car's sticker price in 2025, a figure that will

---

[169] Interview conducted with Professor Enrico Motta, 25 March 2014

[170] IHS, Self-Driving Cars Moving into the Industry's Driver's Seat - January 2, 2014
http://press.ihs.com/press-release/automotive/self-driving-cars-moving-industrys-drivers-seat

drop to around $5,000 in 2030 and about $3,000 in 2035 when no driver controls are available."

According to Dr Mark Handford, who is an expert in aerodynamics; inventor of the Handford Device and famous in Formula One circles; self-driving cars also offer the benefit of travelling much closer together, which would create an aerodynamic effect similar to a peloton in cycling, when cyclists gather in closely bunched groups, achieving aerodynamic benefits.[171]

The biggest barrier to the adoption of self-driving cars will ultimately be with the attitudes of the public and regulation. The public will accept the technology as the Millennial generation ages. Regulators will take longer to change however; sometimes it seems as if they haven't yet caught up with the end of the Stone Age. We may also see resistance from certain industries, for example taxi drivers. In June 2014, traffic across many of Europe's biggest cities was adversely affected by striking taxi drivers over the threat posed to their livelihood by the online taxi app Uber. If we see strikes, not to mention a good deal of resentment aimed at Uber, consider the reaction we are likely to get to the idea of self-driving cars.

Many people also resist the idea of self-driving cars, arguing that humans are better equipped to deal with emergencies. Humans will know, for example, to prioritise stopping in such a way as to avoid hitting a child. Alas, such arguments show their protagonists are victims of what is called the illusion of superiority, or the Lake Wobegon effect, named after the inhabitants of Garrison Keillor's (1985) fictional community of Lake Wobegon, where most people appear to

---

[171] Interviewed by Michael Baxter, 1 February 2014

believe that their skills and abilities are above average.[172] As for driving, one famous study showed that of 161 students surveyed in the US and Sweden, 69 per cent of the Swedish students and 93 per cent of the US students thought they were better than average drivers.[173] You may have spotted the flaw. It is not possible for 93 per cent of people to be better than average. The same logic that insists most of us think we are better than average at most things, surely suggests that a machine can never drive more safely than us. Such beliefs are mistaken, and they are barriers to our wider acceptance of self-driving cars, and before these vehicles are fully accepted our egos may need deflating a little.

Technology that has made self-driving cars possible includes LADAR, sensors, GPS chips, and the internet of things.

Once they do finally garner mass market acceptance, think about the psychology for a moment.

There is something quite special, almost intimate about the relationship between a human and his/her car. As you gently hold the gear stick, you feel the car respond to your movements. You can make it roar into life, and sense its engine, deep inside the car, responding to your gentlest touches. Maybe there is something subconscious going on here – a link between human and car that was once held between rider and horse.

[172] Kruger J.; Lake Wobegon be gone! The "below-average effect" and the egocentric nature of comparative ability judgments. J Pers Soc Psychol. 1999 Aug;77(2):221-32 http://www.ncbi.nlm.nih.gov/pubmed/10474208
[173] Ola Svenson; Are we all less risky and more skilful than our fellow drivers?, Acta Psychologica 47 (1981) 143-148, North-Holland Publishing Company,Department of Psychology, University of Stockholm, Sweden, Accepted March 1980

Remove a human from the driving seat and let the car drive itself, and won't something be lost?

Self-driving cars may well prove to be more efficient and safer than traditional cars, but they will surely be less sexy.

Remove sex from the psychology of owning a car, and will it matter quite so much if you own a red Ferrari, or a little runabout?

There is an implication in self-driving cars that the motor industry has not factored in. The male customer may lose his car related libido.

Electric cars

As the car industry migrates to electric cars, many firms will fall victim to innovator's dilemma.

As they currently stand, most car users would not consider electric cars an attractive proposition. They are expensive, the distance an electric car can travel between re-charges is too short, there are insufficient recharging facilities, and the time it takes to re-charge is too long.

These shortcomings will not always apply. Tesla, the electric car company founded by Elon Musk, is targeting a 50 per cent cut in price within three years starting from the beginning of 2014.[174] The internet is full of scepticism, but what the sceptics overlook is that costs fall over time, especially those related to battery technology.

For example, after a barrage of criticism saying the Tesla plan won't work because batteries are too expensive, the

---

[174] James O'Toole, Musk says cheaper Tesla model 'about three years away' CNN, January 14 2004, http://money.cnn.com/2014/01/14/autos/musk-tesla-cheaper/

company announced plans to invest $5.1 billion in a new lithium ion battery factory.[175]

In other words, before Tesla explained how it would achieve its planned cost reductions, sceptics dismissed the company's plan to cut the cost of its cars, saying the cost of batteries alone make such a plan impractical. Such sceptics can't help themselves. "It's just a pipe dream," they say, totally ignoring the possibility of technological innovation, and failing to heed the lessons learnt by those who are haunted by their embarrassingly short-sighted predictions.

More compelling still are ideas under development, such as for lithium air batteries, that may extend the range of electric cars between refills,[176] or lithium sulphur batteries that may be able to extend the range of electric cars between refuels to 500 miles. Such batteries would also support much faster re-fuelling.[177]

Electric cars are more suited to self-driving than traditional internal combustion engine cars. For example, technology now exists to re-charge electric cars wirelessly. As Enrico Motta said: "They can just automatically drive to a re-charging point and wait there, while the car is re-fuelled."

Self-driving cars will also offer fuel saving benefits, because they will be designed to be driven in fuel efficient ways – gradual acceleration for example.

[175] Will Tesla's $5 Billion Gigafactory Make a Battery Nobody Else Wants? http://blogs.wsj.com/corporate-intelligence/2014/04/04/will-teslas-5-billion-gigafactory-make-a-battery-no-one-else-wants/

[176] ACS, A battery that 'breathes' could power next-gen electric vehicle https://www.acs.org/content/acs/en/pressroom/newsreleases/2014/march/a-battery-that-breathes-could-power-next-gen-electric-vehicles.html

[177] ARPA-E Advanced, Hybrid Planar Lithium/Sulfur Batteries http://arpa-e.energy.gov/?q=arpa-e-projects/advanced-lithium-sulfur-batteries

Sharing cars

But think about the implications of self-driving cars in a sharing economy. Remember, the Zipcar survey finding that "more than 50 percent of Millennials say they would drive less if other transportation options, such as public transit and car sharing, were available".

The success of services such as carpooling.com, which claims to have more than five million registered users and that 65 million people have been transported since its launch, shows how the concept of car sharing is becoming more popular.

Add into the mix self-driving cars, and it is easy to see how the appeal of sharing cars can become compelling. Combine this with the internet of things, and imagine the unfolding scenario.

Professor Motta says: "The current model is not sustainable."

Writing for the Project Syndicate series, Carlo Ratti and Matthew Claudel say: "According to research from the Massachusetts Institute of Technology's SMART Future Mobility team: 'the mobility demand of a city like Singapore – potentially host to the world's first publicly-accessible fleet of self-driving cars – could be met with 30 per cent of its existing vehicles.'" Other researchers suggest this number could be out by even more in New York: "if passengers travelling similar routes at the same time were willing to share a vehicle." [178]

[178] http://www.project-syndicate.org/commentary/carlo-ratti-and-matthew-claudel-foresee-a-world-in-which-self-driving-cars-reconfigure-urban-life#Xd6kiBrpydwmEq7C.99

According to a report from McKinsey, from Stefan Heck and Matt Rogers, the average American car spends 96 per cent of its time parked. Another 0.8 per cent of this time is spent with the driver looking for a parking space, 0.5 per cent is spent sitting in traffic congestion, and just 2.6 per cent of its time is applied to productive use.[179]

The savings that can occur when self-driving cars combine with the sharing economy are fairly self-evident.

The internet of things and big data

Big data is already changing things. Uber, the app referred to above, is made possible by the internet. It enables drivers to become part-time taxi drivers, if they happen to have some free time coming up, or if they happen to be in a certain relevant area.

But imagine if the ideas of smart cities, sharing economy, self-driving cars, the internet of things, and big data combined.

As Enrico Motta asks: "If your bus breaks down, what do you do?" Parents of teenagers across the world might think they know the answer. At least they do if the person in the bus is a teenager. The answer in this case is to call Mummy or Daddy. But, says Professor Motta, if you have an integrated system, with self-driving cars, self-driving pods, bikes, buses, taxis and bus taxi hybrids, with information conveyed over the internet of things, via sensors, multiple options open up. "Your smart phone might tell you that if you walk five minutes, you can take a bike to a place when you can jump on a self-driving pod." It can calculate that there are say, 36

[179] Stefan Heck and Matt Rogers, Are you ready for the resource revolution? March 2014, McKinsey
http://www.mckinsey.com/insights/sustainability/are_you_ready_for_the_resource_revolution?cid=other-eml-nsl-mip-mck-oth-1404

people ahead of you waiting for the next bus, at earlier stops, meaning there may not be enough room. But it can tell you a taxi is two minutes away and that for say three dollars it can take you to another bus."

One form of resistance to the idea of self-driving or sharing cars is that many of us store shopping in our car boot, and stop at one shop and then move on to another. The combination of the internet of things and self-driving pods can remove that issue. We can order a pod to collect our shopping and take it to a pick-up point. Professor Motta talks about the possibility of freight pods – pods just for carrying things, controlled over the internet of things.

Within 15 years, before self-driving cars become dominant, it is possible that all drivers could become part-time taxi drivers. Drivers could get a text, saying someone needs to go in the same direction in which you are driving, and could you collect them? A modest charge might be applied to the passenger as a reward to the driver, but this is done automatically, without the embarrassment of asking for money.

This may alarm you. How do you know the driver is safe? How does the driver know the passenger can be trusted? This is the whole point of the sharing economy. Social media will provide ways of giving this information. Remember the quote from the last chapter, citing Mark Pagel in *Wired For Culture*: "A good reputation can be used to buy cooperation from others, even people we have never met."

Such a system of sharing lifts within a smart city can disrupt, and also create new opportunities in the transport industries by allocating resources more efficiently, and rewarding taxi drivers in different ways – until self-driving cars make them superfluous that is. Uber itself, famous for being a great disruptor, may be disrupted by the changes.

Competition to car industry

In addition to all the factors described previously, the competition posed by Tesla is a threat, and all car companies must dread the prospect of Apple, Samsung or Google entering the market place. (Since these words were written, Google has appointed the former CEO of Ford as a director and in any case has been investing in producing self-driving cars).

Add to that technologies such as Hyperloop, proposed by Elon Musk to transport people over a distance of a few hundred miles travelling at around 750 miles per hour between large cities in "pressurized capsules" riding "on a cushion of air." [180] Incidentally, Musk proposes that Hyperloop would be charged by solar power.

Imagine the disruption caused to the car industry if smart cities combine with hyperloop or other advanced high-speed transport systems operating over a few hundred miles.

Disruption at least similar to what is described here is likely to occur before the end of the next decade.

3D printing and cars

Add to the mix, the potential impact of 3D printing.
Few people are suggesting that all cars will be made entirely by 3D printers, but in the context described here, 3D printing, as it evolves, adds an interesting new dimension.

---

[180] http://en.wikipedia.org/wiki/Hyperloop

Nir Siegel won the Pilkington award for a design he submitted as part of his Masters degree for a car printed in part by a 3D printer.

His idea is for a car that is partially created by its driver using a 3D printer and has some parts ordered in. "The car builds itself, with your help, with some parts 3D printed, some parts made by a specialist," he says.[181] Oddly enough, although Mr Siegel won his spurs, as it were, with his ideas for 3D printing and now works as an industrial designer making use of 3D printing, he thinks the technology is overhyped.

But he says his idea is that if you are more involved with how your car is made, and it is partially customised for your needs, you will have more of an emotional attachment to it. You may keep it for longer.

With his concept, each car will be unique, but many parts will be shipped in. You 3D print parts of the car, with the aid of a robot, and the robot then stays inside, making modifications when required.
He points out that cars today are no cheaper (after inflation) than in the day of the Model T Ford. Today regulation and insurance pushes up the cost of owning a car.

But if it is the case that self-driving cars have the effect of reducing our love for our car, and if the Millennial generation don't share their parents' attachment to the idea of owning a car, then these barriers to car ownership may be partially overcome if each car is in some way customised. The inclusion of a small localised, bespoke 3D printing based car manufacturing facility, which partially assembles parts bought in, may be an answer.

---

[181] Interview with Michael Baxter, 24 February 2014.

If you look at classic cars, they have an elegance and individuality about them. You can see why people loved their 1930s Morris Minor. 3D printing, by offering the ability to provide customised parts in a way currently not feasible, can help to return some of that love just as the ideas of self-driving and sharing, and the attitudes of the Millennial generation threaten to undermine it.

3D printing also offers the opportunity of being able to replace car parts that have been damaged at a fraction of the cost currently charged, thereby undermining an important source of revenue for the car industry.

To meet the needs of the consumers' wish to reduce the cost of car ownership, and in response to the myriad of threats set to descend upon the car industry, the industry may well find its future lies in localised assembly, with some customer parts made locally using 3D printing. Such cars may be made employing a more modular system of car design, allowing less labour intensive assembly systems, which would make it much easier for damaged parts to be made locally and fitted at a much lower cost than is currently normal.

However, if the car industry, in its efforts to survive, is forced to make more use of local manufacturing employing 3D printing to offer a degree of uniqueness and character not seen in cars for over half a century, the car industry will undergo major upheaval.

How many existing car manufacturing companies can survive, after taking into account:

- the industry's arrangements with governments, which create inefficiencies
- massive factories and an emphasis on assembly line production
- a world of peak car
- ageing Millennials

- a sharing economy creating more efficient use of cars, and thus less demand
- self-driving cars, with the resulting leakage of at least some magic in the relationship between humans and their cars
- the move to electric cars with the risk described by innovator's dilemma threatening to undermine business models
- 3D printing creating the possibility of more local production, providing greater customisation?

You can see that the next decade and the one afterwards will see the emergence of the greatest threats to the car industry since its inception.

It is doubtful whether more than a small percentage of current car companies will survive such disruption.

The great energy disruption

The lesson of innovator's dilemma, at least in part, is one of dismissiveness. You can imagine marketing executives at companies producing 12 inch disc drives reacting with exasperation at the latest hair brained scheme from an engineer, with no commercial acumen, for the company to start producing nine inch drives. You can also imagine the exasperation from the engineering gurus at the 12 inch disc drive manufacturers – men and women made wise and a little cynical by their years of experience – as some fresh faced new recruit, barely out of university, makes a proposal for the company to start making toys, otherwise known as nine inch drives.

Such dismissiveness may have seemed wise and sensible, but it is the stuff of which corporate catastrophes are made.

And this takes us to the area where the wise, and the sceptical and the serial dismissers are the most extreme – namely the energy industry.

Let's take two ideas which add to that air of complacency; of dismissing new ideas.

The first idea has its roots in history. Churchill once said: "The further back you look, the further forward you can see," but in some respects at least, Winnie was wrong; dangerously wrong in fact. Sometimes the narrative of history misleads us. We are so caught up with looking at what has happened in the past that we forget that different circumstances can produce quite different results.

Here is the first piece of complacency about the energy industry. You may recall from chapter two that the list of survivors of the world's biggest companies in the early 20th century was dominated by the oil companies. That fact alone has led to complacency. The oil industries always have been the world's mightiest companies, goes the logic, and they always will be. Such logic is flawed.

Secondly, there is the idea of peak oil. For some time, people have been predicting a point in the story of the oil industry when the world's ability to supply this valuable commodity is exhausted. Peak oil relates to that date when the supply of oil stops increasing, and begins to fall. Furthermore, goes the argument, because all economic progress of the last 200 years has relied on oil or coal, once the supply of oil and coal peaks and goes into decline, the world will descend into an economic oblivion, in which a new Stone Age is the best one can hope for.

No doubt the list of people who thought that way in 1865 was pretty long too, when William Stanley Jevons predicted that peak coal production was just decades away. Similarly, in 1909, when the US Geological Survey predicted US domestic oil reserves would be exhausted by 1935, no doubt the doomsayers forecasting the end of the world took to the streets. Likewise in 1956, when M King Hubbert came up with a theory of peak oil, suggesting that continental US oil production would peak in the 1970s, the alarmists were in ascendance. And again in 1995, when M King Hubbert repeated his peak oil theory, but this time said it would occur in 1995, he drew much support. Finally, in 2005 when the Hirsch Report stated that US gas production "appears to be in permanent decline," the peak oilers dominated the headlines.[182]

One day we may indeed run out of oil. However, it's more likely that peak oil will never occur, and it will never occur because our reliance on fossil fuels will diminish.

In the short run peak oil won't occur, because of the combination of technology, and the fact that where we sit in the energy super cycle means that the price of oil and gas is exceptionally high, encouraging investment into exploiting fossil fuels in new and innovative ways.

We live in a time, which people were predicting would be a post peak oil era not so long ago. Yet, according to Capital Economics, we have:

- Heavy, and extra heavy oil – oils with higher density and viscosity than conventional oil and requiring different technologies for both extraction and transport.
- Bitumen – made up of organic components ranging from methane to large polymeric molecules. It is

---

[182] The source for the peak oil predictions is an excellent report published by Capital Economics on 22 November 2012, entitled Global growth prospects beyond 2020

found in oil sands and can be synthetically processed into oil.

- Shale oil – "immature oil" which has not been in the ground long enough to form.
- Conventional oil – containing kerogen and bitumen which can be processed into oil.
- Gas-to-liquids – the conversion of natural gas and other simple gases in liquid petroleum.
- Coal-to-liquids – The liquefaction of solid coal.

This is not to say, that if we carry on as we are the world won't run out of oil eventually, it is just that the date of peak oil is still a very long way off.

But there is another, more important point. We are in any case highly unlikely to carry on as we are.

While our ability to extract oil from the deep, once forbidding places of this planet improves, technology is creating new opportunities. But, once again, we see a characteristic illustrative of innovator's dilemma, and the chorus of scepticism is deafening.

The fact is that the cost of obtaining energy from solar power today is now roughly one per cent per unit of energy of its cost 40 years or so ago. Already, we are approaching grid parity (when the cost of energy generated from solar is comparable to the cost of fossil fuels) in some parts of the world. Thanks in part to nanotechnologies, the pace with which the efficiency of solar improves is not likely to slow down.

Just to make this point clear, the above words were written in the full awareness that we can do nothing to increase the energy beamed down from the sun on any given square metre. While we increase the proportion of energy that can be captured, the scope for improvement in this respect is limited. However, there is plenty of scope to reduce the cost of solar panels themselves, and the ease with which they can be installed. So we have solar paint, windows, MEMS, the devices at the heart of the burgeoning internet of things powered by solar energy, clothing, smart phones and watches that will generate solar power.

Just to make this point clear, the above words were written in full awareness that the supply of renewable energies is unpredictable; wind is not much use when there is no wind, and solar is not much use when it is dark. While we can increase the proportion of energy that can be captured from the sun, either directly in the case of solar, or indirectly from wind, tidal and wave power, none of these technologies work all the time. However, thanks in part to evolving nanotechnologies, energy storage is advancing, and may well be set to advance at a rate commensurate with Moore's Law.

Just to make this point clear, the above words were written in full awareness that in the field of synthetic biology the likes of geneticist Craig Venter – armed with computer processing power that was not available just a few years ago – are working on synthetic solutions to creating carbon fuels in a way that is fully sustainable and does not add to the carbon dioxide in the atmosphere.

In April 2014, Ambrose Evans-Pritchard – a writer for the UK's *Daily Telegraph*, and famous for his bearish views on the economy – took time off from preaching doom, to make some out-of-character optimistic predictions on the future of renewable energy. But he did not drop his bearish ways altogether. Mr Evans-Pritchard did predict a resulting catastrophe for traditional energy companies as a result. "Solar power will slowly squeeze the revenues of petro-rentier regimes in Russia, Venezuela and Saudi Arabia. They will have to find a new business model, or fade into decline," he said. [183]

He made good arguments, yet the comments accompanying his article were scathing – and by the way, Mr Evans-Pritchard is usually the darling of the blogosphere, whose scepticism on the economy draws fans from all corners of the planet.

While a very small number of the comments were well reasoned and took some account of modern technology, most repeated the same old cynicism; the same type of attitude that leads to the creative destruction described in the tale of innovator's dilemma.

They say: but solar is still too expensive; it is no use at night; the weather is too dull in northern Europe and across many states in Northern America.

Psychologists have found that as a species, we humans are more biased than we ever thought. When politics is involved, little things like facts seem to be an irrelevance. As Yale Law Professor Dan Kahan found,[184] when it comes to pre-conceived notions, hard numbers showing those notions are wrong cannot alter beliefs. For example, as an article in *Salon* states: "People who thought WMDs were found in Iraq believed that misinformation even more strongly when they were shown a news story correcting it," or people who

[183] Evans-Pritchard, Ambrose, Solar power will slowly squeeze the revenues of petro-rentier regimes in Russia, Venezuela and Saudi Arabia. They will have to find a new business model, or fade into decline, The Daily Telegraph, 9 April,
http://www.telegraph.co.uk/finance/comment/ambroseevans_pritchard/10755598/Global-solar-dominance-in-sight-as-science-trumps-fossil-fuels.html
[184] Dan M. Kahan, Erica Cantrell Dawson, Ellen Peters, Paul Slovic, Motivated Numeracy and Enlightened Self-Government,
http://www.cogsci.bme.hu/~ktkuser/KURZUSOK/BMETE47MC15/2013_2014_1/kahanEtAl2013.pdf

were highly critical of Barack Obama's management of the economy said that unemployment had risen over the previous 12 months, even when they were looking at a graph which showed the precise opposite. [185] You may be interested to note that intelligence does not affect the outcome. There is no evidence to suggest that people with high IQs are less prone to bias interpretation, or indeed are less likely to ignore data if it does fit pre-conceived notions.

The same principle applies to scepticism about renewable energy.

But it also applies in a more serious form.

In March 2014, a report produced by the IPCC for the United Nations, said that the impact of anthropogenic climate change is likely to be "severe, pervasive and irreversible."[186] The snag with this report is that it may not have gone far enough. Our inborn tendency to bias, combined with a sense of self-serving bias, has led to an enormous level of cynicism over the issues of human made climate change. The weight afforded by the media to those who hold cynical views on anthropogenic climate change is much greater than is justified by their profile within the scientific community.

The UN report had no less than 309 coordinating authors, and 1,729 expert and government reviewers. One scientist who worked on the report decided he disagreed with the conclusions, saying they were too alarmist. The media then focused on the supposed dissent within the IPCC.

---

[185] Marty Kaplan, Alternet, Scientists' depressing new discovery about the brain, Salon, Tuesday, Sep 17, 2013
http://www.salon.com/2013/09/17/the_most_depressing_discovery_abou t_the_brain_ever_partner/
[186] Climate Change 2014: Impacts, Adaptation, and Vulnerability 12 April 2014, http://ipcc-wg2.gov/AR5/images/uploads/IPCC_WG2AR5_SPM_Approved.pdf

The way in which climate change is reported does not reflect the balance of opinion held by climate change scientists. When a very small number offer contrary views, the media focuses on the disagreement.

What it does not do

What it does not do however, is focus on the possibility, which is just as legitimate, that the IPCC may underestimate the possible dangers of climate change.

As Professor Stern said: "Scientists describe the scale of the risks from unmanaged climate change as potentially immense. However, the scientific models, because they omit key factors that are hard to capture precisely, appear to substantially underestimate these risks."

Part of the problem here is that if a minor error is found in a paper warning about the dangers of climate change, the media seize on this error, affording it more weight than could possibly be justified. But if a climate change sceptic makes an error in a paper, the mistakes are ignored by large parts of the media. As a result, some media give non peer-reviewed papers, which cast doubt over the climate change hypothesis, equal weight to that which is given to peer reviewed papers warning of the dangers, and these are subjected to enormous scrutiny.

What we can say is that the proportion of carbon dioxide in the atmosphere in 2014 is at its highest level in four million years, or in other words at its highest level since the days when early humans, such as *Homo habilis*, first evolved.[187]

---

[187] O'Connor, Eddie, The CO2 content of our atmosphere is at its highest point for 4 million years. Is this a coincidence? 19 July 2013 http://eddie.mainstreamrp.com/the-co2-content-of-our-atmosphere-is-at-its-highest-point-for-4-million-years-is-this-a-coincidence/

The case for manmade climate change is not proven, and while it is possible that it will turn out to be far worse than the most alarming report predicts, it may turn out not to be very serious at all. We live in an uncertain world, and nothing, repeat nothing, is certain. We can only deal with possibilities. But it is odd that in an era of health and safety dominated corporate practises, when regulators do their best to remove any form of risk-taking, we are asked to shrug our shoulders about the issues of climate change, and assume that the predictions that best fit what we want to hear are right, and carry on playing Russian roulette with the future of humanity.

Then to cap it all, at a time when the proven and unproven oil reserves are said to be worth around $60 trillion dollars,[188] we are told that there are vested interests behind the renewable energy lobby. We are even told that nuclear, which – unlike renewable energy – becomes more expensive the more we use it, is a viable alternative. This is the case even when the timeframe for adopting new nuclear power stations is such that during the time it takes to build a fully working nuclear power station from scratch, advances in nanotechnology will make the case for renewable energy overwhelming. A more sharing and collaborative economy changes the dynamics too – for example in using heat generated by massive server farms, to heat nearby communities.[189]

Most forecasts on the rate at which renewable energies grab market share from traditional sources of energy assume a very gradual growth trajectory, and even by 2035,

---

[188] James Martin; Meaning of the 21st Century
[189] James O'Toole, Your new heat source: data centers 7 April 2014, CNNMoney,
http://money.cnn.com/2014/04/07/technology/innovation/data-centers-heat/index.html?iid=HP_River

the IEA, for example, assumes fossil fuels will still generate 76 per cent of global energy.

But these forecasts are based on the old way of doing things. They assume that most electricity will be provided via a massive national grid.

However, the combination of renewable energies, especially solar, and the falling costs of energy storage, and smart technology, which enables us to channel our energy in more targeted ways – for example, intermittent energy into devices such as storage heaters that do not need to use energy at specific times – is likely to lead to a localised form of energy control.

More homes and businesses will become energy self-sufficient, and the supply chain will expand to meet demand. Once the provision of energy generation becomes a mass consumer market, the traditional barriers to take-up – the legacy systems held by giant utility companies for example – will be rendered surplus to requirements rapidly.

The combination of complacency, denial, and a blinkered attitude to technological changes that surround us poses a truly massive threat to existing energy companies. Bias can be overcome; indeed, it can be reversed so that the bias points in the opposite direction. If evidence builds to suggest that some of the more alarmist predictions of anthropogenic climate change science looks more plausible, and if the US and northern Europe see many more winters like the one of 2014, we may see a populist backlash against fossil fuels, and climate change denial may become as popular as Betamax video recorders. Even if the alarmists prove to be wrong, the backlash may be hard to reverse.

According to a report published by Citi in October 2013, some gas plants have been running for less than ten days a year in Germany as a result of solar power. This has led to profit warnings from some of the utility companies, even though some of these companies saw "renewables as 'niche' technologies" just two years ago.

It predicts that the "utility industry [will be] split into centralised back-up rate-of-return generation – as was the case pre-privatisation – with smaller 'localised' utilities with distribution generation and storage managing local supply and demand, potentially even on a multi-street basis."[190]

The changes that are occurring in the energy industries, the threat posed by anthropogenic climate change, the issues of peak car and the move towards electric cars described above, pose enormous threats to companies operating in energy industries. As a side effect, the price of oil is likely to drop very sharply, and within ten years will be half or even a third of its current price, having a devastating effect on oil companies and countries that rely on the export of oil and gas.

Their hope lies in going, as it were, beyond petroleum, and in diversifying. Ironically, the ample supply of sunlight, combined with land that is currently largely empty of life, or business – namely desert – does provide an opportunity for many of the countries that currently supply oil to retain their position as suppliers of energy to Europe. Likewise, Russia, with its huge size –perhaps even using its natural resources for hydro energy storage – could yet retain its position as an energy exporter. But these outcomes are far from certain. Technology may yet disrupt energy industries as profoundly as the advent of steam power disrupted the traditional industries of Europe in the 19th and early 20th centuries.

[190] Energy Darwinism, Citi, October 2013
https://ir.citi.com/Jb89SJMmf%2BsAVK2AKa3QE5EJwb4fvl5UUplD0lCiGOO
k0NV2CqNI%2FPDLJqxidz2VAXXAXFB6fOY%3D

The great convergence, when the media and retail become as one, and then there is the great disruptor

The thing that many people don't realise about Google, Amazon, Wal Mart and their favourite paper magazine, is that when you drill down, all four of these businesses operate in a very similar business space. At least they do up to a point, and in the case of the magazine, the convergence with retail is ahead: it's about to occur.

When Google was floated in 2004 many investors looked on aghast. They looked at the company's market cap, they looked at predictions of profits in the year ahead, and either put their head in their hands in an act of despair, or fell about in fits of laughter at such folly. "Dot com bubble two," they said. "How could the markets repeat their errors of the dotcom boom so soon?" Analysts had made assumptions so wild, that "there was a danger they might be hit by a flying pig," they said, or at least words to that effect.

Yet, ten years on and things look very different. At the IPO launch, the share price suggested a valuation of $33 billion for Google. At that time Yahoo! was valued at $39 billion. "Most analysts have argued that Yahoo! should trade at a premium to Google since it is a more diversified company," said an article on cnn.com.[191]

Today Google's market cap is $360 billion, making it the third largest company in the world by valuation. Yahoo!'s valuation is $33 billion.[192]. In its latest quarter, Google made a profit of $3.38 billion, and an annual total of $12.9

---

[191] Google IPO priced at $85 a share, August 19 2004, cnn.com
http://edition.cnn.com/2004/BUSINESS/08/19/google.ipo/
[192] Figures according to Yahoo finance, 13 April 2014

billion.[193] That means the company's PE ratio based on profits ten years ahead was just three – an unambiguously cheap price, although of course no one could have known that at the time of IPO.

The reason, at least in part, why Google did so well is because its AdWords product was, at that time, the most cost effective advertising tool ever invented. The way in which those in the business of advertising could use Google to marry up products to prospective buyers of that product was almost beautiful in its precision.
Because an auction determines the price of AdWords, the process and the forces of demand and supply have pushed upwards on price, so much so that bargains are now hard to come by. Even so, AdWords remains an incredibly effective way of targeting advertising.

But consider what determines the cost of a slot in Google Adwords. Those that are selling a product use the Google service to sell that product, and the price they are willing to pay is a function of how many products they can sell and the profit margin on each product.

Amazon makes a profit in much the same way. The key difference is that Amazon fulfils orders and carries stock.

But always, the key determiner of profit is number of products sold and margin on those products.

This is not new. Advertising budgets have always been a function of how much a company thinks it will affect its sales. To use economic-speak, the marginal cost of advertising should equal the marginal revenue that results. It is just that with the internet and with AdWords, advertising can be linked to sales with a degree of precision not possible before. Thanks to products such as Adwords,

---

[193] https://investor.google.com/earnings/2013/index.html

advertising becomes a variable cost, rather than an overhead, and that is truly crucial.

At core, the big difference between Google and Amazon is that Google sells other people's products on their behalf, while Amazon buys other people's products and sells them on. That difference is quite subtle.

People used to say that the key to success in retail was the three Ps: position, position and position. In the era of the internet, the three Ps are just as important, it is just that the position on Google, social media and apps has become just as important.

Back in 2004, when Google was floated, many analysts didn't take this into account. They saw advertising and the money companies paid for retail space, point of sale advertising, and product packaging as quite different. Today they are all converging. Google is competing with owners of commercial property, packaging designers, and the cost of providing effective shop-window displays.

Google, Wal Mart and Amazon all occupy the same business space; they are all after the same dollars, euros and yen that consumers are preparing to spend. It is just that Wal Mart, with its higher overheads, also takes a bigger slice of those dollars, euros and yen. You could say Google takes a fistful of dollars, and Wal Mart a few dollars more.

Paper magazines are neither good nor bad, and it is clear they are not ugly. These days they can be decidedly beautiful. But can you really say they are chasing the same space targeted by Google and Wal Mart? Sure, advertising budgets are a function of how much spare money companies might have, and in a theoretical world such budgets are directly related to how much profitable revenue they generate. However, in the real world, calculating the benefit of an above the line advertising campaign is more of an art than a science. This is set to change.

In 2004, a company called Powa[194] launched a new app or service that may yet revolutionise the way in which we buy goods. The PowaTag enables shoppers to point their smart phone at a picture of a product in a magazine, on a television, on a poster or in a shop window, and buy it, there and then.

No doubt other products will follow. Thanks to the internet of things, magazines, TV commercials, and posters on street corners have been brought up to date. Now such mediums have become extensions of the till in a shop or the shopping cart on a web site.

Forbes magazine described PowaTag as the product that may eat Amazon's lunch. [195] It is now possible to buy products on display in shop windows when the shop is closed.

In such a world, sales can be directly proportional to specific advertising. In such a world, the position of a poster site, or the positioning of an ad in a magazine or its position on Google or Facebook has become an alternative to positioning on a high street. Advertising media clamour for the same budgets that may once have been allocated to renting premium real estate on a street corner, or in a shopping centre.

Throw big data into the mix, and you can see how advertising has just become different, and how the media

---

[194] http://www.powatag.com/page/powatag-transact-how-it-works
[195] The Secret Technology That Attracted $76 Million And Could Eat Amazon's Lunch 13 September 2013, Forbes,
http://www.forbes.com/sites/karstenstrauss/2013/09/13/the-secret-technology-that-attracted-76-million-and-could-eat-amazons-lunch/

and owners of commercial property compete for the same slice of our disposable income. At one level this is not new, but it is now possible to make the calculations with a degree of accuracy that was once inconceivable, and that is incredibly disruptive.

The impact on retail

The internet of things, a more collaborative economy and big data are set to change retail radically. In December 2013, *Venture Beat* published an interview with Bernie Meyerson, vice president of innovation at IBM. [196] Mr Meyerson predicted that in five years' time buying goods from local suppliers will beat buying goods online. To explain this, he used the example of when you go into your local store to get your groceries. That store might send a message saying "'You haven't bought your favourite non-wheat-based bread in two weeks. I know you buy that every two weeks. You might be running low. The sliced bread is on Aisle 2.'" He said that will be "incredibly powerful."

In April 2014, Deloitte released a report drawing the intriguing conclusion that the high street – that is to say local shopping – has performed better since the finance crisis of 2008 than either shopping centres or out-of-town developments. Its report, which focused on the UK, found that just 20 per cent of high street shops affected by 27 high profile administrations since 2009 were still vacant in early 2004, compared with 37 per cent vacancy rates for retail parks, and 29 per cent for shopping centres.

Ian Geddes, head of retail at Deloitte, said: "Rather than taking shoppers away, the internet is pushing people back to shops with the growth of 'click and collect'. The evidence

[196] Dean Takahashi, Our complete interview with IBM's Bernie Meyerson on the top five predictions for the next five years, Venture Beat, December 19, http://venturebeat.com/2013/12/19/our-complete-interview-with-ibms-bernie-meyerson-on-the-top-five-predictions-for-the-next-five-years/

suggests that we may be entering a new era of 'en route' shopping, powered by mobile shopping and the demand for collection points strategically located at a point between where the consumer is travelling from and to."[197]

All of a sudden, technology can offer functions and information that were once available to only the very biggest companies.

Thanks to the internet of things and big data, local retailers now know more about what their customers want. They will never able to compete with giant retailers for in-store choice, but –thanks to the internet of things and big data – this will not matter as much. Massive choice is available online, which no bricks and mortar retailer, no matter how large a store it has, can match in store. Consumers don't need their local stores to offer choice; they just need them to offer the products they want, products they can find online, and big data can tell local stores what they want.

As for the larger stores, they now realise that success lies in combining online and offline shopping with products such as Apple's iBeacon, enhancing the shopping experience with navigation tools for example.

The traditional advantage held by the large retail giants partly lies with their buying muscle and access to market research.

The collaborative economy created by the internet makes it easier for smaller retailers to pool resources, securing superior buying muscle. The emphasis on transparency will make it harder for bigger retailers to negotiate special deals.

---

[197] Deloitte, Just 20% of high street shops affected by administration in last five years remain vacant $ April 2014,
http://www.deloitte.com/view/en_GB/uk/industries/consumer-business/083873bccb725410VgnVCM3000003456f70aRCRD.htm

For instance, consultants can make their expertise available to local stores via technology such as video conferencing, in which several stores can simultaneously benefit from advice at a price that once made such expertise the exclusive property of the giant retailers.

3D printing will enable a new level of product customisation. The high street in ten or fifteen years from now will be equipped with 3D printing experts, who produce bespoke products – or at least refine off the shelf-products by giving them unique features. The high street of the 2030s will see the 21st century equivalent of the local blacksmith – it is just that these 21st century blacksmiths won't be heavily muscled craftsmen working in the heat of a furnace. Instead, they will be 3D printing experts with specialist skills in the design of clothes, shoes, fashion accessories, or spare parts for cars, or products for DIY. The high street of 2030 will see the return of cottage industries, as bespoke design takes over from mass consumer similarity. Urban legend has it that Henry Ford famously said: "You can have any colour you like as long as it is black," illustrating how in assembly production, specialisation was key. The more identical copies of the original design that can be made, the cheaper they could become. In a mass customisation economy, you will be able to have any shape, size or colour you like, as long as you are prepared to pay for it.

The commercial property mudslide

The world of office rentals faces a dual threat from the sharing economy, partially with the challenge coming from the hotel business, and partially from desk sharing schemes. The hotel economy, in turn, faces a disruptive threat from the sharing economy. Existing transport industries will be transformed as the sharing economy disrupts business sectors as old as industry itself. But even these vicissitudes will be as nothing compared to the changes that will be wrought when augmented reality and virtual reality changes the way in which we perceive the world.

In chapter seven we reported that the hotel chain Marriott is now offering workspace when demanded as part of its conference service. The self-styled Millennial thinker Rachel Botsman said: "Marriott is no longer just a place to stay, it becomes a place to meet people, to work – it brings other customers through their doors."

Then you have companies such as Neardesk in the UK, which supplies a network of desks that can be hired by the hour. Ultimately, on days when many employees at a company are out in the field for example, it will be possible for companies to rent out free desks, via companies such as Neardesk, thereby monetising space otherwise lying idle.

Such ideas make better use of scarce office space, but free up may ultimately space, creating spare capacity, which owners could convert into living accommodation.

The sharing economy will make the use of real estate more efficiently, but it may increase the value of a square foot of space, pushing up prices, or it may lead to over-capacity, which could push down rental charges. The latter outcome is more likely, but either way the effect will be massive disruption.

Hotels now have the opportunity to use the technology that creates a sharing economy to compete with those who rent out office space. Equally, the sharing economy – via products such as Airbnb – enables individuals to rent out spare rooms in their home, and will therefore mean they are competing with the hotel business. The battleground may be between the services and food offered by a hotel versus the individuality and personal human interaction made possible by Airbnb.

The chainsaw economy

The sharing economy will also provide the possibility of making use of products otherwise lying idle. A household may own number of DIY tools, which are used only very rarely, for example a chainsaw.

In a sharing economy, empowered by technology, it will be easier to share such technology. Such a sharing economy may reduce overall demand for cars, office space, hotel rooms, and a massive range of goods sold to the end user and to businesses, which would otherwise lie idle for most of the time.

The internet will create a need for those who can facilitate the sharing economy, and thereby remove the embarrassment factor from the equation; for example handling a situation in which someone borrows your lawn mower and then breaks it.

In a sharing economy, taxi drivers may temporarily find demand for their services rises as the technology that creates smart cities creates a more accurate way of matching demand and supply. But services such as Uber, and beyond that lift sharing, and beyond that the combination of sharing with self-driving cars, may cause massive disruption in transport industries. Cab drivers, bus drivers and lorry drivers may find that technology encroaches on a domain, which had seemed immune to the threat posed by technology. Even great disrupters, such as those companies that are currently disrupting the taxi business in the US, may themselves be disrupted by self-driving cars and lift sharing.

In a sharing economy, social media will become more popular than ever, as both suppliers and customers strive to build an e-reputation. That is to say, as someone that can be trusted to give you a lift, rent out a room in their house or office for one day, or can be trusted to borrow your lawn mower, use your desk, or stay in your home.

Ironically, products such as PowaTag may give paper magazines a new lease of life, as it will enable these mediums to fall within the sphere of shopping. Pushing against that, you will have products such as iBeacon, which will enable coffee shops, restaurants, clubs and libraries to offer premium content to consumers on their tablets or smart phones.

There is hope for paper magazines because these days the paper industry is largely sustainable, with trees that are felled for paper being replaced with new trees. Indeed, in some ways paper has been good news for those who fear deforestation because hard commercial realities have forced sustainable practises to be used.

Nonetheless it is hard to imagine that as the Millennial generation matures, and beyond that as the next generation, the so called 'generation Z' matures, that paper books, magazines and newspapers won't be totally replaced by eReaders, tablets, smart phones, or some kind of combination with augmented reality.

The effects of augmented reality and virtual reality

In some respects, both augmented reality and virtual reality may give traditional ways of doing things a new lease of life. They may give a new benefit to paper media, for example, as users can view an article in a paper magazine and then call up additional supporting information from their augmented reality glasses.

In time, however, both technologies, and virtual reality in particular, will change the way in which we view products online. From our headsets we will have a new way of viewing an item of clothing; for example, in three dimensions, with the item worn by an avatar corresponding to our own unique shape, even with our facial characteristics.

Virtual reality will change the way in which we view a hotel or a holiday complex from our home or from a travel agent. In the short term, virtual reality will provide a new reason to visit a holiday booking store, to view details on a hotel from state of the art VR sets. Such sets will include pull down menus featuring videos of other user reviews. In time, all these benefits will be available at home. As we view holiday ideas from our VR headsets, we can invite travel agents to help us, and we may even communicate directly with an agent, via their avatar, represented in the virtual reality landscape that we view.

Homes will have several VR headsets, for different members of the family. VR will represent the biggest threat yet to the cinema. To date, the cinema has survived the march of technology for two reasons. Firstly, its large screen and advanced sound systems can offer benefits few people can enjoy at home. Secondly, there is a social aspect – it remains a popular venue for dating couples, for example. It may be a very long time indeed before virtual reality can offer the second of these benefits, but it is hard to see how the cinema can compete with VR sets for providing a more immersive film viewing experience.

Virtual reality will transform the way in which we communicate over long distances, and enable conversations in virtual worlds, both for fun, and for business with virtual reality board rooms, in which we are represented by an avatar. Peak car will be brought forward thanks to virtual reality, as remote working becomes more practical, and the need for face-to-face meetings reduces.

The online shopping experience may see the addition of sales agents represented by avatars.

Both virtual reality and augmented reality will enhance theme parks and tourist sites. If you were to visit the Coliseum in Rome for example, or the Athenian Parthenon, virtual reality/augmented reality displays will provide you with overlapping images of what the building you are looking at used to be like.

The disruption to transport, communication, shopping, movies and holidays will be massive. As a part of this process, social media will be radically upgraded, as it supports the currency of trust, which is vital for the sharing economy.

Yet in March 2014, when Facebook announced its deal to purchase Occulus Rift, its share price fell.

Those caught in the sceptical phase of innovation could not see beyond the virtual reality hype of the late 1980s. Sure, it has not yet realised the wildest dreams expressed 15 years earlier, but that does not mean it won't do so, or indeed it won't do so very soon.

Those who write off social media and virtual reality, just as they are set to become vital lynchpins in the 21st century economy, will be left with no alternative but to wipe off large helpings of virtual egg from the face of their VR avatar.

Chapter nine: Disruption of the economy
Will technology create more wealth for all, or send us into a deep depression from which we may never recover?

Suppose the technologies we saw in the TV series *Star Trek* became available overnight: what would the economic implications be? Suppose teleporters removed the need for all other forms of transport. Suppose food replicators created an infinite supply of food without the need for an agriculture industry. Suppose a new energy source was discovered, say dilithium crystals used in *Star Trek*, or we simply cracked the problem of nuclear fusion and all the energy required to fulfil the demands of every man, women and child on this planet became freely available. Suppose a new miracle technology enabled our buildings to self-assemble, without using up scarce resources, and suppose all our clothes were grown from test tubes in our own homes, supervised by robots. Would this be a utopian world or a form of hell? And if such innovations occurred overnight, is it not possible that we might suffer a massive economic recession as a result?

Impressive though modern technologies are and promise to be, they are not even close to all those things described above. But they are evolving so fast that we may only be two decades away from a situation in which our technology lead over the pre-internet world of 1990 is greater than the technology lead the world of 1990 had over, say, Britain at the time of the collapse of the Roman Empire. Relatively speaking, the timeframe over which our technology will be transformed is overnight. This may sound exciting, but it could herald a recession, an economic depression, or something even worse.

The finance crisis of 2008 may in fact have been a dry-run of what we might suffer if technology unravels in a certain way over the next two decades. We can avoid such an economic catastrophe, but only if economists remove their heads from the sand and accept that the technology revolution is occurring, and then start drawing up plans to ensure its economic consequences will be benign, and not catastrophic.

The pros and cons of technology

So will the technology revolutions that are underway be good or bad for the economy? Common sense suggests they should be good, but, as any Luddite will confirm, there is no guarantee of it.

We can sum up the economic dangers of technology as follows:

The pros and cons of technology

	Dangers	Response
Jobs	Technologies, such as 3D printing and robotics, will destroy jobs.	The story of past innovations is that new jobs are created by technology, although time lags occur.
Distribution of income	New technology will reward owners of capital over labour.	The story of the first and second industrial revolutions is that income eventually became more equal, not less. See below.

Demand	An economy needs demand to grow, but if the fruits of growth do not trickle down into higher wages, how can growth occur?	Austrian economists say innovation creates its own demand (for example the Apple iPod).
2008 crisis	Growing inequality may have been the underlying cause of the 2008 crisis. What role did technology have in this? [198]	The argument that growing inequality was the main cause of the 2008 crisis is far from proven.
Affordability	Only the rich will benefit from technology. The advances of medicine, for example, may not be affordable for the majority of the population.	This is not borne out by the history of innovation. In general, innovations are linked with demand, and demand only grows if the price of technology falls. Computers are a classic example: as the price of computers fell, demand rose, investment increased, and price

[198] As Nobel Laureate Paul Krugman said: "There's a pretty good, although not ironclad, case that soaring inequality helped set the stage for our economic crisis, and that the highly unequal distribution of income since the crisis has perpetuated the slump especially, by making it hard for families in debt to work their way out." Krugman, Paul; The Populist Imperative, New York Times, January 23 2014.
http://www.nytimes.com/2014/01/24/opinion/krugman-the-populist-imperative.html?_r=0 24 April 2014

		fell even further. Computers became more powerful as more people could afford them.
Dangers of free and sharing economy	Is there a risk that technology may support our material needs, but that this won't be reflected in rises in GDP? For example, sharing self-driving cars may promote more affordable transport, but lead to less car production.	We need to change the way in which GDP is measured, or find another measure of an economy's strength.
Government Debt	If GDP falls, even though we feel better off, won't that make government debt unaffordable?	Falling GDP may be associated with falling interest rates. Does debt matter if the interest on it is minimal? In any case, in an economy in which there is spare productive capacity, governments could always fund debt by printing money. This may be especially so, if more and more services are free. Let's face it, inflation is hardly a danger in a 'free'

		economy.
Money	Will the rise of virtual currencies, such as the bitcoin, remove the ability of government and central banks to set interest rates, and control the money supply?	A libertarian economist might argue that the control of money should be left to the markets.
Danger of conflict	The rise of technologies, such as 3D printing, robotics, the internet of things, and locally sourced energy, may lead to more local supply with trade limited to the supply of scare resources, such as rare earth minerals, where China is the dominant source of supply.	Technology will create new reasons for trade, and in any case scarce resources that cannot be created by technology may be more widely spread than is generally thought. The opportunity for mining in space, asteroids, for example, may create a new vast supply of minerals.

The importance of technology

It's a key point of this book that technology matters. It is the key driver of growth. Technology also influences distribution of income and wealth. Technology, at least in part, charges the economic cycle, and it may ultimately determine whether we can avoid global conflict.

Here are some key points to bear in mind:
Technological revolutions.

Over the last two hundred and fifty years there have been two, possibly three, industrial revolutions. Two will follow in the next two to three decades:[199]

First revolution:	Mid 18th to 19th century: age of steam, revolution in textiles.
Second revolution:	1867 to 1913: called the Age of Symmetry by Vaclav Smil: dynamite, the telephone, photographic film, electricity-generating plants, electric motors, steam turbines, the gramophone, cars, aluminium production, air-filled rubber tyres, pre-stressed concrete, first aeroplanes, tractors, radio signals, plastics, neon lights and assembly line production.
Third revolution:	Circa 1980s to 2008: Computers, early internet. Of all the revolutions described here, this may be the least effective at creating wealth.
Fourth revolution:	More advanced internet, social media, robotics, internet of things, 3D printing and new energy technologies.
Fifth revolution:	Nanotechnology and artificial intelligence.

---

[199] Clearly dates are approximations, and for the fourth and fifth revolutions, the dates are uncertain, but we can say within the next three decades for both and that both may in fact run into each other.

Big history

There is no economic precedent for current technological evolution from the second half of the century. To try to get a feel for the importance of technology, we need to take a broader perspective on history.

Economic growth is a fragile thing

There is an important point about innovation that we tend to overlook. Until a couple of hundred years ago, it wasn't much use. King Duncan of Scotland was murdered by Macbeth in 1040. Ludwig Van Beethoven died in 1827. The average citizen of planet Earth between those years barely became any better off.

Nearly all growth in GDP per capita that there has ever been has occurred since 1820. Sure, we had growth in total output and the economy got bigger, but so too did the population. Until 1820, the benefits of economic growth were somewhat nullified by population growth. [200]
Drill down and take a look at Western Europe.[201]

---

[200] http://www.mssresearch.org/?q=node/581
[201] According to Maddison, Angus, Contours of the World Economy 1-2040 AD, Oxford University Press, 2007. Back in the year 1000 AD, GDP per capita, after allowing for inflation and at 1990 prices, was US $427. By 1500, it was US $771, meaning that the average European over the 500 years became just 39 per cent better off. By 1820, this same European was worth around $1,200 a year – meaning that between 1500 and 1820 he/she became 55 per cent better off. Between 1820 and 1870, growth leapt, expanding by 63 per cent. By 1913, GDP per capita in Europe was worth $3,457 a year.

The truth is that economic growth is a fragile thing. It is possible that the economic history of the last 200 years was a blip; that soon we will return to living in a world of near zero growth.

Golden age of growth

The golden age of growth in the West occurred during a 25-year period after World War 2. It is possible that this was a delayed effect from the second industrial revolution. The Great Depression of the 1930s and then World War 2 may have delayed it.

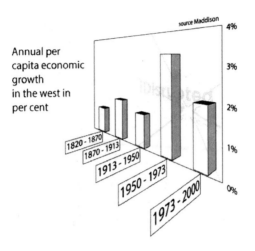

Annual per capita economic growth in the west in per cent

source Maddison

4%

3%

2%

1%

0%

1820 - 1870
1870 - 1913
1913 - 1950
1950 - 1973
1973 - 2000

Distribution of income

The French economist Thomas Piketty took the economic world by storm in early 2014 with the publication of his book: *Capital in the 21st Century*. Reviewers have described the book as the most important economic book of this century so far. [202, 203]

---

[202] Piketty, Thomas; Capital in the 21st Century, The Belknap Press of Harvard University Press, 2014

[203] The book has since come under heavy criticism, with Chris Giles at the Financial Times claiming he had found major errors in the way in which Piketty interpreted the data. Piketty himself responded saying firstly that he put all his data online, and made them freely accessible, so if he did that why would he deliberately misinterpret it? He also suggested the observations made by Giles did not materially affect his conclusions. What we can say, is that regardless of the detail, the overall trend is clear: we have seen growing inequality in the West in recent years. Technology may have been the cause and it may be set to exacerbate this effect. See: Giles, Chris. London, Piketty findings undercut by errors. The Financial Times, 23 May 2014, and for a rebuttal of Giles's rebuttal of Piketty, see: The Daily Piketty: May 30, 2014, http://equitablegrowth.org/2014/05/30/daily-piketty-may-30-2014/ 23 June 2014

The book is important for three reasons: the extensive data it contains, a theory about the rate of return on capital, and its policy recommendations. We will take a brief look at the recommendations in the conclusion of this book.

The data show that that there was a sharp fall in inequality during the period, both in income and wealth, from roughly the start of World War 2 to the mid-1970s. Inequality has since increased. This chart below is fairly typical.

It is clear that we saw a sharp decline in inequality during the golden age of growth.

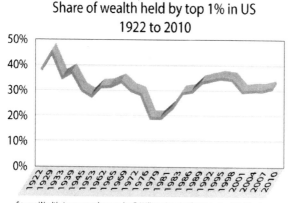

Source Wealth, income and power, by G. William Domhoff, University of California

Sometimes mathematical equations can be famous. Einstein is perhaps as famous for the equation $E=MC^2$ as anything else. Piketty has an equivalent: R>G. It means return on capital is greater than economic growth. Examples of return on capital include interest on cash on deposit in a bank or from renting out property/land.

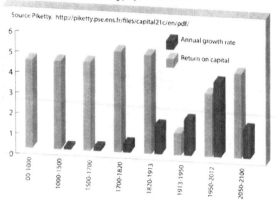

Return to capital after tax and
Capital destruction vs global growth
Including projections to 2015

Source Piketty. http://piketty.pse.ens.fr/files/capital21c/en/pdf/

204

Piketty's core point is that inequality falls when growth is greater than the return on capital.

His charts do appear to overlap with technological evolution. If technology promotes growth, and if equality rises when growth is significant, then that may explain the link.

Those who say that technology will lead to more inequality may be right, but this is not borne out by the experience of the last 250 years. If anything, it suggests that technology promotes equality, but with time lags.

However, there are two caveats. Firstly, a superficial analysis of Piketty's data may support the economist Robert Gordon, who says that the age of technological evolution

---

[204] Technical appendix of the book Capital in the 21st century. Thomas Piketty.
http://piketty.pse.ens.fr/files/capital21c/en/Piketty2014FiguresTablesLinks.pdf 23 June 2014

peaked several decades ago. However, this misses a core point. This book is not about the technology of recent years, it is about technology that is developing and this is about to affect the economy. It may have been that the technologies of the last 50 years have had less economic impact than previous innovations, but this does not mean that the technologies of the next ten to 30 years will not have a major economic impact. To put it another way, you may or may not agree that innovations of the last few decades have not impacted on the economy in the same way as the advances of the 18th, 19th and early 20th century industrial revolutions did, but it seems probable that many of these recent advances have paved the way for the great industrial revolutions yet to come. These revolutions are only just dawning.

Secondly, there is no reason to assume that the story of technology will be the same this time around. Just because the first and second industrial revolutions created more jobs than they destroyed, it does not necessarily mean this will happen the next time around.

Why did the technological revolution occur?

This all begs the question: why? Why did the economic turnaround from 1820 occur? How important was technology? Will technology lead to even more growth, or will it peter out?

Here are some possible explanations for the period of economic growth:
- It was technology led. Technology created growth.
- Discovery of the New World.
- Growth in the money supply after the discovery of gold in the New World.[205]

---

[205] The discovery of gold in the New World may have come too soon for Spain and Portugal. Because the discovery of gold came before Europe was

- Evolution of banking system based on debt.[206]
- Evolution of a capitalist system, and the decline of mercantilism and cronyism. [207]
- The development of the so-called Protestant work ethic, coupled with the idea of savings, creating the funding for investment, and also combined with the idea of philanthropy. [208] For example, as exemplified by Andrew Carnegie, and the Quakers of 19th Century Britain.
- Western imperialism, slavery and exploitation of countries with less advanced military capabilities.

The importance of trickle down

For an economy to grow, demand must rise. This is an incredibly important point often missed by non-economists. In economics, demand has a very specific meaning, and one that is often misunderstood. We all have wants. Most of us want to live in a nicer house, eat out more often, and have better holidays. This is not the same thing as saying we all demand. Demand – at least the economic definition of demand – depends on how much money we have, and how much money things cost. Demand is a function of what we can afford. Without it, we cannot have growth.

---

technically ready for an industrial revolution, the consequence of gold finds was a rise in the money supply leading to hyperinflation and a possible loss of economic pre-eminence for these two countries.

[206] Niall Fergusson argued in his book Ascent of Money that the reason why the industrial revolution first occurred in the UK, and not France was that the UK saw the development of a banking system based on debt, whereas France, after one of its richest citizens suffered after the bursting of the Mississippi bubble, developed an aversion to debt.

[207] Repeal of the Corn Law in the UK in 1846 is an example of putting an end to legislation that put the interests of food producers over consumers.

[208] As advanced in the book The Protestant Ethic and the Spirit of Capitalism of 1904, by Max Weber.

Maybe, technological advances create their own demand. Maybe for an economy to grow in the long term, it needs a mechanism by which demand and technology can support each other in tandem. Two famous stories, both involving Ford, illustrate the point. A third story relating to Moore's Law hammers the point home.

Let's begin this story in 1958 when Walter Reuther, a US trade union leader, was taken on a tour of a Ford car factory, and shown the latest developments in automation. The manager conducting the tour asked Mr Reuther: "Aren't you worried about how you're going to collect union dues from all these machines." Mr Reuther is said to have replied: "The thought that occurred to me was how are you going to sell cars to these machines?"[209]

The second story takes place further back in time, during the early days of Ford. Henry Ford doubled the wages at his factories to $5 a day, in the hope, or so it is often said, that other manufacturing companies would follow suit, and that as a result wages would rise across the economy and more people would be able to afford to buy his cars.

The third story dates from around 1964, when Gordon Moore at Intel is supposed to have made his bold claim that the number of transistors on an integrated circuit would double every 24 months. Moore's Law is a good example of how technology does not evolve automatically but needs growth in demand for the technological advances to occur. In the case of Moore's Law, technological progress and growing demand worked together. As the price of computers fell, demand rose, encouraging greater investment, then economies of scale were realised, prices fell further and computer power increased, making the technology more accessible so that demand rose again,

[209] Quote taken from Steve Johnson, Capital gobbles labour's share, the FT 13 October 2013

encouraging even more investment and the realisation of even more economies of scale. Moore's Law was made possible as computers moved from the corporate computer room to sitting on every desk, to sitting in pockets and handbags. It will continue to be advanced thanks to computers appearing in our clothes, in our consumer durables, and in the packaging of products for sale in shops. The more we demand computer technology, the more it advances. The more it advances, the more we demand it. As John Scully was quoted as saying in Chapter One, Apple's startling resurgence of the last decade was made possible by the homogenisation of technology.

This is an exceedingly important idea. Those who suggest that technology may create a world of extreme inequality may be right, but equally it may be that unless the profits from technology trickle down, pushing up wages and creating demand, then further technological evolution may be impossible. If technology leads to more inequality, it may have the effect of suffocating demand from the economy and can become self-destroying, making further technological evolution redundant as only the few could afford it.

This does not mean that a capitalist system will inevitably implode, as Marx predicted, but neither does it mean that there no dangers. To try to ensure that wealth trickles down and enables technology to spread out among the entire population within a capitalist system is neither a policy of a Marxist nor a socialist; it can be equally be the policy of a capitalist.

Profits to GDP

Piketty focused on the return on capital relative to growth. Here is another twist on that argument.

The ratio of US corporate profits to GDP hit its highest level ever recorded in 2006, just before the global economy imploded. [210] However, since the 2008 crisis, after initially falling, this ratio has climbed, hitting a new high.

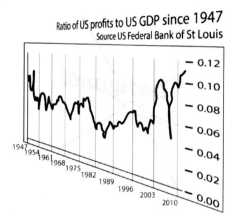

Ratio of US profits to US GDP since 1947
Source US Federal Bank of St Louis

Quarterly data do not go back before the 1940s, but year on year data do go back to 1929. During this period, the ratio of profits to GDP hit three plateaus: in 1929, 2006 and right now. On each occasion, the plateau was higher than the previous one. [211] [212]

It may be a coincidence of course, but US corporate profits to GDP peaked just before the 1930s Great Depression and before the economic downturn of 2008. In other words, profits to GDP hitting a new high, and wages to GDP hitting a new low preceded the two biggest economic catastrophes of the last 85 years.

---

[210] US Federal Bank of St Louis

[211] Fox, Justin; The Real Story Behind Those "Record" Corporate Profits, Harvard Business Review, November 24, 2010
http://blogs.hbr.org/2010/11/the-real-story-behind-those-re/, 18 April 1014

[212] In fairness we don't really know what happened before 1929; it is assumed here that as the ratio fell sharply soon after, and that as 1929 was the year of the Wall Street crash, the level in 1929 was at a high point.

It is possible that technology was the underlying driver. To remind you, there are time lags between innovation and its impact on the economy. In 1873, John Stuart Mill said that that the industrial revolution had not yet had much impact. According to economic historian Brad DeLong, between 1800 and 1870 real working class wages grew at just 0.4 per cent a year, but tripled to 1.2 per cent from 1870 to 1950. [213]

First industrial revolution mid 18th century to circa 1840

But workers did not benefit at first. We had the Luddites

By 1870 wages for workers were rising much faster as a result of delayed impact of first industrial revolution

---

[213] See Gavin Kelly, The robots are coming. Will they bring wealth or a divided society? *The Observer*, 4 January 2014 http://www.theguardian.com/technology/2014/jan/04/robots-future-society-drones

Second industrial revolution from around 1861 to 1913

But workers did not benefit at first. We had the US Great Depression of the 1930s

But by the 1950s ordinary families were at last benefiting from previous innovations

When wages began to rise in 1870, this may have been a result of innovations that occurred up to a century earlier. The second industrial revolution ended around the year 1913. The First World War delayed the impact of these innovations on the economy. The 1920s saw economic boom in the US, but greater inequality as the reward to capital exceeded the rewards to labour. Instead, debt levels rose until we had the crash of 1929. Is it not possible that technology initially had a negative impact on the economy, destroying jobs and sucking demand out of the economy?

By the end of World War 2, the economy had finally found a way of turning technology into economic growth. Just as workers in 1870 had only just begun to benefit from innovations that had occurred in the late 1700s, is it not possible or indeed likely that it took until the 1950s before workers benefitted from the innovations of the second industrial revolution?

Maybe greater equality enabled the possibility of converting technology into growth by ensuring that demand kept growing. After World War 2, there was a feeling of dissatisfaction. In countries such as the UK, the poor had made a kind of tacit agreement with the elite. The agreement went something like this: 'We will fight for you. We will pull together, but when this is over we want an economy in which reward is based on merit, rather than privilege; an economy that sees full employment, decent wages, and some form of welfare state.' In this way, the conditions in which demand could rise were set, enabling the full exploitation of technology.

In the West, from 1973 to 2008, economic growth was much lower than from the period 1948 to 1973. Maybe by the mid-1970s, we had just about used up the potential created by the innovations of the late 19th and early 20th centuries, and so growth slowed down. Demand, however, continued to rise, creating inflation and exacerbating union activism.

Four important points about inequality and globalisation

But in the story of inequality, and amongst the theories as to the identity of the underlying cause of the 2008 crisis, technology has a rival. Many say that globalisation, and not technology, has been the main driver of the economy, both good and bad, in recent years.

There is surely little doubt that globalisation had the effect of increasing the rewards to capital and decreasing the rewards to labour, but bear the following four points in mind:

318

- Firstly, technology, and the internet in particular, may have made the recent wave of globalisation possible.
- Secondly, while there has been an increase in inequality from one point of view, from another it has fallen. Thanks to globalisation, in recent years the global economy has seen hundreds of millions – maybe even more than a billion people – leave poverty altogether.
- What we have seen, however, is that the wealth pertaining to the richest 1 per cent has risen and the richest 0.1 per cent have experienced an even bigger rise.
- It is important to emphasize that we are not suggesting here that globalisation and technological innovation are negative things, merely that they can have negative as well as positive impacts.

Technology and jobs

Since the time of the Luddites, and maybe before, there has been an assumption that technology destroys jobs. We now know that the first and second industrial revolutions created more jobs than they destroyed. There were time lags, however, and mass unemployment and poverty has occasionally been the short-term result of technological innovation.

But will the next industrial revolution, made possible by the internet of things, robotics and 3D printing – or indeed the one that will come afterwards, made possible by nanotechnology, artificial intelligence, and maybe virtually reality – follow the pattern of the past?

We know that the advance of computers may have destroyed some industries, but it created new ones. At first glance, it is hard to see how robotics or 3D printing can do anything other than destroy jobs. For example, if the internet of things makes it possible to pay for goods in a shop without even passing a till, how can the result of this be anything other than job losses?

On the other hand, one of the probable benefits of 3D printing will be customisation. While we may see automation cause a loss of jobs, we may see the creation of new jobs, following a cottage industry style format, in which local designers tailor-make products to the requirements of each customer. There was a time when every village had its blacksmith. The industrial revolution destroyed this worthy profession. The next one may create the 21st century equivalent of the blacksmith: designers/craftspeople/3D printing experts creating bespoke products for a local market. So net job losses may not be the result of new technology, but disruption in the labour market will undoubtedly result.

It is generally assumed that the big profits from technology will accrue to those who understand it, and especially to those who can create it. So it is assumed we will need superior education; the creation of more PhDs in robotics, and nanotechnology. It is assumed that the big money will go to those with MBAs, the business strategists, the captains of 21st century industry.

These assumptions may not be wholly accurate.

Firstly, there will also be a limit to how many new recruits with PhDs companies will require; on how many MBAs are necessary. If we focus our education system on creating highly educated engineers/ potential business leaders, by 2030 we may end up with a large number of extremely disappointed products of the education system.

Secondly, the requirement of customisation will create jobs for skilled crafts people, who are adept at technology.

Thirdly, the need for a service economy will not abate. Wearable technology may provide us with regular updates on our health, but this is likely to create the need for more, not less medical expertise, as we demand more medical support for each and every ailment to which technology alerts us.

As we age, and the prospects of us living into very old age rise, we will demand services to maintain our health. We will demand physiotherapists, and experts in training us in how to use prosthetics; experts in fitting enhanced exoskeletons, experts in communicating to us the results achieved from sequencing of our respective genomes, personal trainers, carers to support us in our old age, experts in skin care...the list goes on.

Technology may create as many jobs as it destroys.

A Downton Abbey economy

Back in October 2012, the economist Roger Bootle, writing in the British newspaper *The Daily Telegraph*, looked back at the 19th century and early 20th century, at the type of economy with which viewers of the TV hit Downton Abbey will be familiar. In this world, a small number of the society's richest people had a virtual army of servants, who didn't earn much, but they were kept in employment. This ended with industrialisation, and in the post war years millions left school with very little in the way of qualifications, yet they earned a good living. Mr Bootle asked: "Is the current situation an aberration? Or was the aberration rather the immediate post-war period?" He speculated that that we may return to a situation in which once again millions of people are either employed by the rich, "or are indirectly employed by them to cook, clean and look after them, albeit often in separate commercial establishments such as restaurants, dry cleaners etc."[214]

He may be right. On the other hand, it depends on the extent to which the fruits of technology trickle down.

It also depends on how government regulators handle the issues of patents. A powerful case can be made for saying that in most cases patents do not promote innovation; rather they hinder it. But what they unambiguously do achieve is to ensure the profits from innovation accrue to larger companies and their owners.

It is possible that there are occasions when patents can enhance the innovation process, for example under certain circumstances within the pharmaceutical industry. But, as was argued earlier in the book, more often than not, patents slow the innovation process up. Indeed, even within the pharmaceutical industry, also as pointed out earlier in the book, an open source drug discovery platform has been created and GSK has opened up its research data and laboratories to outside scientists in the fight against malaria.

The existence of patents may mean that the majority of wealth created from innovations boosts the wealth of the very richest in society, but restricts the extent of trickle down.

A 21st Century economy, which sees the domination of patented technology continue, may well see the creation of a *Downton Abbey* type economy, in which most of the wealth in society is owned by the richest 1 or 0.1 per cent.

---

[214] Roger Bootle: Cutting prices to raise living standards is just a waste of energy, The Telegraph, 6 October 2013,
http://www.telegraph.co.uk/finance/comment/rogerbootle/10359344/Roger-Bootle-Cutting-prices-to-raise-living-standards-is-just-a-waste-of-energy.html

Maybe we don't want to see the emergence of an economy in which the super-rich once again lose the ability to dress themselves. In addition, such an economy may be self-defeating, because as a result of the way in which wealth is skewed in favour of the super-rich, demand may be sucked out of the economy.

A 21st century which sees the curtailing of the ruthless adoption of patents, and encourages free access to knowledge and use of the science behind innovations to all, will be more egalitarian, and more dynamic.

The Dangers of Free

It was pointed out in chapter two, a knowledge economy may result in more goods being offered free. Economic theory says price is a function of marginal cost. The marginal cost of digital products is typically zero. This seems to provide the theoretical explanation for products over the internet being free. We get the exception, such as eBooks, which are often no cheaper than paper books, or premium content from newspapers such as the *Financial Times (FT)*.

The jury is out on whether the internet will inevitably lead to more free digital products, or whether the fight-back led by the likes of the *FT* will win through.

The problem with a free economy is that advertising becomes just about the only means of funding digital products. And advertising revenue is becoming increasingly dominated by a handful of companies; Google and Facebook, for example. Without the enormous volume of content on the internet, there would be little point in either search or social media. Yet the revenue from this content accrues to the companies that provide search and social media, not the producers of content.

Whether this is sustainable in the long run is not clear. It is possible that it is only if the providers of search and social media are in some way taxed, with the proceeds being distributed to the producers of free content.

It is clear, however, that in a service economy, in which individuals provide bespoke services for others, marginal cost is far from zero. This is why such an economy may be vital to long-term creation of prosperity.

The problem with bitcoins, and other virtual currencies

During the banking crisis of 2008, journalists frequently drew comparisons between the woes at banks and the famous story of the emperor who had no clothes. Banks, it was suggested, had been outed like the emperor.

But it is just possible that a growing economy needs an element of naked emperor about it. This is why.

Companies do not produce more unless demand has risen, but demand cannot rise unless income goes up, and this cannot increase unless companies produce more. To put it another way; in an economy output equals demand. Demand is a function of income. Income is a function of output. In such a scenario how can growth occur?

It is possible that the only way we can overcome this problem is either via debt or via a boost in the money supply. In this way, demand can rise in advance of salaries going up, and in advance of output rising.

Such a strategy can be dangerous. An economy that needs debt or a rising money supply is vulnerable to debt bubbles or inflation. When bubbles burst, the economic activity that led to the bubble bursting may seem like a sham. People may say: "Look, the economy is like the emperor who wore no clothes." Maybe an economy that has neither debt nor a growing money supply cannot grow. Only fans of English football will get the next point. A growing economy may be a little like West Ham Football Club: forever blowing bubbles.

This is why the discovery of gold in the New World leading to an explosion in the money supply may have made the continuation of the industrial revolution possible. This is why the development of a banking system based on debt may have created the foundations of the industrial revolution in the UK, and a lack of banking system based on debt could explain why such a revolution did not occur in France, even though the two countries were similar in many other respects.[215]

Bitcoins are massively popular with those who subscribe to libertarian philosophy; those who believe that central banks should not control the money supply. The same school of thought has called for the return of a gold standard.

But a growing economy needs a growing money supply, and central banks are responsible for ensuring this growth in the money supply. The supply of gold and bitcoins is limited by arbitrary, external factors.

Contrary to belief, if central banks no longer controlled the money supply and instead we had a fixed money supply, for example via bitcoins, such a system may act as a tourniquet on growth. If we had a bitcoin type monetary system, we may see a static economy, with growth being suffocated; one in which inequalities persist.

But in one sense, the critics may have a point about central banks; maybe they are not the right institutions to be left in control of the money supply.

---

[215] Although the French revolution may have played just as big a part.

Consider for example the policy of quantitative easing, also called QE, introduced in 2009 by the US Federal Reserve and adopted soon afterwards by the Bank of England.

Many warned that QE would lead to hyperinflation, and a deep rooted fear of this in Germany meant that the European Central Bank was itself reluctant to indulge in QE.

The policy was not especially effective, but neither did it lead to hyperinflation. This is because QE did not create money as such; rather it made the cost of government borrowing cheaper and drove up asset prices. There is little economic benefit of making it easier and cheaper for governments to borrow money if those same governments are trying to impose austerity at the same time.

If instead governments funded their spending by the creation of money – for example in the US there was talk about the US treasury issuing a trillion dollar platinum coin, which it could hold on deposit at the Fed, and withdraw money against it – it could fund tax cuts or spending. Many fear that such an approach would be disastrous. They fear it would lead to inflation, maybe hyperinflation. However, there was little danger of this in 2008, when deflation rather than inflation was a bigger threat.

And there would be little danger of this in a 21st century enjoying an industrial revolution in which 3D printing, robotics, the internet of things, nanotechnology, artificial intelligence and virtual reality increased potential output.

If the bitcoin became the dominant international currency, the money supply would probably not grow at a pace sufficient to support potential growth in output from innovations. A virtual currency linked to a basket of goods, such as kilojoules of energy, or data bandwidth, would be an improvement because its supply would rise with output, but it would not be ideal because it would remove governments' ability to print money.

The dangers of a sharing economy and energy self-sufficiency

In a sharing economy – for example in a chain-saw economy as described in chapter eight, in which the internet makes it easier for people to share the same goods; for example chainsaws, lawn mowers, cars, spare rooms in their homes, their drive, spare desks in an office – it is possible that people's needs would be catered for more effectively than ever before, but with a simultaneous decline in output. A sharing economy may be better for consumers but may appear to show that GDP has contracted.

Currently, energy generated by householders, for example via photovoltaics, is fed into the national grid and shows up in energy bills and is counted towards GDP. But as photovoltaics become more efficient combined with advances in energy storage, we may see a situation in which many households become almost fuel self-sufficient. In this scenario, it is possible that householders' own energy production might increase but this will be invisible to government. In this instance, GDP may appear to contract. The problem in part may relate to how we define GDP.

Regardless, in a sharing economy, in which a high proportion of households are energy self-sufficient and in which digital products are free, people may be better off, but GDP may fall.

This may pose a particular problem for governments. Declining GDP is bad news for government tax receipts.

It is hard to see how government spending can be funded in an economy that sees declining GDP, even if households are no worse off.

This may not appear to matter, but bear in mind that governments across the world are currently highly indebted. It may be impossible for them to repay debts if GDP is declining. The repercussions of governments defaulting are serious; wars have been fought over less.

If governments cannot raise money, how can they pay for education, health care, and care of the elderly and disabled?

But in an economy made more efficient by a sharing mantra, and energy self-sufficiency, inflation is less likely to be a danger. Governments could fund spending by the printing of money. But the evolution of virtual currencies may make this impossible.

Regulators may hit back

To an extent, governments may try to fight against a sharing economy via rules and regulations. A trivial example of this fight back is provided by the attitude of local government towards parking in the UK. Among drivers in the UK, there was a kind of unspoken agreement. If you parked your car in a pay and display car park, and there was still time left on your parking ticket when you left, you gave it to another driver. This is an example of the sharing economy, but working under the baby boomer generation and without the internet. It was and indeed is a delightful practice. It is one in which drivers support other drivers for no obvious gain. Now, however, across many car parks authorities have made it very difficult to follow this practice, because a growing number of car park ticket machines require you to type in your car's number plate, so it removes the possibility of handing parking tickets to other people. This is an example of local government acting to try to stop a sharing economy, and trying to stop altruistic behaviour. Such attempts are shameful, but illustrative of how government and regulators, perhaps egged on by businesses,[216] may try to insert barriers in the way of the development of a sharing economy.

Similarly, we may see resistance to new technology from the workforce, as was demonstrated in 2014 when taxi drivers across much of Europe went on strike in protest over Uber.

The dangers of conflict

A benefit from trade is that it can make the cost of war prohibitive. It is an advantage of globalisation not commonly understood. The more the economies of different countries are intertwined with each other, the less likely it is that they will declare war on each other. Economic links may be what stands in the way of an armed conflict between NATO and Russia in the Ukraine.

But in an economy that shifts to more localised production, in which robotics and 3D printing, and then nanotechnology and artificial intelligence potentially evens out any competitive advantage one country may have over another, exports may be restricted to certain very rare, but important mineral/metals. An example may be rare earth minerals such as cerium – used in self-cleaning ovens; neodymium-iron-boron used to make magnets in a computer's hard drive, europium oxide, used as a red phosphor in television sets and fluorescent lamps; or lanthanum (inside catalytic converters in an exhaust system) or samarium, praseodymium, neodymium, promethium, samarium, gadolinium...the list goes on.

---

[216] In this case, local government may sub-contract the process of administering parking charges and fines, and the sub-contractors may have urged the implementation of this anti sharing policy.

Such rare earth minerals may be vital for the next industrial revolutions to occur and may well be the source of potential conflict. This is the sort of conflict that will be fought by robots rather than humans.

To sum up

Technology can make the world a better place. It can be used to make the average person much better off, and can be used to eliminate poverty altogether. But it may destroy jobs, and may act to concentrate wealth into a very small percentage of the population. On the other hand, for it to evolve, technology needs demand, and demand may not increase unless the fruits of innovation trickle down into higher median wages. One solution is greater government spending funded by the creation of money. But virtual currencies may make this impossible.

Technology may also create an economy with more customisation and services, which may lead to job creation.

It is possible that, in the past, technology revolutions may have temporarily led to economic crises, recession or even depression. By distorting distribution of income, and increasing profits at the expense of increases in wages, it is even possible that technology played a role in the crisis of 2008.

In the past when the ratio of profits to GDP peaked, economic slowdowns often followed, for example 1929 preceding the 1930s depression, and in 2006 preceding the economic troubles post 2008. In 2014, the ratio of profits to GDP hit an all-time high.

A sharing economy and energy self-sufficiency may be good for households, but may have the effect of apparently leading to lower GDP and fewer tax receipts.

Chapter ten: Disruption in healthcare

Change: it can be frightening! It is never predictable. But it sometimes turns out to be for the best. Healthcare is set to change, that is certain. For many diseases, this is bad news. But then again, viruses don't seem to have that much public support. A lot of people, however, especially those who work in healthcare related areas, do have reason to worry about change.

When you consider that, among fortune 500 companies, between 1999 and 2009 there was a 65 per cent increase in the number of jobs in healthcare, while the rest of the workforce increased only 16 per cent, you can see why it is important that we understand these changes.

The traditional players in the industry will be almost as energetic in their resistance to change as some bugs are to antibiotics. These players will lobby and goad. They will use their influence and money to intimidate doctors and regulators into rejecting innovation. Indeed doctors themselves will be amongst those resisting the march of technology.

Such a response is inevitable, but we must reject it.
Take as an example the UK's National Health Service delaying plans for a national electronic health record scheme.

Pharmaceutical companies stand accused. Critics say they push marginally different drugs instead of potentially better generic solutions, because they want you to be a drug subscriber and generate recurring revenue for as long as possible. Also in the dock are medical device manufacturers. They don't want to cannibalize sales of their expensive equipment by providing cheaper, more accessible monitoring devices – or so say the critics.

Technology is changing the rules, and regulators may be the biggest barrier.

Computer modelling techniques may transform the speed and cost of developing new drugs. Armed with data that we can now obtain more cheaply and quickly from sequencing the genome of bugs, bacteria, and the micro-organisms that can either work as our allies or our enemies deep within our biological system, the healthcare industry now has the potential to accelerate the development of treatment and solutions.

The old way of doing things was profitable for many, and we will hear many reasons why change is not required. The new way of doing things will be profitable for us in two key respects: it will help to both make us healthier, and to live longer.

The pharmaceutical companies, along with other healthcare verticals such as medical devices, have developed a very shrewd new technologies scouting model over many decades. They are able to identify and evaluate innovations. Deep pockets have enabled the industry to acquire these technologies to sustain their own growth. Visionary leadership, greater risk taking and placing the right bets, will drive the continued success of their businesses.

Disruptive innovation is however driving change along the four following themes:
1.   The value network and the way in which companies collaborate. In the pharmaceutical industry in particular, we've seen new players emerge, especially smaller and medium-sized companies.
2.   The business model has evolved from a single uniform model to a plethora of models. Very often, the same company will have a range of different business

models – one which obeys the current rules, while the others follow disruptive models.

3.	The arrival on the market of new entrants, which follow entirely different rules. This is similar to the music industry, where a variety of business models based on the internet have proliferated, yet the major players continue to make money with the same old business model. It took the arrival of iTunes from Apple to change the rules of the game indefinitely. The small players don't have the clout to change the rules. One assumes that a proven 3D printing orthopaedic product manufacturer will become the centre of attention for the established incumbents, such as Johnson & Johnson.

4.	A change in the type of value proposition is helping to transform the medical industry. The value proposition is no longer based on a single product aimed at very large markets, but on providing services and solutions. The industry is now looking to develop a care ecosystem, for instance with medicines plus video games.

The big pharmaceuticals have money, distribution and marketing clout. As such, they may be able to employ these strengths to survive and indeed even flourish in an industry, which sees more and more innovation coming from smaller companies and other sectors. However, the giants of the industry want to cling to old ways, to an approach with patents that may no longer be appropriate in an age of advanced computing power.

Even doctors may find they have to re-define their careers and roles in society.

Recently Vinod Khosla, founder of Sun Microsystems, gave the keynote speech at a health innovation summit where he made the staggering claim that "technology may replace up to 80 per cent of what doctors do!"– that algorithms will be able to do a great deal of what doctors have been doing up to now.

He said that medicine needs disruption. He suggested that entrepreneurs focused on consumers are most likely to do the disrupting and that since doctors are part of the system that is the problem, they're not likely to create the solutions.

The medical community welcomed Mr Khosla's prediction with the kind of warmth normally reserved for welcoming a new virus.

Close your eyes and think about what happens when you visit a doctor. You feel unwell one morning so you have to physically go to the hospital or some office, where you wait (with no real idea of how long), and then the nurse probably takes you in and checks your vitals. Only after all this, does the doctor show up and, after some friendly banter, asks you to describe your own symptoms. The doctor assesses them and hunts around (probably in your throat or lungs) for clues as to their source, provides the diagnosis, writes a prescription, and sends you on your way.

The entire encounter should take no more than 15 minutes and usually takes probably less than that. Sometimes a test or two may be ordered. And, as we all know, most of the time, it turns out to be some routine diagnosis with a standard treatment.

The truth is that a computer algorithm could carry out much of this work. A lot of the vitals being tested (for example, blood pressure, pulse) can now be routinely done at home or even with the help of a smart phone. An explosion of additional heath related applications of technology will emerge during the course of the next decade.

Consider the inefficiency. You have to give up time to visit the doctor, when wearable technologies could carry out most of the tests, without you having to do much at all. You are the one telling the doctor your symptoms, the doctor has to enquire (probably every time) into any possible history of each symptom, test results, and illnesses. The prescriptions are still done on paper, requiring you to, again, physically go to a pharmacy and pick up what you need there.

Within a few years, the vital signs could all be determined with the help of mobile devices. Their operation will not require years of training and certification. You will be able to do it yourself. [217] Telemedicine is accelerating. For example, a subsidiary of Qualcomm is measuring heart rates using an iPhone. Devices such as phones that display your vital signs and take ultrasound images of your heart or abdomen are in the offing, as well as genetic scans of malignant cells that match your cancer to the most effective treatment. Ear infection and skin rash pictures will all be mobile phone based, often supplemented by the kind of (fractal) analysis that skin scan does, and more than what the doctor's naked eye could usually see.

The history of symptoms, illnesses, and test results could be accessed, processed, and evaluated by a computer to see any correlation or trends with the patient's past. You are the one providing the doctor with the symptoms anyway.

Any follow-up hunt for clues could again be done with mobile devices.

---

[217] Philips already is using the iPhone camera to try to measure vital indicators; others will be even more innovative and it would be cost-effective for an insurance company to give them to every insured person free of charge.

The prescriptions—along with the medical records—could relocate to electronic and digital methods, saving paper, reducing bureaucracy, and easing the healing process. A little like an airline app holds your travel itinerary and e-ticket.

Does this mean we won't be needing doctors any longer?

The comedian Tommy Cooper once told about a trip he had to the doctor. The medic said that he had some bad news. "You have just 3 minutes left to live," he said. To which the hapless comedian said, "But that is terrible! Is there nothing you can do?" The doctor replied: "Well I could make a boiled egg."

In reality, doctors cannot know everything about every disease type, treatment and the latest advancements in medicine. Indeed, we don't really expect them to know. Diagnosis can seem cold and scary when done by computer. Sometimes you can misinterpret data, and get your own diagnosis wrong. At least doctors can act as a go-between, sitting between us and the machine.

Of course, we will always need specialists. Maybe, however, there will be a premium on doctors with a good bedside manner. Doctors who can re-assure us, translate the results of data and counsel us on our wellness and disease prevention. This would be a better use of their training and skills!

Disruption in healthcare is inevitable and will be a positive force where all stakeholders will benefit but will need to adopt and adapt in order to benefit.

The economics of Healthcare

Will the medical advances in the offing be too expensive for the majority of people? Will we see an economy emerge, in which only the super-rich can afford transformative medicines and other advances?

It is indeed the case that on occasions new medicines are developed that are too expensive for all but a few to use. After all, many of these new technologies and discoveries have required substantial investment and so are likely to be priced richly. We have seen this with new drugs such as the very newly launched Hepatitis C treatment from Gilead, which is USD 84,000 per person for a daily 12-week treatment. This is prohibitively expensive in a country such as India where the average annual wage is USD 10,000 and the number of people infected with Hepatitis C exceeds the tens of millions (roughly three times that in the US).

However, technology is changing the way things are done. Drug research and development is being reshaped to include in-house, outsourced and crowd sourced research. GSK, for example, as mentioned earlier, is collaborating with the Path Malaria Vaccine Initiative, and has opened up its research data and labs to outside scientists. They are using GSK's massive collection of data on 13,500 other compounds that seem to offer promise against malaria. It is likely that GSK will launch a malaria vaccine soon, following a very positive trial data in Africa. Such a novel approach is helping to address curing or preventing diseases such as malaria or dengue fever in those low-income countries with huge medical need but which offer small profitability.

The economics of healthcare in the developing world

Although developing countries face many challenges in the 21st century, in some respects they have advantages. They are typically less burdened by legacy; they are not stuck with old infrastructure, and ways of doing things, and may find it easier to implement new disruptive technological innovations, alternative operating and financing models and new legal frameworks that were not previously evident or even possible for developed countries. Thanks to the internet and digital technologies, the costs of starting a new venture are much lower too.

These countries have a fantastic opportunity to leapfrog their existing infrastructure to deliver first world type healthcare to the population of these nations. Things are already changing. General Electric is now selling an ultra-portable electrocardiograph machine in the US at an 80 per cent markdown against similar products. GE Healthcare originally built the machine for doctors in India and China!

There is also the opportunity to use mobile phone technology to offer mobile-phone-based health education and awareness programmes. For example by offering advice by text and phone-based counselling Project Masiluleke in South Africa was able to advance preventative measures against HIV/AIDS and TB prevention. To take another example, in Kenya the Integrated Mobile MNCH Information Platform provides pregnant women with mobile phone based health information to promote safe pregnancy.

Chapter eleven: Will technology even disrupt what it is to be human?

When we look back at an older age, such as the 1960s with women wearing miniskirts, or the teddy boys of the 1950s, it feels somehow alien. With TV programmes such as *Downton Abbey*, we are given a peek into what life was like long ago. Go back into the dim and distance past, to Victorian Times, the Middle Ages, or if you really want to think about truly ancient times, look at life in Ancient Rome or Greece. Things have changed so much since then. Well, maybe they have, but truth be told, if we were to pull back, and look at history from a genetic point of view, or from the point of view of evolution, we realise that the era when Ancient Egyptians constructed pyramids was hardly any time ago at all.

Think of the period when we humans have inhabited the Earth as a 24-hour clock. And by we humans, we mean the species we refer to as Homo Sapiens Sapiens, as opposed to our cousins Homo Sapiens Neanderthalensis.

This 24-hour day commences as the time passes midnight, and early Homo Sapiens Sapiens appear to have emerged as a distinct species in East Africa around 200,000 years ago.[218] As a species, we are incredibly young, but to us, living in the early 21st century, that seems like a long time ago. By 1am 2am, 3am, nothing much had changed. At some point, probably between 10am and 1pm, we saw the first exodus of our species from Africa.[219] Apologies for those timings being so vague, but we really don't seem to have a much of a clue when the African exodus occurred. By around

---

[218] How long have we been here? Natural History Museum, http://www.nhm.ac.uk/nature-online/life/human-origins/modern-human-evolution/when/index.html, 26 April 2014

[219] Benton, Adam; When did humans leave Africa? Evoanth, 28 March 2013, http://evoanth.wordpress.com/2013/03/28/when-did-humans-leave-africa/ 26 April 2013

6.15pm, early human explorers reached Australia, and the racial group we call Australian Aborigines diverted from the other early humans in the South East. By about 7pm, the first Homo Sapiens reached Britain, but it may not have been until around 11.55 pm that the first humans reached America.

The world's first city, which was probably Jericho[220] in what we now call the Palestinian West Bank, was built at around 11.45pm; Julius Caesar was assassinated at around 11.56; Christopher Columbus rediscovered the Americas at around one minute to midnight, and Captain Cooke rediscovered Australia a few seconds later.

As the last chapter said, we have only seen growth in GDP per capita since 1820, so to put that in terms of the 24-hour clock that is tracking the story of our species, we only begin to get significantly better off during the last second.

Genetically, we are pretty much the same. If we could somehow take a new-born baby, from say 1am in the story of our species, and through some wizardry transport it into the 21st century, bring it up with a modern family and send it to a modern school, it seems likely that you would be hard pressed to tell the difference between that child and any other.

In short, we have jumped through an extraordinary period of economic, social and technological change, without any material physical changes. Add to that, the technologies described in this book and the idea that social/economic/technological change is set to accelerate. We will be the same, however.

---

[220] Tristam, Pierre, Jericho,
http://middleeast.about.com/od/glossary/g/me090314.htm, 26 April 2014

At least, it is assumed we will stay the same, unless we go down the route of designer babies; only allowing foetuses that happen to be configured with what we consider to be the ideal combination of genes. In that case, we could, through artificial selection, create more genetic changes to our species over the next few seconds of the 24 hour clock, than occurred in the previous 23 hours and 59 minutes.

All this begs the question: are we genetically adapted for the new technology world?

Many scientists laugh at the idea that somehow we may not be able to cope with modern technology. The brain, they say, is extremely pliable; we can adjust to just about anything.

Is that right?

Think about this from a common sense point of view. We evolved to live in small communities, perhaps of around 148[221] people, living a hunter-gatherer lifestyle. Evolution has hardwired our brains to work in a certain way.

It is possible that for early humans, group cohesion was so important that we developed all kinds of foibles in our make-up to help to cement the efficiencies of our group.

Psychologists have found a raft of ways in which we are not as well developed as we think we are. We comply with the group, even when the group is clearly wrong – studies show this. Put us in a position in which we are asked to say out loud, in front of our peers, what the right answer to a question is, and even when the correct answer is obvious,

---

[221] See Dunbar number.

we will often get the answer wrong if all our peers also got the answer wrong before we are asked.[222]

We are lousy with probability. The likes of Leonard Mlodinow [223] show how we misunderstand numbers time and time again. We incorrectly misunderstand probability and consequently we think we have seen a causal link between unrelated items. We get ideas such as if we wear a 'lucky jumper' we are more likely to have good day, or if we wear our 'lucky socks' we are more likely to do well in a job interview. From this failure to distinguish randomness from causality, we get superstition, and maybe early religious rituals grew out of this. But such rituals help to promote group cohesion. Maybe evolution has made us poor at probability because our resulting beliefs helped to promote our survival during our hunter-gatherer past.

Will such limitations act as a bonus or a hindrance in the era that is fast approaching?

Anthropologist Robin Dunbar reckons we are designed to live in communities of 148. This has given rise to what is called the Dunbar number, defined as the 'cognitive limit to the number of people with whom one can maintain a stable

---

[222] Sherif, M.; A study of some social factors in perception, Archives of Psychology, 27, 1935.

[223] Mlodinow, Leonard; The Drunkard's Walk, Pantheon, 2008. He gave examples, and this case, the example is taken from Michael Baxter's book The Blindfolded Masochist when he is writing about Mlodinow. "Someone invents a test to check for breast cancer. They claim a nine in ten chance the test is accurate. What does that mean exactly? This example was given by Mlodinow: assume that one in a hundred women aged around forty develop breast cancer. Also, assume that the test never fails to identify cancer when it is in fact present. If the test is 90 per cent accurate, it means that one woman in ten will be wrongly identified as having the disease: that is to say the test will yield a "false positive" result. If one woman in one hundred has cancer and is accurately diagnosed, then ten per cent of the remaining ninety-nine will be falsely diagnosed. That's one accurate diagnosis out of 10.9 positive results. Apparently, this is a nuance of probability that doctors often do not grasp."

social relationship.'[224, 225] But how many friends do you have on Facebook? How many contacts do you have on LinkedIn? In an era in which we may communicate with people using virtual reality, how many people will we mix with? Can we cope? Will the result be that we know thousands of people but not have many, if any, true friends? Will technology make us lonely?

Psychologists are now familiar with such concepts as groupthink, when groups of people start to think as one. Groupthink is blamed for a disastrous attempt by the US government, under President Kennedy, to orchestrate a coup in Cuba at the time when Fidel Castro came to power. The President later remarked: "How could I have been so stupid?" The truth was that a team of highly skilled advisors got sucked into groupthink.[226] We can all think of examples, such as the conviction that there were weapons of mass destruction in Iraq, or the view formed by the IMF that the

---

[224] Dunbar, Robin; How Many Friends Does One Person Need?: Dunbar's Number and Other Evolutionary Quirks, Faber and Faber, 2011

[225] The anthropologist Robin Dunbar found a correlation between the skull size of certain primates and the typical size of the community in which they lived. Gibbons, for example, which boast quite small crania, live in communities of five to six. The bigger-brained chimps typically mix in communities of between 50 and 80. Extrapolating the trajectory Dunbar believed he had identified, he concluded that the cognitive limit to the number of people we can hold stable relationships with is 148. This number has been rounded up so that the Dunbar Number is said to be 150. Contemporary hunter-gatherers live in groups of around 150. Early Neolithic villages — the remains of which have been found in Mesopotamia — had accommodation for approximately 150. The smallest unit of independent troops in the army is close to this number: 135 in the British Army and 200 in the US Army. This begs the question: Why? Dunbar reckons it all boils down to social bonding. Chimps promote social cohesion via grooming. For humans, living in larger communities, grooming is not practical. Instead, we need language, which is a superior communication tool.

[226] Janis, I. L.; Victims of groupthink: A psychological study of foreign policy decisions and fiascos, Boston: Houghton Mifflin Company, 1972

innovation called mortgage securitisation meant a banking crisis was less likely.[227]

There is also something called group polarisation. Put a group of relatively risk averse individuals together, and as a group this tendency towards risk aversion is exaggerated, whereupon the group becomes paralysed by indecision. Put a group of individuals who are included to take mild risks – modest gamblers if you like – into a group and the group can become insanely reckless.[228]

But supposing the internet creates huge groups, communities of thousands, communicating via avatars in virtual reality landscapes. Are the dangers of groupthink or group polarisation less or more likely?

We are subject to certain biases. For example, confirmation bias is where we ignore all evidence that contradicts our own view of the world, and we only consider evidence that supports it. We then say: "Look, I must be right, the evidence is overwhelming."[229] Dan Kahan, a leading scholar in the field of criminal law, has produced a paper, which

---

[227] IEO, IMF Performance in the Run-Up to the Financial and Economic Crisis IMF Surveillance in 2004–07, http://www.ieo-imf.org/eval/complete/pdf/01102011/IEO_full_report_crisis.pdf, May 27 2011 IMF The influence of credit derivative and structured credit markets on financial stability – Chapter II

[228] Moscovici, S. and Zavalloni, M.; The group as a polarizer of attitudes, Journal of Personality and Social Psychology, 12, pp. 125-135. (1969). Forsyth, Donelson R.; Group Dynamics, Wadsworth, Cengage Learning, 2009 http://www.cengagebrain.com/shop/content/forsyth99522_0495599522_01.01_toc.pdf, May 27 2011 Stone, James A. F.; Risky and cautious shifts in group decisions, Journal of Experimental Social Psychology, Volume 4, Issue 4, October 1968, pp. 442-459 Massachusetts Institute of Technology.

[229] Kahneman, Daniel; Slovic, Paul; Tversky, Amos,(edited by) Judgment under uncertainty: heuristics and biases, Cambridge University Press, Cambridge, 1982

appears to show that we simply ignore facts if they contradict our preconceived notions.

He took a slightly tricky puzzle.

In Kahan's experiment, he took a fictitious example of two groups of people comprising individuals who had a skin rash. The two groups were not the same size. One group was given a cream. Here are the results of this fictitious experiment:

Dan Kahan Motivated Numeracy and Enlightened Self-Government.

	Rash got better	Rash got worse
Group A: Patients who did use the cream	223	75
Group B: Patients who didn't use cream	107	21

He then asked people to select one of two possible conclusions relating to his fictitious study:

1: People who used the skin cream were more likely to get better than those who didn't.
2: People who used the skin cream were more likely to get worse than those who didn't.

The answer is not obvious, but if you look at the ratio of 'rash got better' 'to rash got worse', for each of the two groups, you realise that actually people who used the skin cream were more likely to get worse than those who didn't. As a rule, those who were better at maths tended to get the answer right.

He then set precisely the same puzzle, but in a different context. Instead of rash and cream, the subject of the study concerned the link between carrying guns and crime in the US. In this case, reasoning went out of the window. If the numbers were fixed so that a quick look suggested carrying guns reduced crime – when a more careful look revealed the opposite finding – it was irrelevant how good the test subjects were at maths. If they held liberal view on crime, they were more likely to get the answer right. Then Kahan flipped the stats, to show the opposite finding. In this scenario, those with more conservative views on carrying guns got the answer right.[230]

Now see this limitation of the way in which we reason in the context of the internet.

As search becomes more sophisticated, we will only be fed the information we want. We may end up being inundated with information that supports our preconceived notions. [231]

If we hold a sceptical view on climate change for example, or on immigration, we may be fed a stream of information that supports this view. Search when combined with artificial intelligence may make us more biased.

Moving beyond group dynamics, there is the question of whether technology may change the very nature of what it is to be human. Do you recall an occasion when you were trying to remember something? "Agh, it's on the tip of my tongue," you might, say, and then suddenly – maybe an

[230] Kahan, Dan M. Dawson, Erica Cantrell. Peters, Ellen, Slovic, Paul; Motivated Numeracy and Enlightened Self-Government, The Cultural Cognition Project.
http://www.cogsci.bme.hu/~ktkuser/KURZUSOK/BMETE47MC15/2013_2014_1/kahanEtAl2013.pdf 26 April 2014
[231] Eli Pariser; The Filter Bubble: What the Internet Is Hiding from You. Penguin Press HC, 12 May 2011

hour or so later – it comes to you like a bolt out of the blue. You have an Aha! moment.

But when was the last time you did have such an experience? Instead, did you pull your smart phone out of your pocket or handbag, and get the answer from the internet, rather than from your own memory. But is such practice good for us, or does it make our brain lazy? Has anyone even considered applying rigorous study into answering that question?

Then there is the process of learning a language. If augmented reality devices advance so much that when we hear someone speaking in a language we do not know, they can translate the words on the fly, and even applying the same nuances and vocal tones of the person we are speaking to, will we need to learn foreign languages anymore? Or, for that matter, if we listen to people speaking the same language, but with a strong regional dialect, will augmented reality translate the words. Will such debates as whether we pronounce the word bath, as in calf or as in math, be made redundant by augmented reality? Will that Fred Astaire song with the line: "You say tomato, I say tomato" become as meaningless when spoken out loud as it is when written down?

But will such developments be positive or negative, hinder or promote cultural understanding, make us lazy, or simply provide us with more information from which we can draw more elaborate understanding?

Then there is the evolution of brain interfaces with the internet. Will we become permanently connected to the internet, initially with information fed to us via text displays on our augmented reality glasses or whispered into our ears via wearable technology, but then replaced by direct brain interfaces to the internet where information is fed directly into our brain?

In time we will be able to download learning modules into our brain, so that we wouldn't need to learn how to drive, the knowledge would be downloaded instead – not that we will need to drive when we have self-driving cars. Will we be able to download knowledge of a foreign language – not that we will need to learn a foreign language when augmented reality gives us the real world equivalent of Douglas Adams' Babel fish, from *The Hitch Hikers Guide to the Galaxy*.

And if we are permanently connected to the internet, how many relationships might we form? Will we exceed Dunbar's cognitive limit? Will the dangers of groupthink, group compliance, and group polarisation be exacerbated?

In his book *The Shallows*, Nicholas Carr suggests the internet is damaging our ability to contemplate. [232] He says: "Our growing use of the Net and other screen-based technologies has led to the 'widespread and sophisticated development of visual-spatial skills.' We can, for example, rotate objects in our minds better than we used to be able to. But our 'new strengths in visual-spatial intelligence' go hand in hand with a weakening of our capacities for the kind of 'deep processing' that underpins 'mindful knowledge acquisition, inductive analysis, critical thinking, imagination, and reflection.'"

He also says: "What the Net seems to be doing is chipping away my capacity for concentration and contemplation. Whether I'm online or not, my mind now expects to take in information the way the Net distributes it: in a swiftly moving stream of particles. Once I was a scuba diver in the

[232] Carr, Nicholas; The Shallows: What the Internet is Doing to Our Brains, W. W. Norton & Company, 6 June 2011

sea of words. Now I zip along the surface like a guy on a Jet Ski."

Before the invention of writing, the story teller was a highly prized artist, but we all relied on our memory for storing information. With the evolution of writing this changed. By Victorian times, an era when many of us were new to reading, books were often drawn out affairs, replete with long, long sentences.

Dickens wrote: "It was the best of times, it was the worst of times, it was the age of wisdom, it was the age of foolishness, it was the epoch of belief, it was the epoch of incredulity, it was the season of light, it was the season of darkness, it was the spring of hope, it was the winter of despair, we had everything before us, we had nothing before us, we were all going direct to Heaven, we were all going direct the other way—in short, the period was so far like the present period, that some of its noisiest authorities insisted on its being received, for good or for evil, in the superlative degree of comparison only." That is just one sentence. Did the Victorians enjoy the challenge of deciphering such long sentences, or paragraphs that meander on for an age?

Alternatively, take this sentence from Charlotte Bronte in *Jane Eyre*: "Blanche Ingram, after having repelled, by supercilious taciturnity, some efforts of Mrs Dent and Mrs Eshton to draw her into conversation, had first murmured over some sentimental tunes and airs on the piano, and then, having fetched a novel from the library, had flung herself in haughty listlessness on a sofa and prepared to beguile, by the spell of fiction, the tedious hours of absence." What was she on when she wrote that?

It is not difficult to realise that modern literature tends to have much shorter sentences. Web sites have much shorter paragraphs. Maybe, when we were more used to listening to stories and with the concentration this required, we were more able to cope with longer sentences, and more drawn out explanations.

Then there is the issue of social skills. We are social animals; we are designed to talk to others. Communication is enhanced by face to face conversion, with body language sending subtle messages of which we may not even be conscious. We learnt socials skills by playing. If kids play by playing video games, or communicate via social media, and – beyond that – via virtual reality, will we lose some of the core social skills that pretty much define us as humans?

Looking beyond that, there is the field of enhancement. Will the internet, combined with artificial intelligence, become so much an integral part of our thought processes that it will be as though our brains are enhanced? Will the advances in prosthetics eventually be applied to healthy individuals to make them stronger and faster via exoskeletons, like bionic men and women? And given this, will the need for exercise diminish? Will this lead to a greater sedentary lifestyle, obesity and the onset of lifestyle diseases?

Will the combination of 3D printing, robotics, artificial intelligence, wearable technology and stem cell research make us healthier and longer lived, and in the process lock us in technology that augments our abilities and protects us?

Will the appeal of video games played via virtual reality be so great that we increasingly retreat into virtual worlds – not exactly like the world portrayed in the film *The Matrix*, but moving in that direction. [233]

---

[233] Bostrom, Nick; Future of Humanity Institute, Faculty of Philosophy & James Martin 21st Century School, University of Oxford. Nick Bostrom has proposed we may already be living in a 'Matrix' type environment.

Looking even further ahead, will the advances in artificial intelligence and brain interfaces develop so that the neurons in our brains will eventually form synapses with neurons in other brains, and in this way totally change what it is to be human?

We know that 150,000 years when we were hunter-gathers in the Rift Valley, we rarely found sugar. On the odd occasions when we did, we may well have binged, getting a year's worth of intake in one sitting. Today sugar is so common that it sometimes feels as if it is hard to find food that doesn't have too much sugar content. And so we eat chocolate and sweets and fats, and those very same tendencies that caused us no harm 150,000 year ago now work against us, as we overindulge in these things that are bad for us given our sedentary lifestyle, and we get ever higher levels of obesity. This is a clear example of how our evolution has given us traits that are not well suited to modern living.

It seems implausible that evolution gave us the tools to help us ensure we did not misuse the applications that come with augmented reality, virtual reality, artificial intelligence, nanotechnology and prosthetics.
We cannot know the answer to any of these questions.
We can say one thing for sure, and that's that these issues are not being given sufficient consideration.

If the banking crisis of 2008 taught us anything, it should be that there is no benign secret organisation looking after our interests, ensuring that we don't stumble into disaster.

Technology is changing fast. Its implications are not easy to predict but we can say that it will impact upon us much faster than we are ready for.

It is time we started to take these considerations more seriously. There is no guarantee that the results of technological change will be benign, but unless we accept that technology is changing at a pace for which there is no precedent, rather than hide behind absurd theories that suggest technology evolution has peaked, we are stumbling forward in the dark.

Those stuck in the sceptical view of technological development threaten us. Innovator's dilemma can apply to humanity as a whole, and in such a scenario 'pragmatic realism' poses a threat to our survival.

Technology can make us healthier, richer, more social, and happier. It can help us to migrate into a modern day garden of Eden.

It may also disrupt us in ways that we can only really guess at. Humanity itself may be changed. If Homo Sapiens Sapiens had a voice, it may say: I have been disrupted.

Conclusion:

Chapter twelve: What can we do about it?

"Thou aimest high, Master Lee," said Queen Elizabeth the first. She looked sternly at her subject and paused; her stare seemed to delve deep into his soul. She continued: "Consider though what thy invention would do to my poor subjects." Inside, Lee trembled. His great invention, a device for knitting stockings, was disruptive technology for Elizabethan England. Her voice, like steel on soft flesh, the Queen concluded: "It would assuredly bring to them ruin by depriving them of employment, thus making them beggars." She refused Mr Lee's request for a patent. Turning to her advisor, Lord Hunsdon, her face an image of authority, the Queen of England remarked: "Had Mr Lee given me a machine that could knit silk stockings, I would have perhaps been justified in granting him a patent." She added: "To enjoy the privilege of making stockings for everyone is too important to grant to any individual."[234]

So it was that almost 450 years ago that the authority, who in this case was one of England's most famous monarchs, delayed the onset of the machine.

"Thou aimest high, Uber," said the London cabbies, who went on strike over the threat the taxi app posed to their jobs, or at least words to that effect. "Consider though what might happen to those who work in the hotel business," said the pressure groups operating in New York trying to halt Airbnb, the room rental service which enables ordinary folks to hire out spare rooms to strangers for one or more days. "It would assuredly bring independent car dealers to their ruin," said the representatives of the US auto retail trade In New Jersey, who were fuming about Tesla's policy of owning the car dealers that sold its cars. "Your plans may make

[234] William Lee, http://calverton.homestead.com/willlee.html, 5 July 2014

beggars of staff who work on London's Underground," said Rail Unions in response to Transport for London's plans for automatic ticket machines, or at least you could paraphrase their response in those terms.

Queen Elizabeth the first, great Queen though she was, had no understanding of economics. She failed to grasp that devices that increased the productivity of labour led to higher earnings, creating demands for services that up to that point few people could have afforded.

What she had failed to grasp is that labour saving devices would spark a revolution that would one day make even silk stockings affordable by millions.

There is always resistance to technology and change.
Doctors will resist attempts to let machines take on part of their role. They will resist the idea that patients may be able to employ new technologies to self-diagnose. But new technology does not threaten to remove the need for doctors. Rather, diagnostic and therapeutic technologies furnish them with the opportunity to provide services to patients at the local level that are more accurate by contributing to their knowledge, which is the preserve of specialists working in hospitals.

It has been speculated that one of the key factors that enabled Britain to enter the industrial age before any other country was legislation passed in 1769, which made the destruction of machinery punishable by death, or so says Carl Benedikt Frey and Michael Osborne from Oxford University in their paper *The Future of employment: how susceptible are jobs to computerisation?*[235]

---

[235] Carl Benedikt Frey and Michael A. Osborne The future of employment: how susceptible are jobs to computerisation? September 17 2013, http://www.oxfordmartin.ox.ac.uk/downloads/academic/The_Future_of_E mployment.pdf, 5 July 2014

The Backlash

There is always resistance to new ideas. We are seeing it today; from a backlash by EU lawmakers against the rise of digital companies to rules requiring Google to 'apply the right to be forgotten' by complying with requests from individuals to have links to articles concerning them removed from the search engine. Financial regulators are even trying to restrict the extent to which they allow ordinary investors to take part in crowd sourced funding ventures.

If the digital age puts the emphasis on cooperation, collaboration, transparency, trust and honesty, the fight back against technology is indiscriminate. It fails to differentiate between technology that makes the world a better place, and technology that poses a threat to our future survival.

We have two options. One is to understand what is happening, and try to adopt an approach that ensures technology makes us better; that it creates more prosperity, fairness and enhances the very qualities that make us human. The second is to bury our heads in the sand and, like a latter day King Cnut, try to stop the tide of technology, and in the process find we are ill equipped to survive in the digital age. The lesson of innovator's dilemma is partly that companies that resist technology advances eventually stumble; they go bust. This lesson does not only apply to businesses, it applies to those who want to have a job in ten years' time. It applies to policy makers who are trying to ensure the country that they govern can compete in the digital age, and it applies to us all.

Take as an example resistance to social media within companies. You hear the critique so often: Facebook is a distraction, and it is a waste of employees' time. What bosses who try to ban social media within their companies fail to grasp is that firstly it is a communication tool, a method of supporting the flow of ideas. Secondly, they fail to grasp that a company that has a positive attitude to social media is one that has taken a step towards embracing technology. Thirdly, they fail to appreciate that social media is a powerful marketing tool, and that you can hardly expect to exploit this benefit if you don't practise what you preach. Above all, they fail to grasp that in the 21st century there is a shift in the way in which the workplace operates. Corporate structures are changing from hierarchical, in which the boss sits in an office on the top floor, to a flat management structure, in which seniors managers place their desks in the centre of offices and become a part of the culture rather than above it.

The future of jobs

Let us turn to you, and your job or your children's jobs.
Do you want a job in ten years' time? Not understanding computers, refusing to adopt social media, ignoring the technologies that are developing is simply no longer viable. As we age, we all have a tendency to resist change, to think that 'it used to be better'. Such attitudes are as old as humanity. However, understanding social media and certain other digital technologies is not terribly difficult. It only requires a willingness to learn and collaborate.

Stuart Elliot, an expert in these matters, conducted a detailed study looking the kind of jobs that are in danger of being replaced by technology. He envisages that over the next few decades up to 80 per cent of current jobs will be lost to technology, but that the workforce covering the remaining 20 per cent of jobs can expand to "absorb the entire workforce." He believes technology will have a devastating effect on employment in sales, management, administration, construction, maintenance, and food service work, but that there will be a massive explosion in the number of jobs in healthcare, education, science, engineering, and law.[236]

In their paper referred to previously, Frey and Osborne suggest that the type of jobs most likely to be replaced by computers and robots are jobs involving manual dexterity, finger dexterity, and working in cramped spaces. They say jobs that involve a high level of social intelligence are less likely to be disrupted. Occupations that are likely to be safer include those which involve developing ideas, originality, negotiation, social perceptiveness, and assisting or caring for others.

They are very specific too. They suggest that the type of job that is most likely to be done by machines is telemarketing. Other jobs that sit high in their list of occupations they identify as likely to be replaced by technology include insurance appraisers, insurance underwriters, and tax preparers. On the other hand, occupational therapists, mental health counsellors, healthcare social workers and teachers seem quite safe from disruption.

As for timing, they say that in 2030 the types of jobs that are least at risk from technology will be jobs that involve social intelligence, creativity or working in a complex and unstructured environment, including choreographers, physicians and surgeons, and podiatrists.

It is possible that these studies underestimate the move towards customisation and the production of bespoke products. It was predicted earlier in this book that certain technologies may do away with the advantages of scale in

---

[236] Elliott, Stuart W; Anticipating a Luddite Revival Issues in science and technology, http://issues.org/30-3/stuart/ 4 July 2014

production.[237] Jobs that involve manual dexterity may not vanish altogether, but such jobs will be a part of a new localised bespoke production industry that will also employ robots and 3D printers to produce unique products on demand. As we will see in a moment, we may also see the development of tailor made services in education and healthcare.

Equally, these studies may underestimate the possible impact of computers on education and the teaching profession.

What can people do?

They say there is more than one way to skin a cat. Likewise, there is more than one way to try to safeguard your career, and keep your skills relevant as we head into the next industrial revolutions. But whatever you do, if you are to be successful, skills promoting collaboration, networking, and engaging are likely to feature.

One solution to the challenge of staying relevant lies in the host of online courses that are now available.

The rise of MOOCS (massive open online courses) could change the nature of higher education fundamentally. They are beginning to open up access to new forms of teaching

---

[237] We are already seeing it in the print business. There was a time when the cost of printing 50 copies of a book was prohibitively expensive; it only made sense to print in quantities of 1,000 plus. This is no longer the case. Some books are even printed on demand, meeting customer orders as and when they come in. But printed books are themselves being disrupted by ebooks. The result of this is that the start-up costs of producing a book are much lower, paving the way for a greater variety of books available, catering for niche markets.

and learning, including those available to the under privileged. These MOOCs are often free;[238] they employ multimedia techniques to convey information and ideas, and make learning accessible in a way that was not possible before. They are also proving to be incredibly popular. More people are now signing up for a MOOC produced by Harvard University in a year, than attended the university in its entire 377-year history.[239]

An important part of MOOCs is communication. The courses allow students to engage with each other, and share ideas. This is what makes them so very much a part of the 21st century ethos.

Andrew Law, director of the open media unit at the Open University, was interviewed on this very subject. "Are MOOCs the 'Napster moment' for Higher Education?" he asks, and continues, "As with the music industry, it may be difficult to tell the scale of impact until the disruptive wave has actually passed over. Will it rise above our ankles – or wipe the landscape clean for fresh new approaches? The key is to make sure we are all ready and willing to participate in finding the positive outcomes of this wave for our learners, whatever its size. Those outcomes might be concerned with more equitable access to education. They might include more engaging, communicative, participatory and effective forms of teaching and learning, and they might even end with a truly radical change to a 500 year old tradition – and transform the nature of how and where qualifications and skills are acquired in higher education."[240]

---

[238] But they usually generate some revenue for the course provider and platform owner by providing a certificate or statement of activity, or fees for additional support. At present, there are no known examples of MOOC platforms directly providing formal qualifications.

[239] Coughlan, Sean; Harvard plans to boldly go with 'Spocs', BBC, 24 September, http://www.bbc.co.uk/news/business-24166247 7 July 2014

[240] Statement by email sent to Michael Baxter, 18 July 2014.

In this digital age, willingness to embrace technology is crucial. Business is becoming more social; social media is a key part of ensuring that you don't find that your skills are disrupted into irrelevance. Of course, privacy issues loom large too. This is a complex topic, and would need a book in its own right to fully explore the issues. Bear in mind, however, that digital technology is about a new way of doing things: of openness, honesty, transparency. Providing this is a two way street, and both the users of technology and its masters – the likes of Google and Facebook, big companies and governments – apply the same standards of openness and transparency that technology forces upon us. Lack of privacy may be the price we pay for living in a safer, more trusting and honest world.

Remaining relevant entails communicating. The more you engage, and the more open you are in communicating with others, the better.

It is a two way process. Don't expect to greedily absorb ideas from others without giving something back.

IBM found that by engaging with the Linux community as transparently as possible, and in providing ideas and offering its expertise, it was able to secure trust. Its engineers found the Linux community was more willing to collaborate. Indeed, IBM became part of that community, and the company's own expertise increased as a result. It was subsequently able to sell the expertise it gained to companies as part of its consultancy service.

The lesson of IBM may not seem relevant to individuals trying to safeguard their future, but it is.

Rupert Jupp is a director in Princedown Partners, a recruitment/headhunting firm for board and commercial leaders for digital and multichannel clients. In an interview,[241] he was asked what advice he would give to individuals trying to ensure that their own skill sets are not disrupted into irrelevancy.

He said: "I think it is incredibly important to have as many strings to your bow as you possibly can by experiencing stuff in different ways." He talks about MBAs, but said that while they are a good way to go off-site and learn, "You don't need to wrap up this learning in an expensive $50,000 a year MBA." Rather he says: "You need to do that socially or within your business. I think that when people go off for MBAs they always come back saying they have met loads of really good people. Most people have not learnt how to plot a better spreadsheet or how to become Prime Minister, most people have really enjoyed the perspective they glean from different people about functions in different sectors."

He continued: "My advice to anyone is to try and learn about different job functions and industries, by writing a blog, following certain people on LinkedIn, or for example setting up a wine and cheese evening with PAs from different companies." He added: "But learn about the breadth and perspective of how other people work, what they do, what works what doesn't work, and of course at the heart of this, how does technology make a play on all these areas. I think that de-risks everyone, it keeps them interesting."

Turning to social media, Jupp draws upon an idea expressed in chapter six: your online reputation. He said: "For certain roles in business and society, I think it is very important to understand your social reputation, and how to use it to your advantage."
But how do you gain a social reputation?

---

[241] Interview with Michael Baxter, 10 December 2013

There is an analogy with how you gain a good credit rating. These days if you are the type of person who does not like borrowing, and likes to pay for everything as they go along, you become invisible to the system and you are at a disadvantage. Sometimes you need a good credit rating to consume certain products; for example, a mobile phone contract or rent a property. If you don't use credit, your rating is non-existent and you are at a disadvantage. The same principles apply to gaining an online reputation. You can only achieve this if you are active. That does not just mean being on Facebook or LinkedIn and passively observing other people's content, it means commenting on social media, and on online articles by liking, reviewing, and by blogging if you can.

Maybe there is a slight contradiction between the ideas behind a MOOC, and Jupp's ideas for networking and engaging with others, but it is not that significant.
The truth is that it may help to do both.

If you want to have a job in ten years' time, you need to be willing to learn new future-relevant skills, and you can do this partly by taking online courses – be it via a MOOC or perhaps a degree at the UK's Open University – but also by engaging with others both in person and online.

Your social reputation may be the key, and you can only achieve this by doing things online.

Online anonymity may be the route to being disrupted out of work.

The disruption of antibiotics and the disruption of MRSA

You probably don't want to see us all descend back to the dark ages. We have already described how we are losing the war against some bugs – the so-called super bugs, such as MRSA. Doctors in some countries prescribe antibiotics too easily. Some patients don't complete the course of medicine, and in so doing allow certain bacteria to fester and gain time to build-up an immunity. In farming, over-use of antibiotics applied to livestock is a major issue. These practices threaten to send medicine back to an age when dying from diseases such as tuberculosis was common. In July 2014, the British Prime Minister David Cameron said: "If we fail to act, we are looking at an almost unthinkable scenario where antibiotics no longer work and we are cast back into the dark ages of medicine where treatable infections and injuries will kill once again." He announced a review headed by Jim O'Neil, who was the former chief economist at Goldman Sachs – not to mention the man who first coined the acronym BRICs to describe Brazil Russia, India and China.[242]

Technology can lead the fight-back, but regulators and governments can help.

In time, it will be possible for wearable technology, big data and the internet of things to be used to drastically limit the indiscriminate and inappropriate use of antibiotics.

Nanotechnology fixes to the problem are already in the pipeline. IBM, for example, has been developing tiny polymers, which they refer to as Ninja Polymers. To quote Jim Hedrick, a polymer chemist at IBM Research, "The

---

[242] Department of Health, Prime Minister warns of global threat of antibiotic resistance, Department of Health and Prime Minister's Office, 2 July 2014,

polymer attaches to the bacteria's membrane and then facilitates destabilization of the membrane. It falls apart, everything falls out and there's little opportunity for it to develop resistance to these polymers." This is quite different to how antibiotics, which mimic the body's own immune system, work. [243]

Researchers at the University of Strathclyde have worked out a way to make a type of virus, called bacteriophages, eat bacteria while leaving human cells intact. In fact, applying bacteriophages in this battle is not new. They were, for example, used to treat bubonic plague and cholera, but were largely disrupted out of use by antibiotics, and have not been widely used for many decades. One of the snags with bacteriophages is that they can only survive in water. The researchers at the University of Strathclyde have investigated applying a cleaning material, such as a detergent, which contains small particles with bacteriophage attached to them. These particles allow the bacteriophage to survive drying.[244]

Moving away from nanotechnology, researchers at the University of East Anglia have discovered a type of ant that evolved its own form of antibiotic 50 million years ago. The leafcutter ants of South America eat fungi that they first nurture. An antibiotic-producing bacterium grows on the ants, which the ants use to protect themselves and their fungi against infection. Lead researcher Dr Matt Hutchings said: "We have also discovered that the ants use multiple drug combinations to prevent drug resistance from arising,

[243] IBM; Nanomedicine that can destroy antibiotic-resistant bacteria, http://www.research.ibm.com/articles/nanomedicine.shtml#fbid=MQ3mK Gt4zzb 7 July 2014

[244] University of Strathclyde, Catching up with the 'superbug', Prism, November-December 2004, http://www.strath.ac.uk/media/publications/prism/2004/media_77413_en .pdf, 7 July 2014

So by using multiple antibiotics at once, we can slow the rise of antibiotic-resistant superbugs."[245]

Genome sequencing technology will also play a vital part in this war. By sequencing a bug's genome, it will become possible to use computer modelling techniques to develop a customised approach to treatment.

But one of the snags with developing a new cure for superbugs lies with economics. The cost of developing drugs versus the potential economic returns does not appear to justify the required investment by the large pharmaceutical companies. The partial issue here is that most of us only use antibiotics rarely, say for two weeks once every few years. For the pharmaceutical companies this means fewer profits, and makes it hard for them to justify the necessary investment to develop treatments in this area. This will definitely leave the big pharmaceuticals at a disadvantage, encumbered as they are by a huge cost base, but does not necessarily limit the smaller biotech player. We will continue to need medicine to combat superbugs, so it is likely that we will see new superbug antibiotics being developed, but they may not come from the usual incumbents and may not be promoted or distributed in the same way that drugs are now. In short, we can win the battle against superbugs, but disruption amongst pharmaceutical companies may result.

It is tempting to conclude that governments need to provide stronger patent protection to companies that develop new cures for superbugs. It may be tempting to conclude this, but such a policy would surely be wrong.

---

[245] UEA, Antibiotic research to find next-generation drugs unveiled in London, Mon, 30 Jun 2014.
http://www.uea.ac.uk/mac/comm/media/press/2014/june/ants-royal-society, 7 July 2014

A more effective approach might be to encourage open programmes in which researchers around the world can contribute towards advancing cures. Governments can help to accentuate this process by offering prizes to key contributors. Collaboration tools make it more practical to develop systems that measure contribution. At its simplest level, they could measure contributions by how many likes they receive. At a more complex level, governments could develop algorithms, applying similar ideas to those inside search engines, which rank web sites in terms of relevance to search enquiries. They could then develop a kind of system to various ideas and contributions. For example, they could take into account what suggestions gained likes or led to comments, and also who the people were who liked and commented on the suggestions.

How business can survive

When a company is in crisis, when its share price is crashing and it is in debt and new technology threatens to disrupt the very features of that company that once made it successful, is there any hope?

If you take the example of Thomas Cook, a giant travel company that can trace its roots back to 1841, it would appear that the answer to that question is yes.

Technology may well disrupt many businesses out of existence. In chapter eight, we suggested that only 19 of the world's 100 largest companies in 2012 will be in that list in 2042, and there may be a good deal fewer. However, companies can survive, and this is how.

The Green approach

In 2011, the Thomas Cook Group was in crisis. A series of over-ambitious acquisitions and mergers, combined with a series of political and environmental global events, had drained its finances and brought the iconic brand to its knees.

There are perhaps even some parallels with the story of Kodak, which we highlighted earlier in the book.

Thomas Cook, a true innovator, founded his travel company in 1841. The company has helped to transform the face of leisure travel by inspiring personal journeys and fuelling our desire to explore the world. Cook's early inventions include hotel booking coupons and circular notes, which ultimately became the traveler's cheque, and of course the concept of package holidays.

Like every other business, technology drove change in the travel sector.

Technology creates but it also changes and those who don't evolve and embrace it are at risk of being destroyed by it. Moore's Law and the homogenisation of computer technology meant that by the beginning of the new millennium, it was easy to achieve innovations that had previously seemed impossible. For many businesses, technology threatened their raison d'etre.

The internet helped to take the mystery out of travel, and make it more accessible. The ease of obtaining information and dealing directly with suppliers made DIY holidays increasingly popular. Technology removed barriers to entry, and the consumer was offered choice on a scale that had once seemed inconceivable. How could traditional travel companies like Thomas Cook survive in such an environment? To many outsiders, it seemed that travel agents and tour operators were living on borrowed time.

Against this backdrop in 2011 when the company issued three profit warnings and delayed the release of its full year results, many onlookers began to mentally write the company's obituary. The share price crashed from 335p in 2007 to just 14p in early 2012.

The board appointed a new Chairman and he quickly set about recruiting a new CFO and CEO. He looked outside the travel industry to find a CEO who would bring different experience and skills to the much-needed transformation. Harriet Green took over as CEO of the troubled group in July 2012.

With her leadership team, she set about defining a profitable growth strategy for Thomas Cook, which they took to the capital markets just eight months later. Pace and urgency were their watchwords – during that first year the group measured results not in weeks or months but in days.

The final strategy had many layers to it, but a digital evolution was at its heart. At the time of writing (25 August 2014), Thomas Cook has achieved remarkable results. Within the first 300 days, it successfully achieved a recapitalisation of the business, which resulted in the market capitalization soaring to more than £2 billion, from a lowly £150 million less than a year earlier.

The eruption of an Icelandic volcano in 2011, with its attendant dust cloud, caused flight cancellations, and major disruptions to holidays. This was nearly the final straw for Thomas Cook, but the real disruption surely came from technology.

In 2007, the technological forces that were set to disrupt the business of Thomas Cook and many others like it were already well advanced. The idea that that the internet could disrupt traditional companies was not new, or even surprising. Maybe the real mystery is why Thomas Cook's leadership in 2007 was not ready to embrace the growing disruptive force. They were not alone.

Maybe the capital markets, along with previous management of Thomas Cook, were victims of that same trait we have described before in this book: underestimating how rapidly technology can disrupt, and threaten even the most tried and tested business models. Maybe the dot.com bust had lulled the markets into a false sense of security and they were still in denial about the effect that the internet would have?

The plan to save Thomas Cook was not just about embracing technology. Strong financial control, restructuring, cost reduction, a brilliant strategy, moving at speed, rebuilding belief internally and externally, and bold recruitment were all part of the transformation. Companies looking to survive the ravages of technology and transform for the future can learn from this approach.

Technology, and finding a way to embrace it, was the key to working more effectively and giving customers what they wanted. Delighting customers at every stage of their experience – from planning and booking to returning home – was vital. Every part of the business could be improved, and so the high tech, high touch vision developed – an omni-channel commitment to being there for customers wherever, whenever and however they wanted to connect with the company. It harnessed the power of technology to improve every part of the business, whether this was the way in which it purchased hotels or how the group's airlines worked together – there were efficiency, service improvements, and cost savings to be had.

With 23 million customers a year and a turnover approaching £10 billion, Thomas Cook had plenty of clout.

Historically, its individual businesses and brands operated with a fair degree of independence. Each business, for example, used to source its own hotel capacity. Under the new plan, it introduced a unified hotel purchasing system. Likewise, it brought together the airline side of the business to operate as one, instead of four separate ones. When they merged, it created Europe's 11th largest airline. The concept of 'Groupness' was born; they shared best practice and welcomed technology welcomed, which made it possible to do things that previously seemed hard to manage.

The emergence of Online Travel Agents (OTAs) had led to many of the more traditional businesses keeping their online business totally separate. This created internal competition, and confused customers, most of whom use more than one channel in the booking process.

During the transition, Thomas Cook learned a valuable lesson, which is relevant to all those who work in or invest in retail. The internet and traditional shopping are not separate. They work best when they are integrated and supporting each other. Customers who go online to look at holidays expect an in-store travel agent to offer a complementary service, not a competing one. With increasing levels of data and more choices, customers want guidance and advice from specialists, who can help them to sift through the data.

Insight into customer needs and beliefs is crucial. Sometimes myths need to be exploded. In the formulation of its new strategy, Thomas Cook surveyed almost 18,000 customers, looked at its own data gleaned from 23 million travellers, and the experience and insights from across the group. It turned out that around half of the company's customers felt overwhelmed by the volume of information and choice, and around two thirds of customers wanted help in choosing a holiday. 70 per cent wanted a provider they could trust – one who would support them in the event of a problem, not leave them stranded, which many had experienced when they organized their own holiday. In the 2011 ash cloud, the thousands of affected Thomas Cook customers were put up in hotels and flown home eventually. Many independent travellers found themselves stranded when airlines cancelled scheduled flights and travel insurance was invalidated. Even in the internet age, trust matters.

The truth is that the internet is powerful, but it can also be a force for confusion and the cause of that terrible affliction most of us these days have experienced: information overload.

Most of us check reviews on Trip Advisor now before booking a hotel. Many of us have experienced the frustration of struggling to find a hotel that has not received an "awful" or "stay clear" comment amongst the many rave reviews. Too much information can be a challenge to us all. The internet is impersonal. If you make an error in a booking form, for example, having that error corrected once booked can be a nightmare of complexity.

Chances are you will understand the problem. The internet can be wonderful tool, but it is not without its downsides. Social media has amplified this problem – for business too. Monitoring, vigilance and rapid response to customers are demanded nowadays, and Thomas Cook has responded by deploying a Care team to provide support pretty much round the clock.
Traditional retailers, companies with high street, town centre or shopping mall space, do not have to be displaced by the internet.

In a funny kind of way – although this was surely more luck than judgment – the markets did not misjudge Thomas Cook in 2007. Retailers, be they sellers of clothes, food or holidays, can offer the best of both worlds: the personal service, advice, and security that comes with face to face retail, with the choice, and research capability that the internet can provide.

Virtual reality may yet change the rules again. Virtual Reality itself may disrupt the way in which we rely on customer reviews when booking a hotel – after all, who needs a review when we can see the hotel for ourselves in glorious virtual space? Will we need to visit a store, when we can visit in a virtual reality landscape instead?

The answer to that question will probably be the same as the lesson learnt by many retailers facing the challenge wrought by the internet. The successful ones have learnt how to combine online with offline shopping. Virtual reality will not replace the need for face-to-face contact, but it may enhance it. It will form a part of the shopping process, not replace it – at least it will if we are able to stop computers changing the very nature of what it is to be human. And it is rather important that we achieve this.

Companies need to be at the pioneering end of new technologies. Thomas Cook is itself testing the Oculus Rift virtual reality set in-store, ensuring that the spirit of innovation, which began with that first rail journey in 1841continues today.

As Alan Kay, the computing pioneer, said: "The best way to predict the future is to create it."

A willingness to embrace new technologies in this way is the key to survival for most companies – and Thomas Cook's continuing transformation is evidence of this.

The comeback kid: Seagate

In March 2013, Seagate announced it had sold its two billionth hard disc drive, which is not bad for a company that was once verging on failure.

Seagate is one of the classic examples of how technology can disrupt your business and leave you fighting for survival. A giant of the disc-drive industry in the 1980s, it was a victim of disruptive technology. In fact, the tale of Seagate was one of the key parts in Christian Clayton's book: *The Innovator's Dilemma*.

But there is good news for companies that think the fight against such disruption is unwinnable; that the technologies that disrupt you are not predictable, because Seagate is back.

In fact, it has been back for a while. In 2001, for example, it increased profits tenfold. In 2014, its share price was almost six times greater than the IPO share price in 2002.

You may recall, innovator's dilemma describes what happens when companies listen to their customers too carefully. Question: "Should we start making 5¼ inch disk drives?" Client answer: "It depends if you want to make toys: nine inch drives are where the money is." The client was wrong of course. The PC became more popular, and companies such as Seagate became rather good at making 5¼ inch disc drives for it. Gradually, the nine inch market lost traction, eventually becoming irrelevant. By the time the superstars of the nine inch market had spotted the change it was too late, the likes of Seagate had too great a lead.

However, Seagate did not learn the lesson of its own success and lost a huge amount of market share with the advent of 3½ inch disk drives.

The company was not finished, but it was most certainly diminished. It was a tale of how the mighty can fall.

The turnaround appeared to occur with the appointment of a new CEO: Stephen J Luczo. It sold disc drives for the game console market; for example Microsoft's XBox, and today it focuses on the storage solutions for Cloud. In March 2012, it announced the first ever 1TB/square inch density hard drive.

It has come up with a way of disrupting the disrupters.
How did it manage it?

In 2001, George Anders penned an article for fastcompany.com in which he outlined five ways Seagate achieved this.[246]

That was 13 years ago, so what has that to do with 2014? Well, quite a lot actually. With the benefit of hindsight, we can see whether the plan worked.

The fact that Seagate has seen its share price increase almost sixfold since the Anders article shows that the plan did actually work.

Here are the five methods:
- First off, it moved one step on in the research process. Instead of looking to customers for new ideas, it looked to their customers. **It surveyed its customer's customers.** You can see how that might help. With hindsight, if it had listened to end users maybe it would have predicted the rise of laptops

[246] Anders, George; The Innovator's Solution, Fast Company, May 31, 2002, http://www.fastcompany.com/44935/innovators-solution 7 July 2014

and 3½ inch disk drives. As part of this process, it got its engineers more involved in the consumer intelligence process – remember in the tale of innovator's dilemma, engineers at companies often had ideas for new products that were dismissed out of hand by marketing departments. Marketers often look down their noses at the techies, but these are the guys who are often best placed to guess where technology is going.

- Secondly, it looked further ahead with its research, trying to predict what would be successful five years down the line.

- Thirdly, it introduced a more flexible supply chain; one that was less specialised and that could adapt to new ideas faster. As part of this, it worked more closely with suppliers. It collaborated with them, incentivising them to support the development of new ideas, rather than merely attempting to screw them down on price.

- Fourthly, it put more emphasis on teams that crossed functions. In this respect, the emphasis was on team work, and on team members supporting each other – in other words it became very collaborative, which is very much the digital way. And because it implanted these ideas in the early noughties, it was way ahead of its time.

- Finally, it deliberately produced some products – if you like separate product lines – that sold for much lower costs. Such a strategy helped its move into the XBox market for example, and may have helped it to avoid the disruption caused by the rise of laptops and 3½ inch drives.

The Clayton remedy

Clayton M Christensen, the man who came up with the concept of innovator's dilemma in the first place, teamed up with Michael E Raynor in 2003 to write *The Innovator's Solution*.[247]

You may recall from the chapter on the sharing economy, Guy Rigby from Smith and Williamson said: "If ain't broken, break it."

To avoid being disrupted out of business, companies need to develop their own disruptive projects.

Christensen and Raynor discuss four steps.

Firstly, a company looking to avoid disruption needs to start before it needs to. Maybe it would be more accurate to characterise this as really meaning a company needs to develop strategies to avoid disruption before it thinks it needs to.

Secondly, it needs to put a senior manager in charge of these disruptive projects.

Thirdly, it should create a team of people that do not use the company's core planning strategies; who operate as if they are almost separate from the rest of the company.

Fourthly, it needs to train staff within marketing, sales and engineering functions in the idea of disruption.

---

[247] Christensen, Clayton and Michael E, Raynor; The Innovator's Solution, Harvard Business School Press; 2003.

Move away

Christensen and Raynor talk about a team of people operating as if they are separate from the rest of the company. The lessons of Kodak and Blockbuster are not to be scared to invent something that could put you out of business and to stop investing in dying business models.

Sometimes you need to rebuild in parallel. For example, in the banking industry, many so-called challenger banks are at an advantage because they are not restricted by their legacy IT systems. The best option for traditional banks may be to build a new core IT system in parallel, perhaps as part of new ventures, while their old system still operates.

Companies that try to move with disrupted technology, without either a major change to the company or one working in parallel are more likely to fail. For example, in attempting to compete with the budget airlines, BA launched Go, but the company was subject to the same BA overheads and legacy systems. The venture was not a success. In contrast, Qantas enjoyed better results with its budget airline Jetstar Airways, and Singapore Airlines with Silk Air. In both cases, the parent companies kept their budget subsidiaries at more of an arm's length. In this way, the subsidiaries were able to embrace a new disruptive way of doing things, without disrupting the core business out of all recognition. The key point here is that both airlines felt they needed to respond to the threat posed by budget airlines, but neither felt their existing business model was dead. So, by keeping the new ventures at a distance, they could have the best of both worlds.

The Microsoft way

Microsoft chose a different approach, although it may have forgotten its own lesson more recently.

When MS DOS was nearing its end, Microsoft faced the challenge of coming up with a new strategy. It is tempting to say it just created Windows, but that is not true; it experimented, and Windows evolved as the experiment that worked best.

Microsoft tried many approaches. Firstly, it looked at beefing up MS-DOS. Secondly, it agreed a joint venture with IBM to develop the OS/2 operating system. Thirdly, it looked at forming joint ventures in the Unix market. Fourthly, and to quote Eric D Beinhocker from his excellent book *The Origin of Wealth*,[248] "In addition to playing the Unix alliance game, Microsoft bought a major stake in the largest seller of Unix systems on PCs, a company called the Santa Cruz Operation. Thus, if Unix did take off, Microsoft would at least have a product of its own in the market." Fifthly, it agreed a deal with Apple to supply software for its hardware, and finally it invested in Windows.

Microsoft did not know which strategy would work; it found out by mirroring evolution. It did this by placing bets, knowing that not all of its projects and ventures would work out. This is an ethos that is alien to many corporates.

At the time, the company came under heavy criticism. The critics said it didn't know what it was doing; that it lacked focus.

Such critiques are often made by the very people who are most likely to be affected by disruptive technology. They throw stones from glass houses.

Focusing too much on one plan and sticking to it is a very risky thing to do when disruptive technology is so unpredictable.

---

[248] Beinhocker, Eric D; The Origin of Wealth

Microsoft has appeared more focused in recent years, with Windows being the lynchpin of most of its activities. Maybe such an approach has cost it; maybe it has forgotten the lesson of MS DOS.

The Corporate VC model

You could say luck comes into it, but you can make your own luck by experimenting.

Not every project works. Sometimes a company is so far gone down one route that it is hard to see how it can change internally.

It is not easy to imagine how Kodak could have reinvented itself. Its overheads were such, and its revenue model was such, that to have made the necessary changes to avoid bankruptcy would have required radical re-invention. Few boards or shareholders have an appetite for such change, and even if they did, the strategy may not have worked.

By setting up several quite distinct businesses, which in some way build on a company's expertise and resource, but at the same time do things very differently, companies may survive, no matter how disruptive technology becomes. There is a good chance that some of these businesses that they back will work, and in time may even become bigger than the original company.

In other words, stack the odds in your favour, and you are more likely to get lucky, as Microsoft once did.
There is another way, and it is called corporate venture capital.

At first glance you might think that venture capital and corporate venture capital are much the same, but there is a subtle but important point. The purpose of venture capital is to make investments that will return a profit. Corporate venture capital wants to do this too, but it is also interested in investing in areas that have a strategic fit with the company. In this way, corporate venture capital can enable companies to place bets on the future without disrupting the core.

In many cases, the purpose of a corporate venture capital firm is to gain knowledge in a certain market sector. They may also look towards acquiring outright some of the companies in which they invest at a later stage.

BP, Bosch, and Panasonic are examples of corporate venture capitalists that look to invest directly into companies for the main purpose of gaining experience and expertise in emerging areas. Unilever Ventures, Reed Elsevier Ventures, and Bloomberg Beta have corporate venture capital arms for which return on investment is a slightly higher priority, and Siemens Venture Capital (SVC), and Physic (Unilever) focus almost entirely on return on investment.[249]

However, these days, companies such as Google, Facebook and the big pharmaceuticals provide venture capital in all but name.

Increasingly, the big pharmaceutical companies let smaller companies carry out the R&D, and take the risk at the early stages of drug development and then either buy the companies out or form joint ventures. The pharmaceuticals bring more to the table than just money though; they also provide regulatory and marketing clout.

---

[249] as Corporate Venture Capital, BVCA,
http://www.bvca.co.uk/Portals/0/library/documents/BVCA%20Guide%20to%20Corporate%20Venture%20Capital.pdf 8 July 2014

Facebook has been buying other social media companies, such as WhatsApp and Instagram, and in both cases, these companies operate in a similar space to Facebook. But the companies are kept at arm's length, and given relative autonomy.

No one knows what the next big social media products will be, but Facebook knows this market better than anyone else. It is hedging its bets, but it is doing so from a position of strength. Facebook may also be buying other social media companies in an attempt to create a stronger advertising force. The rationale for its purchase of Oculus Rift is less clear, but even in this respect, the purchase does fit in with its strategy – and probably anticipates a day when social media communication occurs via avatars in virtual reality space. In any case, Facebook would like to become a dominant player in video games, especially as they now have a strong social media element to them.

As for Google, it too is behaving like a corporate venture capitalist; indeed it has its own VC arm: Google Ventures, but its focus is search and big data. The purchase of DeepMind technologies, for example, was about developing artificial intelligence to enhance search.

Business disruption and you

There is not much difference between how individuals and businesses can avoid disruption. The advice offered by Rupert Jupp on how individuals can ensure their career is not disrupted is not particularly different to what businesses can do.

Collaborate, move out of your comfort zone, talk to people you might not usually talk to or even meet, diversify, and broaden your skills. Familiarise yourself with technologies, such as social media.

And learn. You can learn via online courses or MOOCs. Thomas Cook set up what it calls iClinics.

Disrupting us

Here is your question for the moment. If computers can do quadratic equations, why do we need to learn them?

Well, actually there is a reason, and the reason will be revealed.

It is not clear whether the next industrial revolutions will fall on us all like manna from heaven or like acid rain. They may create as many jobs as they destroy, but one thing is for sure, we won't all need to be experts on physics, or computing, or neural science, or quantum mechanics; only few of us will. So in that case, why teach science at school; why not teach it to the minority? Well, there is a reason why we should teach it to the masses.

If wearable technologies might in time be able to translate spoken foreign languages on the fly, will there be any point in learning a foreign language? Well, actually there will be.

In the age that we are set to enter, education will be more important than ever before, but there is a real risk, a very serious and quite scary risk, that we will mess up.

Computers, the internet and the ingenuity of humanity are revolutionizing learning.

Take video games as an example. Kids love them, and they can be addictive - too addictive sometimes.

But supposing we could turn learning into a video game. One man who seems to be qualified in this area is Nolan

Bushnell. His claim to fame is that he founded Atari. His latest venture, a company called Brainrush, adopts a video game type format to teaching. It turns learning into a game. In an interview on BBC Radio 4 back in February, and as part of a programme entitled *My teacher is an app*, he said that he had run a study in which he divided people into two groups. One learnt Spanish the conventional way, the other by dressing the learning experience up as if it was a video game. He said that using the former approach, students learnt 150 words. Using the second approach, they learnt 1,500 words.

There is no shortage of cynics. [250] They say that using the Brainrush technique is not proper learning. Are they being serious? Learning is learning. Maybe the only time we learn a language properly is when we are babies, but does that mean the techniques we use to learn when we are older don't count?

There is nothing wrong in learning through video games, providing such techniques are combined with other experiences. Great, you now know 1,500 Spanish words, and now start talking to Spanish people. Now imagine this type of game within a virtual reality context and you could simulate being immersed in that country.

In that same interview on BBC Radio, Bushnell told the show's presenter that if you really want a permanent memory: "You want review what you learn today after a good night's sleep, and then review it in a week, and then review it in a month." He said: "If you are in the software environment that we are developing for 20 to 30 minutes a week you will be able to remember 100 per cent of everything you learned for the rest of your life."

---

[250] *My Teacher is an App,* was broadcast on BBC Radio 4 on Monday Feb 24 2014

What is wrong with that?

Alternatively, take a product called Amplify. This is a tablet computer aimed at educating. One cunning aspect of this product design is that if you are reading and see a word that you don't know, you can click on it to get a translation. The software then makes sure you see the same word several times when you use the product again to ensure you really do learn what it means.

Some people find that scary, but are they merely afraid of change? Are they no different to our ancestors who thought reading would damage our brains; that learning to ride a horse made us lazy, and that climbing down from the trees to traipse across the Rift Valley was an unnecessary and dangerous step?

Not all teachers like the idea behind Amplify.

However, we could look at Khan Academy, a form of learning by interactivity and video. The key point is that the teachers featured in the videos are rather good. And you can pause. Imagine if you could have done that when you were at school – pause the teacher that is. The thing about Khan Academy is that it is the most popular school in the world – it has 10 million users a month. Bill Gates is reportedly a fan. It is also used by some schools in a practice known as flipping. The Khan Academy replaces the teacher standing in front of a blackboard, but the teacher still has a job acting as a mentor, giving the students interactivity, and one to one support. The kids are taught at home, in front of their computer, but they do homework at school. The dream of the Khan Academy is free education for anyone, anywhere. And what is so great about it is that, because it uses computer technology, it tailors education for the students, sets tests and works out what the student doesn't understand and then focuses on that. It is a school for ten million, but each student receives a unique experience.

The Rocketship takes another approach. It works in schools in disadvantaged areas, where students learn mainly online. The school employs fewer teachers but pays them more, with a view to only employing the very best teachers.

These are all very exciting ideas.

Technology promises to make learning easier, more effective. The trouble is that there are downsides.

Technology cynics do themselves a disservice. Their argument often loses credibility because they automatically react in horror to the very ideas described above.

However, the jobs that most of us will do in the new technology age will be jobs that involve empathy and creativity.

We don't go to school just to learn facts; maybe a more important part of school is learning social skills.
It has become fashionable to belittle the teaching of music, drama, dance and the like. We are told that what matters is maths, science and being able to communicate in our native language, and maybe other languages.

But technology can help kids to do that – at least it can up to a point.

Technology may never be effective at teaching creative skills.

It most certainly cannot teach social skills, or sport – although it can help.

The danger is that we are seduced by the benefits of technology, and forget about the social aspects of education.

Play needs to be re-introduced to schools.

Maybe the Scandinavian model of delaying formal education until kids are a bit older – such as seven in Sweden and Finland (a similar practice is followed in some eastern European countries) – is more appropriate. Up to that age, school should be all fun, all play and very little computer usage.

As children get older, we could introduce technology to make learning more fun, and effective. However, we need to place emphasis on sport, creative subjects, practical subjects, and above all communication as well.

There is a product called the Wolfram Problem Generator. It can solve quadratic equations for you. So what is the point of learning them?[251]

The answer to that comes in two parts.

The first answer is that we have to understand technology. If we create technology that only machines can understand, we tread a dangerous path.
The second answer builds on the first. It may be that only a very small proportion of us will work in jobs that entail understanding technology, but we don't know in advance who will be best suited to this.

That is why learning quadratic equations will remain an important part of school. Let everyone learn the basic science stuff, and the people who will take this to a further level will eventually choose themselves.

---

[251] http://www.wolframalpha.com/pro/problem-generator/

As for learning second languages when technology can do the translations for us, well, the dangers are clear. We may face a kind of Monty Python scenario in which translation tools get it embarrassingly wrong, such as with Monty Python's famous sketch involving a Hungarian phrasebook consisting of inaccurate translations:

Hungarian:	I will not buy this record. It is scratched.
Clerk:	Sorry?
Hungarian:	I will not buy this record. It is scratched.
Clerk:	Uh, no, no, no. This is a tobacconist.
Hungarian:	Ah! I will not buy this tobacconist. It is scratched.
Clerk:	No, no, no, no. Tobacco...um... cigarettes (holds up a pack).
Hungarian:	Ya! See-gar-ets! Ya! Uh... My hovercraft is full of eels.
Clerk:	What?
Hungarian:	My hovercraft (pantomimes puffing a cigarette)... is full of eels (pretends to strike a match).

Learning a language helps to teach people about other cultures, promotes understanding, and it may be just too tempting to rely on technology to do the job instead.

This is why foreign languages should be taught in school, and if technology makes it possible to learn 1,500 words quicker, so much the better.

By creating an environment in which the emphasis is on learning social skills, we will need teachers more than ever.

There may even be a case for longer school days, and raising the school leaving age, but only if play, social learning and the learning that technology provides are included. We may need a lot more teachers.

Healthcare

Likewise, we read in chapter ten, that up to 80 per cent of the tasks carried out by doctors may be replaced by technology, but that does not mean we won't need doctors. Far from it, we may need them more than ever, along with nurses, physiotherapists, occupational therapists, and...well the list goes on.

But at the moment, and across much of the world, doctors have a disincentive, for diverse reasons, to move patients on to specialists. This is not a good thing, and can lead to medical errors. Technology will enable doctors to – as it were – move upstream, and offer medical services that are currently the preserve of specialists, and to offer a higher standard of care.

Technology can also translate jargon. Too many doctors hide behind a mist of terminology. In a more collaborative digital world, the patient doctor relationship will change, and the patient will have more control. Not all doctors like this idea.

Just as bankers, lumbered with their legacy IT systems, are struggling to compete with challenger banks, many hospitals and medical centres are living with outmoded practices and institutions. Inevitably, the resistance to change from within will be enormous. However, such institutions need to be subjected to the same ideas and pressures that permeate business. Medical industries need to be opened up to entrepreneurs, venture capital firms, people with a willingness to take risks and to try new ideas within the limits of patient safety.

It's inevitable that the need for medical support and care will move beyond doctors.

The need for carers as we age will, if anything, grow.

Customisation

Just as industry may be transformed so much that we will see more localised production, education will be more tailored to individual needs. Algorithms will work out with which subjects pupils need help. Teachers will focus more on one-to-one support. Already, some teachers find that Khan Academy dashboard tells them more about pupils than they ever dreamed possible.

In healthcare, wearable technology and genome sequencing will lead to more customer specific medicine.

Technology may lead to an impersonal world, but if we apply it right, it will create a more personal world; one of collaboration. Users of Facebook will understand this next point; technology can make you closer to your friends.

Trickle Down

But there is a danger.

There may be plenty of things for people to do in a digital age, but who will pay for them?

The wealth generated from technology has to trickle down.

It is not clear why recent years have seen a growing gap between the very richest in society and the rest. Do they get richer because they work harder? Of course not. Plenty of people work hard but live in poverty.

Is it because they are risk takers? Well yes, to an extent, but by definition some risk takers are poor – it wouldn't be risky if all risk takers were rich. In any case, wealthy risk takers can take risks as they are small relative to total wealth. The very poor take risks as they have all to gain and nothing to lose. Those in the middle are most risk averse and sadly most likely to be facing the challenge of managing change in business and in society.

One lesson of Moore's Law is that once technology is affordable, it becomes more powerful and cheaper.

If wealth becomes ever more concentred in the top 0.1 per cent, where will the consumer demand come from to make the economy grow? Where will the demand come from to incentivise companies to invest, and thus lead to more powerful technology?

And where will the consumer demand come from to pay the wages of the army of teachers, doctors, nurses, occupational therapists, mental health counsellors and healthcare social workers?

Who will pay for the carers?

Recall the section above looking at the jobs that Frey and Osborne believe are less likely to be disrupted by technology. Typically, these are skilled jobs, but they don't pay particularly well. Indeed, the voluntary sector performs many of these jobs. If the fruits of technology are to trickle down, and we are to see consumer demand rise across the economy, the remuneration for these types of jobs must rise. Indeed, in some cases, there must be remuneration for these jobs.

Somehow, a way has to be found to ensure the money that is generated by innovation trickles down into mass market demand.

If technology also means that people are forced to change careers more often, won't that mean the natural rate of unemployment will rise?

It has become fashionable for tabloids to demonise people on benefits, but who knows how technology will affect you? Will the greatest critics of benefits claimants end up claiming benefit themselves?

If the challenge of reducing unemployment during the technological revolution becomes insurmountable, should we consider introducing a four-day week?

Taxation and money printing

In an age in which corporate profits to GDP rise and there is a worldwide savings glut – which is perhaps the underlying reason why interest rates are so low – taxation needs to be adjusted.

Taxation on the creation of wealth needs to be as low as possible.

Taxation on the hoarding of wealth needs to be increased.

We should maximise incentives to work and invest, and minimise incentives to live off property, savings, and other forms of rent seeking.

At the same time, we must encourage the ownership of capital amongst those who might otherwise be squeezed out of capital ownership. Let taxation incentivise the pension payments for those at the lower end of the income scale, so that a higher proportion of the population has ownership of capital.

And if technology leads to vast increases in productive potential, in which there is a real risk that economies may be constantly running below potential with minimal risk of inflation, governments can always fund spending to create demand via printing money – assuming bitcoins do not remove this ability from central banks.

Innovation

We need to look at ways in which we can radically reform patent law.

Just before these words were written, Elon Musk – the founder of Tesla –announced that he was going make Tesla's patents on electric cars open to the electric car industry. He said that he hopes that by doing this, innovation in the industry will increase, which will be good news for Tesla as the world's leading electric car company.

A recent paper from MIT's Sloan Business School said: "Investment would have been at least $8.1 billion higher over the course of five years but for litigation brought by frequent patent litigators." [252]

---

[252] Mullin, Joe; New study suggests patent trolls really are killing start-ups, Arts Technica, June 12 2014, http://artstechnica.com/tech-

In this era of collaboration, patents are an anachronism; an idea that needs to be disrupted out of sight.

But some say there has to be a way to fund innovation.
Instead of patents, consider following the example set by the music industry. Pay those responsible for the key inventions a royalty based on shares of net receipts from the products to which they contributed. Maybe introduce an 'innovation added tax', a little like VAT, but a tax that distributes proceeds to innovators. Alternatively, less radical reform may entail keeping patents, but incentivising those who hold patents to lower the barriers to allow third parties to apply their patented technology.

How do you work out who are the people that contribute to this innovation process? How do you weigh up the value of each person's contribution?

As was alluded to in the discussion on antibiotics and superbugs, social media and algorithms applying the principles that underpin search engines can help.

If innovation forums are set up in which people are invited to contribute toward the innovation process, technology can provide a way to ascertain who the key contributors are. It can do this by looking at ideas that receive the most likes, the most comments, or are cited the most. It can weigh likes, comments and citations depending on who made them. If certain individuals who themselves are widely cited, cite or like an idea, the person who put forward that idea could achieve a higher ranking than if their idea was cited by someone who hadn't done anything else. There are potential problems with this associated with peer review fraud, but such barriers can be overcome by the promotion of transparency and this could be achieved by innovation forums being open rather than closed rather like a social research platform.

Using computer algorithms in this way it will be possible to calculate the value of certain ideas to an innovation. Innovators could then receive a financial reward without clogging up the innovation process.

By doing this, we also find a way to ensure the fruits of innovations trickle down, rather than stay with large companies.

This time it is different

When you hear the phrase "this time it is different," you are meant to assume that phrase is being used ironically; as meaning it is never different and beware when people make that claim. Alas, civilizations collapse because people refuse to think that something is different. When Vesuvius erupted, the Romans of Ancient Pompeii had no way of responding; that time it really was different.

Technology is making a permanent change, and when and if we come out at the other side, the world will be different. How we handle that change is perhaps the greatest challenge we will ever face. How we handle it matters more than almost anything.

We have to find a way of ensuring that minimal pain results from new technology in the short run, and that the maximum benefit is realised in the long run. Those two aims may be mutually exclusive.

Technology is accelerating at an accelerating rate

The issues discussed in his book are about as important as you can get, but rarely do you hear or read about them being discussed in the media, by politicians, or indeed in academic circles.

Some dismiss the idea that technology is changing the world. The effect that technology has had upon the economy and indeed on all of us over the last decade or two may be open to debate. You may or may not think its impact has been dramatic.

But that is not the point.

The impact that technology has had up to now will be as nothing compared to the impact it is about to have. Certainly, this is a point that few economists seem to understand. In economic text books, technology seems to play a bit part. How often do economists refer to the phrase Moore's Law? The answer is surely not often enough.

You could say that the technology we have seen over the last one or two decades is like the tip of an iceberg compared to what we are about to see. The truth is, however, that such a statement would be massively understating the reality. The technology we have seen over the last one or two decades is like a snow flake sitting on the tip of an iceberg compared to what we are about to see.

The rate of technological change is not merely accelerating. It is accelerating at an accelerating rate. And this leaves us with some questions.

Some questions

2008 and all that. While the impact of technology to date may be little more than an early rehearsal of what we are about to see, it has had an impact. How great has this impact been?

Is technology the underlying cause of rising inequality in the developed world?

Has technology had the effect of increasing the reward to capital and decreasing the reward to labour? Has it, in turn, led to a global savings glut, and is this the underlying reason why we have such low interest rates?

Was it the underlying cause of the financial crisis of 2008?

Watching the machine

Science fiction is just that – fiction right? It is just a bit of fun. Such an attitude may be a problem. If you were to say to someone that you are worried about machines taking over from us, they might laugh and say: "You have been watching too much science fiction." Such attitudes may lead us into a sense of complacency; of not taking the threats of technology too seriously, because 'it is just science fiction.'

The truth is that there is a very real danger that technology will more than disrupt us; it will make us irrelevant It doesn't have to be like that. Technology can enhance us, improve the quality of our lives, and make us healthier, cleverer, and more complete.

How do we ensure technology has this benign effect? Are enough people even asking this question? It may seem glib to recommend dusting off an old book by Asimov, and introducing the three laws of robotics, as indeed others have, but it may not be such a bad idea, all the same.

Will technology change the very essence of what it is to be human? Is it already affecting our ability to think deeply?

If technology brings us closer together and encourages greater collaboration, will this have a positive or negative effect? Will we benefit from a kind of wisdom of crowds writ large, or is there a danger of groupthink, group polarisation, and madness of crowds?

Supposing in a decade or two we are always linked to the internet, and that by then we are on 6G or 7G and we can get just about any information we need instantly. Is that exciting or frightening? What are the implications of that?

Looking further forward, what about the possibility of brain interfaces providing us with seamless access to the internet, so that the internet feels like an extension to our brain? What would the implications of that be, especially in view of the questions posed in the above paragraph about group psychology?

If there will be a need for jobs such as teachers, and carers, and artists etcetera, but the profits from technology only accrue to small number of people, how do we create the aggregate demand for these jobs to be paid? In other words, how do we ensure the profits from technology trickle down?

How can we get our schools to apply technology in a way that gets the best out of it, without us losing social skills?

Above all, can we afford to sit back and hope for the best? Do we need to draw up plans to ensure the effect of technology is benign?

Augment, rather than replace

It is just human nature to fear that computers and robots may replace us. A more likely scenario is that instead they will enhance us via augmented reality; for example, by making us stronger, healthier and giving us rapid access to information providing the impression of greater intelligence. These changes will be disruptive, but not necessarily destructive.

We will still need people to work

At the beginning of this book Buckminster Fuller was quoted as saying "We should do away with the absolutely specious notion that everybody has to earn a living." He was not entirely right. There will always be a need a need for jobs; jobs in areas that require empathy, social skills, human interaction. But while these jobs will be needed, a question mark relates to whether they will be affordable. Only if the profits from technology trickle down can this happen.

Warnings

Here are two warnings.

Firstly, you can't make sure the effect of technology is benign by ignoring it. Resisting technology is pointless. As the Borg might say 'resistance is futile'. If we turn our back on it, all of us — business, you, me, and humanity — will become victims of a kind of innovator's dilemma. We will be disrupted into irrelevance.

Secondly, the speed with which technology is changing is very fast and will get faster. Its impact may be sudden. And if we play it wrong, we may not get a second chance.

Epilogue

Imagine this scenario.

I have some dead trees at the end of my garden and I make the decision to cut them down.

I visit my local DIY store and buy a chainsaw for £80.00. I cut down the tree on a Saturday afternoon.

The chainsaw goes into the shed. It stays there collecting dust.

Now imagine the effect the sharing economy will have.

I am easily able to rent the chainsaw via the internet.

A few weeks later someone in the same village finds my chainsaw on the internet and comes to borrow it for £30 – half the price of hiring it from a company, causing further disruption in the retail hire business.

The disruption caused by the internet of sharing in this case causes a number of chainsaw manufacturers to fail.

If I want to buy a chainsaw all I now need to do is download a schematic from the internet, add the functionality I require and email it to Amazon who will 3D print it for me (using disruptive new material science from LiquidMetal Technologies) for a pittance.

A little later an industrial designer invents an entirely new method of cutting technology based on graphene. In the process he makes the design of the new saw totally free to download for 12" blade models – for anything larger you pay a licence fee to download it and arrange to have it 3D printed. A whole new industry is born.

3D printing combined with robotic technologies have massively taken off by this point and a looming problem becomes a major political issue – raw materials for 3D printing are running out...a territory war breaks out between America and China.

But that's OK because no one is killed – it's fought by robots. This may sound like an implausible statement, but bear in mind that usually (and with some obvious exceptions) the object of war is not to kill people, but to destroy or damage infrastructure. The more sophisticated the technology, the lower the risk of human casualties.

As an aside – unfortunately, the person who borrowed the chainsaw had an accident and they cut their leg badly. But that was solved in a few hours – their stem cell profile was already known by their local private doctors' surgery (state run medical services have ceased to exist because they were over-run by folk self-diagnosing due to new information provided by the new Apple iPhone and Google Health), who then proceeded to print new replacement skin that was knitted together using an injection of nanobots.

As for reading books, or learning a new language, will we need to do that when our brain interface to the internet is so fast we can download all we need to know in seconds?

As for worrying about the tree in our garden, with virtual reality, maybe we would be better off sitting in our virtual garden?

And the challenge to you

It matters not if you are the President of the United States, the CEO of a global corporation or a school leaver. The issues covered in this book are as important as you can get.

We all – that's all of us: you, me, your friends, Romans and countrymen – need to familiarise ourselves with technology, and we need to talk about it and its possible consequences more often.

There will be a need for jobs in the era we are entering, but only if enough people can afford to pay for the services that computers cannot provide. In addition to the many jobs we have already talked about, we will need life coaches, personal trainers, and modern day equivalents of blacksmiths, who produce bespoke products for us using 3D printing and robot technology. We will also need those who understand technology, and it is essential that we are all taught the rudiments of technology.

But the jobs will only be created if the profits from technology trickle down. If the profits from new technology do not translate into higher wages, demand may be suffocated out of the economy, in turn crushing future innovation. Equally, in a globalised world, if the taxation from profits only accrue to governments that operate low taxation regimes, the impact on government finances across the world, and thus aggregate demand created by government spending, may be catastrophic.

In 1919, shareholders in Ford tried to stop its boss Henry Ford from implementing his now famous strategy. Ford said: "My ambition is to employ still more men, to spread the benefits of this industrial system to the greatest possible number, to help them build up their lives and their homes. To do this we are putting the greatest share of our profits back in the business." [253]

Shareholders said Ford's duty was to them not his workers, hence the legal action. The court held in favour of

[253] http://en.wikipedia.org/wiki/Dodge_v._Ford_Motor_Company

shareholders, forcing the company to pay out dividends. While this presented Ford with a setback, he did eventually get his way and paid his workers higher wages. Today we see Ford's strategy as a stroke of genius. By paying workers at his factories more money, Ford forced rivals to follow suit, and higher wages led to wealthier consumers. Wealthier consumers demanded more cars. Ford grew on the back of this policy, but it was a policy that was almost halted in its tracks.

A latter day equivalent of such a policy may be a sharp rise in the minimum wage.

In the UK, British Prime Minister David Cameron has coined the phrase Big Society, by which he refers to the voluntary sector taking a bigger role in society. Yet many of the roles that his Big Society is meant to offer free of charge are precisely those tasks that the computer might never be able to provide. If we make the jobs that computers can't do unpaid, then the number of paid jobs in existence may reduce dramatically.

We need a latter day Henry Ford, or someone – or better still, a great many someones – who shares his vision. We also need leaders who have a better understanding of the importance of collaboration in a digital world, and how patents are often an anathema to the digital ethos.

Maybe what we need is techno-politics and techno-economics – that is to say policy that is set with disruptive technology in mind.

The day a prospective US President has as his or her core policy, 'ensuring technology works to all our benefit', and is elected on that ticket is the day we have woken up to the challenge posed by technology. Let's hope such a day does not come too late.

References

3ders.org; 3D printing hype overdone, says Nomura's Kim, 9 December 2013, http://www.3ders.org/articles/20131209-3d-printing-hype-overdone-says-nomura-kim.html

AAPL Investors; iPad versus iPhone versus iPod, http://aaplinvestors.net/stats/iphonevsipod/

ACS, A battery that 'breathes' could power next-gen electric vehicle, 16 March 2014, https://www.acs.org/content/acs/en/pressroom/newsreleases/2014/march/a-battery-that-breathes-could-power-next-gen-electric-vehicles.html

Airbnb; https://www.airbnb.com/economic-impact

Allen, Bob; Hedrick, James; Coady, Dan; Engler, Amanda; Narayan, Spike; Pitera, Jed; Ninja Polymers: Nanomedicine that can destroy antibiotic-resistant bacteria, IBM, http://www.research.ibm.com/articles/nanomedicine.shtml#fbid=MQ3mKGt4zzb, 7 July 2014

Allen, Nick; Why 3D Printing Is Overhyped (I Should Know, I Do It For a Living), Gizmodo, 17 May 2013, http://gizmodo.com/why-3d-printing-is-overhyped-i-should-know-i-do-it-fo-508176750

Anders, George; The Innovator's Solution, Fast Company, May 31, 2002, http://www.fastcompany.com/44935/innovators-solution 7 July 2014

Anderson, Chris; Free: How today's smartest businesses profit by giving something for nothing, Random House Business, 6 May 2010

Andreesen, Marc; Why Bitcoin Matters, New York Times, 21 January 2014, http://dealbook.nytimes.com/2014/01/21/why-bitcoin-matters/?_php=true&_type=blogs&_r=0

Anthony, Sebastian; The wonderful world of wonder materials, Extreme Tech, 27 August 2013, http://www.extremetech.com/extreme/164594-the-wonderful-world-of-wonder-materials, 29 January 2014

Apple Museum, Apple History Timeline, 18 December 2013

Armstrong, Doree; Ma, Michelle; Researcher controls colleague's motions in 1st human brain-to-brain interface, University of Washington, August 27 2013, http://www.washington.edu/news/2013/08/27/researcher-controls-colleagues-motions-in-1st-human-brain-to-brain-interface/, 31 January 2014

ARPA-E Advanced, Hybrid Planar Lithium/Sulfur Batteries, http://arpa-e.energy.gov/?q=slick-sheet-project/advanced-lithium-sulfur-batteries

Asymco; Television History - A Timeline, The University of Texas School of Law Tarlton Law Library 1878-2005 http://www.asymco.com/

Atherton, Kelsey B.; How Robo-Bees Could Save America's Crops, Popular Science, 19 September 2013, http://www.popsci.com/technology/article/2013-09/true-bee-or-robot-be

Azonano.com., Comprehensive Report on Global Market for Nanoelectromechanical Systems, 24 October 2012 http://www.azonano.com/news.aspx?newsID=25791, 31 January 2014

Bailey, Ronald; Post-Scarcity Prophet Economist Paul Romer on growth, technological change, and an unlimited human future, Reason, December 2001

Banwatt, Paul; 3D Printing Patents Expire – RepRap Moves In http://lawitm.com/3d-printing-patents-expire-reprap-moves-in/, 21 January 2014

Barr, Alistair; Amazon testing delivery by drone, CEO Bezos says, USA Today, 2 December 2013, http://www.usatoday.com/story/tech/2013/12/01/amazon-bezos-drone-delivery/3799021/

Basiliere, Pete, The Future of 3D Printing, Gartner, 26 February 2014

Baxter, Michael; The Blindfolded Masochist, Hothive, 2011

Baxter, Michael; The Wind Farm Bias, Investment and Business News, 27 August 2013,
http://www.investmentandbusinessnews.co.uk/economic-news/the-wind-farm-bias/5131

BBA; The way we bank now,
https://www.bba.org.uk/landingpage/waywebanknow/

BBC; Millions tune in for Doctor Who 50th anniversary show,
http://www.bbc.co.uk/news/entertainment-arts-25076912, 28 December 2014

BBC; The Classroom of the Future: My Teacher is an App, BBC Radio 4, 24 February 2014,
http://www.bbc.co.uk/programmes/b03w02sj

Beinhocker, Eric D; The Origin of Wealth as Corporate Venture Capital, BVCA,
http://www.bvca.co.uk/Portals/0/library/documents/BVCA%20Guide%20to%20Corporate%20Venture%20Capital.pdf, 8 July 2014

Bellew, Corby Lenn; An SOI Process for Integrated Solar Power, Circuitry, and Actuators for Autonomous Microelectromechanical Systems, University of California, Berkeley, Spring 2002,
http://robotics.eecs.berkeley.edu/~pister/publications/dissertations/BellewColby.pdf

Bellis, Mary; Inventors of the Modern Computer ARPAnet - The First Internet. About.com
http://inventors.about.com/library/weekly/aa091598.htm/ 18 December 2013

Bellis, Mary; The Birth of Fibre Optics, about.com,
http://inventors.about.com/library/weekly/aa980407.htm, 19 January 2014

Benkler, Yochai; Open-source economics, TED,
http://blog.ted.com/2008/04/16/yochai_benkler_1/   18 December 2013

Benkler, Yochai; The Wealth of Networks How Social Production Transforms Markets and Freedom,
http://www.benkler.org/Benkler_Wealth_Of_Networks.pdf, 18 December 2013

Bennett, Drake; Clayton Christensen Responds to New Yorker Takedown of 'Disruptive Innovation', Business Week, http://www.businessweek.com/articles/2014-06-20/clayton-christensen-responds-to-new-yorker-takedown-of-disruptive-innovation, 20 June 2014

Benton, Adam; When did humans leave Africa?, Evoanth, 28 March 2013, http://evoanth.wordpress.com/2013/03/28/when-did-humans-leave-africa/ 26 April 2013

Biever, Celeste; Free trade may have finished off Neanderthals, New Scientist, 1 April 2005

Biology Online; Answers to all your Biology Questions, Stem cell, http://www.biology-online.org/dictionary/Stem_cells, 21 January 2014

Bonsor, Kevin; Fenlon, Wesley How RFID Works, http://electronics.howstuffworks.com/gadgets/high-tech-gadgets/rfid.htm 19 January 2014

Bootle, Roger; Cutting prices to raise living standards is just a waste of energy, The Telegraph, 6 October 2013, http://www.telegraph.co.uk/finance/comment/rogerbootle/10359344/Roger-Bootle-Cutting-prices-to-raise-living-standards-is-just-a-waste-of-energy.html

Bostrom, Nick; Future of Humanity Institute, Faculty of Philosophy & James Martin 21st Century School, University of Oxford

Brack, Jessica; Maximising Millennials in the Workplace, UNC Kenan-Flagler Business School, 2012, http://www.kenan-flagler.unc.edu/executive-development/custom-programs/~/media/DF1C11C056874DDA8097271A1ED48662.ashx

Brandon, Alan; New type of rechargeable battery – just add water, http://www.gizmag.com/rechargeable-battery-freshwater-seawater/18565/, 30 January 2014

Breaux, Justin H. S.; Silicene: To be or not to be?, Argonne National Laboratory, http://www.anl.gov/articles/silicene-be-or-not-be, 24 July 2014

Brewster, Signe; How do you manufacture huge amounts of graphene for a fraction of the cost? Printing presses, Gigaom, http://gigaom.com/2013/09/30/how-do-you-manufacture-huge-amounts-of-graphene-for-a-fraction-of-the-cost-printing-presses/, 26 January 2014

Brumfiel, Geoff, The Insane and Exciting Future of the Bionic Body, Smithsonian Magazine, Septmber 2013, http://www.smithsonianmag.com/innovation/the-insane-and-exciting-future-of-the-bionic-body-918868/?no-ist, 12 May 2014

Bryzek, Dr Janusz; Roadmap to a $Trillion MEMS Market VP MEMS Development, Fairchild Semiconductor, Mancef, Board Member, http://meptec.org/Resources/Roadmap%20to%20a%20$Trillion%20MEMS%20Market,%20Meptec.pdf

Buckley, Sean; Solar cell that can receive data transmitted through light waves. Engadget, http://www.engadget.com/2014/01/06/wysips-connect/?ncid=rss_truncated, 30 January 2014

Buller, David J.; Evolution of the Mind: 4 fallacies of evolution, Scientific American, December 2008

Bumiller, Elizabeth; Nagourney, Adam; Bush: 'America is addicted to oil', New York Times, 1 February 2006, http://www.nytimes.com/2006/02/01/world/americas/01iht-state.html?pagewanted=all&_r=0

Butler, Nick; Peak oil? The trend to watch is peak car, Financial Times, 15 December 2013, http://blogs.ft.com/nick-butler/2013/12/15/peak-oil-the-trend-to-watch-is-peak-car/?ftcamp=published_links%2Frss%2Fcompanies_energy%2Ffeed%2F%2Fproduct

Bylund, Anders; Wikipedia didn't kill Britannica – Windows did, Wired, 14 March 2012, http://www.wired.com/business/2012/03/wikipedia-didnt-kill-brittanica-windows-did/

Car Pooling; http://www.carpooling.co.uk/

Carr, Nicholas; The Shallows: What the Internet is Doing to Our Brains, W. W. Norton & Company, 6 June 2011

Casey, Tina; Caution: Wet Solar Power (New Affordable Solar Paint

Research), Cleantechnica, 15 May 2013,
http://cleantechnica.com/2013/05/15/caution-wet-solar-power-new-affordable-solar-paint-research/

CERN; The birth of the web, CERN
http://home.web.cern.ch/about/birth-web, 18 December 2013

Channell, Jason; Jansen, Heath R.; Syme, Alastair R.; Savvantidou, Sofia; Morse, Edward L.; Yuen, Anthony; Energy Darwinism: The Evolution of the Energy Industry, Citi, October 2013,
https://ir.citi.com/Jb89SJMmf%2BsAVK2AKa3QE5EJwb4fvI5UUplD OICiGOOk0NV2CqNI%2FPDLJqxidz2VAXXAXFB6fOY%3D

Chozick, Amy; As Young Lose Interest in Cars, G.M. Turns to MTV for Help, New York Times Business Day, 22 March 2012

Christensen, Clayton; Raynor, Michael E.; The Innovator's Solution, Harvard Business School Press; 2003.

Christensen, Clayton; The Innovator's Dilemma: When New Technologies Cause Great Firms to Fail, Harvard Business Review Press, Reprint edition 19 November 2013

Christensen, Clayton M.; Bohmer, Richard; Kenagy, John; Will Disruptive Innovations Cure Health Care?, Harvard Business Review, 2000 http://hbr.org/web/extras/insight-center/health-care/will-disruptive-innovations-cure-health-care

Clements, Isaac Perry; How Prosthetic Limbs Work, How Stuff Works, http://science.howstuffworks.com/prosthetic-limb.htm, 21 January 2014

Clermont, Ryan E.; Standards of Living in Britain during the Industrial Revolution (1770-1820) (pp. 3-11), Western Undergraduate Economics Review, Western University, Ontario, Canada,
http://economics.uwo.ca/undergraduate/undergraduatereview/un dergraduatereview02/1_Clermont.pdf

Clinton, Bill; Text of Remarks on the Completion of the First Survey of the Entire Human Genome Project, The White House Office of the Press Secretary, June 26, 2000,
http://clinton5.nara.gov/WH/New/html/genome-20000626.html,

21 January 2014

Clover, Ian; US solar power costs fall 60% in just 18 months, PV Magazine, http://www.pv-magazine.com/news/details /beitrag/us-solar-power-costs-fall-60-in-just-18-months_100012797/, 21 January 2014

CNN International; Google IPO priced at $85 a share, 19 August 2004, http://edition.cnn.com/2004/BUSINESS/08/19/google.ipo/

Cohen, Daniel; Sargeant, Matthew; Somers, Ken; 3-D printing takes shape, McKinsey Quarterly, January 2014, http://www.mckinsey.com/insights/manufacturing/3-d_printing_takes_shape?cid=other-eml-nsl-mip-mck-oth-1402

Cohen, Dr Joe; An effective vaccine against malaria may at last be in sight, Financial Times, http://www.ft.com/intl/cms/s/0/21788c96-be6d-11e3-a1bf-00144feabdc0.html#axzz30RFpAdPZ, 12 May 2014

Cohen, Tyler; The Great Stagnation: How America Ate All The Low-Hanging Fruit of Modern History, Got Sick, and Will (Eventually) Feel Better: A Penguin eSpecial from Dutton, 2011

Collins, Jim; Articles - The Secret of Enduring Greatness, Jim Collins, May 2008, http://www.jimcollins.com/article_topics/articles/secret-of-enduring-greatness.html

Coughlan, Sean; Harvard plans to boldly go with 'Spocs', BBC 24 September 2013, http://www.bbc.co.uk/news/business-24166247, 7 July 2014

Crucible, 3D printing, http://www.crucibleid.com/3d-printing/

Cuthbertson, Anthony; Scientists develop the first ever low-cost 3D metal, http://www.itproportal.com/2013/12/09/scientists-develop-first-ever-low-cost-3d-metal-printer/#ixzz2ryQoULV4 31 January 2014, December 2013

Danova, Tony; Morgan Stanley: 75 Billion Devices Will Be Connected To The Internet Of Things By 2020, http://www.businessinsider.com/75-billion-devices-will-be-connected-to-the-internet-by-2020-2013-10#ixzz2uPxWxeL3

Davies, Professor Dame Sally; Grant, Dr Jonathan; Catchpole, Professor Mike; The Drugs Don't Work: A Global Threat, Penguin, 2013

Dawkins, Richard; The Selfish Gene, Oxford University Press, 1976

Dediu, Horace; A Dollar a Day, Cumulative iOS units sold, July 25 2014, Asymco, http://www.asymco.com/2014/07/25/whats-apple-worth/ 5 September 2014

Deloitte; Just 20% of high street shops affected by administration in last five years remain vacant, 4 April 2014, http://www.deloitte.com/view/en_GB/uk/industries/consumer-business/083873bccb725410VgnVCM3000003456f70aRCRD.htm

Delong, Brad; The Daily Piketty: May 30, 2014, http://equitablegrowth.org/2014/05/30/daily-piketty-may-30-2014/ 23 June 2014

Department of Health, Prime Minister warns of global threat of antibiotic resistance, Department of Health and Prime Minister's Office, 2 July 2014

Domhoff, William; Wealth Income and Power, Who Rules America, University of California at Santa Cruz, http://www2.ucsc.edu/whorulesamerica/power/wealth.html 3 September, 2014

Dorrier, Jason; DNA Origami to Nanomachines: Building Tiny Robots for the Body and Beyond, Singularity Hub, http://singularityhub.com/2014/01/27/dna-origami-to-nanomachines-building-tiny-robots-for-the-body-and-beyond/ 30 January 2014

Dorrier, Jason; Genomic Studies Sift Centenarian DNA for Genes Protecting Against Age-Related Diseases, Singularity Hub, 29 December 2012, http://singularityhub.com/2013/12/29/genomic-studies-sift-centenarian-dna-for-genes-protecting-against-age-related-diseases/ 31 January 2014

Downes, Larry; Nunes, Paul F.; The Big idea Big-Bang Disruption, Accenture, March 2013, http://www.accenture.com/SiteCollectionDocuments/PDF/Accenture-Big-bang-Disruption.pdf, 30 December 2013

Dunbar, Robin; How Many Friends Does One Person Need?: Dunbar's Number and Other Evolutionary Quirks, Faber and Faber, 2011

Dvorak, Paul; Wind energy blowing life into global carbon fiber industry, Windpower Engineering and Development, 3 July 2013, http://www.windpowerengineering.com/design/mechanical/blades/wind-energy-blowing-life-into-global-carbon-fiber-industry/

Efrati, Amir; In online ads, there's Google and then everyone else, Wall Street Journal, 13 June 2013

Elgan, Mike; Why the Internet of Things may never happen, Computer World, 18 January 2014, http://www.computerworld.com/article/2487816/emerging-technology/why-the--internet-of-things--may-never-happen.html

Elliott, Stuart W.; Anticipating a Luddite Revival, Issues in science and technology, http://issues.org/30-3/stuart/ 4 July 2014

Evans-Pritchard, Ambrose, Global solar dominance in sight as science trumps fossil fuels, The Telegraph, 9 April 2014, http://www.telegraph.co.uk/finance/comment/ambroseevans_pritchard/10755598/Global-solar-dominance-in-sight-as-science-trumps-fossil-fuels.html

Evans-Pritchard, Ambrose; Solar power will slowly squeeze the revenues of petro-rentier regimes in Russia, Venezuela and Saudi Arabia. They will have to find a new business model, or fade into decline, The Daily Telegraph, 9 April, 2014

Evilyoshida.com; Robert Johnson and the Crossroads Curse http://www.evilyoshida.com/Thread-Robert-Johnson-and-the-Crossroads-Curse , 19 January 2014

Fallows, James; The 50 Greatest Breakthroughs Since the Wheel, The Atlantic, 23 October 2013

Farmer, Andrew; One in three UK consumers 'can't see the point' of 4G, YouGov, July 11 2013, http://yougov.co.uk/news/2013/07/11/4g-third-uk-consumers-cant-see-point/ 29 December 2013

Farrimond, Stuart; The Man Who Could Never Forget, Doctor Stu's Science Blog, 24 October 2010, http://realdoctorstu.com/2010/10/24/the-man-who-could-never-forget/

Fehrenbacher, Katie; How battery improvements will revolutionize the design of the electric car, Gigaom, 2 February 2014, http://gigaom.com/2013/02/10/how-battery-improvements-will-revolutionize-the-design-of-the-electric-car/, 26 January 2014

Ferguson, Kirby; Rise of the Patent Troll, Everything is a Remix, 8 April 2014, http://everythingisaremix.info/

Ferguson, Niall; The Ascent of Money: A financial history of the world, Penguin, New York, 2008

Field, C.B.; Barros, V.R.; Dokken, D.J.; Mach, K.J.; Mastrandrea, M.D.; Bilir, T.E.; Chatterje, M.; Ebi, K.L.; Estrada, Y.O., Genova, R.C.; Girma, B.; Kissel, E.S.; Levy, A.N.; MacCracken, P.R.; Mastrandrea and White, L.L. (eds); Climate Change 2014: Impacts, Adaptation, and Vulnerability Summary for Policymakers, IPCC, Cambridge University Press, 12 April 2014, http://ipcc-wg2.gov/AR5/images/uploads/IPCC_WG2AR5_SPM_Approved.pdf

Fiol, Taryn; Why 83 per cent of Millennials sleep with their phones, Apartment Therapy, http://www.apartmenttherapy.com/do-you-sleep-with-your-cell-ph-127903, 18 December 2013

Fisher, Adam; Inside Google's Quest To Popularize Self-Driving Cars, Popular Science, http://www.popsci.com/cars/article/2013-09/google-self-driving-car 19 January 2014

Fong, Danielle; Making Economical Clean Energy at Planet Scale, Lightsail, http://www.lightsail.com/blog/making-economical-clean-energy-at-planet-scale/, 30 January 2014

Forsyth, Donelson R.; Group Dynamics, Wadsworth, Cengage Learning, 2009 http://www.cengagebrain.com/shop/content/forsyth99522_04955 99522_01.01_toc.pdf, 27 May 2011

413

Fox, Justin; The Real Story Behind Those "Record" Corporate Profits, Harvard Business Review, 24 November 2010, http://blogs.hbr.org/2010/11/the-real-story-behind-those-re/, 18 April 1014

France-Presse, Agence; Fighter Jet Flown with 3-D-printed Components, Industry Week, January 5 2014,http://www.industryweek.com/emerging-technologies/fighter-jet-flown-3-d-printed-components, 31 January 2014

Frankl, Paolo; Renewable Energy 2013 World Renewable Energy Outlook 2030-2050, International Energy Agency, 3 October 2013, http://www.celluleenergie.cnrs.fr/IMG/pdf/intro_i3_paolo_frankl.pdf

Freeman, Clinton; What sort of patents are have been granted against 3D printing?, http://reprage.com/post/47776307526/what-sort-of-patents-are-have-been-granted-against-3d/, 21 January 2014

Frey, Carl Benedikt; Osborne, Michael A.; The future of employment: how susceptible are jobs to computerisation? University of Oxford, 17 September 2013,

http://www.oxfordmartin.ox.ac.uk/downloads/academic/The_Future_of_Employment.pdf, 5 July 2014

Fuller, Richard Buckminster; We must do away with the absolutely specious notion..., http://en.wikiquote.org/wiki/Buckminster_Fuller

Garrett, Laurie; Biology's Brave New World. Foreign Affairs Magazine, November/December 2013, http://www.foreignaffairs.com/articles/140156/laurie-garrett/biologys-brave-new-world

Gartner; Gartner Hype Cycle, 2014, http://www.gartner.com/technology/research/methodologies/hype-cycle.jsp, 20 September 2014

Gibbs, Samuel; Metal 3D printing and six key shifts in the 'second industrial revolution', The Guardian, 9 December 2013, http://www.theguardian.com/technology/2013/dec/09/metal-3d-printing-key-developments-second-industrial-revolution

Giles, Chris; Piketty findings undercut by errors, The Financial Times, 23 May 2014

Good, Jonathan; How many photos have ever been taken? 1000 Memories blog, http://blog.1000memories.com/94-number-of-photos-ever-taken-digital-and-analog-in-shoebox 18 December 2013

Goodwin, Phil; Peak Car' Where did the idea come from? And where is it going?, Centre for Transport and Society and The University of the West of England (UWE), CTS Winter Conference 2012

Goodwin, Phil; Peak Travel, Peak Car and the Future of Mobility Evidence, Unresolved Issues, Policy Implications, and a Research Agenda, OECD, October 2012

Goodwin, Phil; What about 'peak car' – heresy or revelation?, TransportXtra, 25 June 2010, http://www.transportxtra.com/magazines/local_transport_today/opinion/?id=23221

Google; Investor Relations 2013 Quarterly Earnings, https://investor.google.com/earnings/2013/index.html

Gordon, Robert J; Is US economic growth over? Faltering innovation confronts the six headwinds, Centre for Economic Policy Research, September 2012

Graves, Philip; Predicting the Future with Market Research?, Marketing Week, 9 September 2010

Gray, Richard; Stem cell study raises hopes that organs could be regenerated inside patients' own bodies, Telegraph http://www.telegraph.co.uk/science/10302341/Stem-cell-study-raises-hopes-that-organs-could-be-regenerated-inside-patients-own-bodies.html, 12 May 2014

Greenemeier, Larry; Scientists use 3-D printer to speed human embryonic stem cell research, Nature, 5 February 2013, http://www.nature.com/news/scientists-use-3-d-printer-to-speed-human-embryonic-stem-cell-research-1.12381, 30 January 2014

Greenstein, Shane; Devereux, Michelle; The Crisis at Encyclopaedia Britannica, Kellogg School of Management, May 2010, http://www.slideshare.net/renerojas/case-study-encyclopedia-britannica

Grynol, Benjamin; Disruptive Manufacturing: The effects of 3D printing, Deloitte, 2013, http://www.deloitte.com/assets/Dcom-Canada/Local%20Assets/Documents/Insights/Innovative_Thinking/2013/ca_en_insights_disruptive_manufacturing_102813.pdf

Hampton, Keith; Sessions Goulet, Lauren; Rainie, Lee; Purcell, Kristen; Social networking sites and our lives, Pew Research Internet Project, 16 June 2011, http://www.pewinternet.org/2011/06/16/social-networking-sites-and-our-lives/

Hannah, Leslie: Marshall's "Trees" and the Global "Forest": Were "Giant Redwoods" Different?, University of Chicago Press, January 1999, http://www.nber.org/chapters/c10235.pdf, 8 January 2013

Harris, Siân; Lasers in Medicine, SPIE Professional, https://spie.org/x43738.xml, 12 May 2014

Heck, Stefan; Rogers, Matt; Are you ready for the resource revolution?, McKinsey, March 2014, http://www.mckinsey.com/insights/sustainability/are_you_ready_for_the_resource_revolution?cid=other-eml-nsl-mip-mck-oth-1404

Hensley, Russell; Newman, John; Rogers, Matt; Battery Technology Charges Ahead, McKinsey Quarterly, July 2012, http://www.mckinsey.com/insights/energy_resources_materials/battery_technology_charges_ahead

Herper, Matthew, The $1,000 Genome Arrives -- For Real, This Time, Forbes, http://www.forbes.com/sites/matthewherper/2014/01/14/the-1000-genome-arrives-for-real-this-time/, 12 May 2014

Himberg, C.J.; Zipcar's annual millennial survey shows the kids are all right, Zipcar, 27 January 2014, http://www.zipcar.com/press/releases/fourth-annual-millennial-survey

Hong, Hung Le; Fenn, Jackie; Emerging Technologies Hype Cycle for 2013: Redefining the Relationship, Gartner, 21 August 2013, http://www.gartner.com/it/content/2546700/2546719/august_21_hype_cycle_fenn_lehong.pdf?userId=73417090

Horn, Rachel; Consumer Digital Health Care, Five Technology Trends to Watch 2014, Consumer Electronics Association, p14, http://content.ce.org/PDF/2014_5tech_web.pdf

Huetlin, Thomas; Modern mobility: car sharing gears up in German cities, Spiegel Online International, 28 August 2013, http://www.spiegel.de/international/zeitgeist/car-sharing-increasingly-popular-in-german-cities-a-913891.html

Hyperphysics, Laser Applications, http://hyperphysics.phy-astr.gsu.edu/hbase/optmod/lasapp.html, 19 January 2014

IHS; Self-Driving Cars Moving into the Industry's Driver's Seat, 2 January 2014, http://press.ihs.com/press-release/automotive/self-driving-cars-moving-industrys-drivers-seat

Illinois Oil and Gas Association; History of Illinois Basin Posted Crude Oil Prices, July 2013, http://www.ioga.com/Special/crudeoil_Hist.htm

IMF; Global Financial Stability Report, April 2006: Chapter II. The Influence of Credit Derivative and Structured Credit Markets on Financial Stability , 11 April 2006, http://www.imf.org/external/pubs/ft/gfsr/2006/01/pdf/chp2.pdf

Incorrectpleasures; Luria's "S" the synaesthete wasn't face-blind, 10 September 2011, http://incorrectpleasures.blogspot.co.uk/2011/09/lurias-s-synaesthete-wasnt-face-blind.html

Intel; Moore's Law and Intel Innovation, http://www.intel.com/content/www/us/en/history/museum-gordon-moore-law.html, 30 December 2013

International Hapmap Project; October 2002,
http://hapmap.ncbi.nlm.nih.gov/thehapmap.html.en

Ivanova, Olga S.; Williams, Christopher B., Campbell, Thomas A.;
Additive Manufacturing (AM) and Nanotechnology: Promises and
Challenges, University of Texas, 17 August 2011,
http://utwired.engr.utexas.edu/lff/symposium/proceedingsArchive
/pubs/Manuscripts/2011/2011-56-Ivanova.pdf

Janis, I. L.; Victims of groupthink: A psychological study of foreign
policy decisions and fiascos, Houghton Mifflin Company Boston,
1972

Johnson, Steve; Capital gobbles labour's share, but victory is
empty, The Financial Times, 13 October 2013

Johnson, Steven; Where Good ideas come from, Allen Lane,
London, 2010

Johnson, Todd; What is the 787 Dreamliner, about money,
http://composite.about.com/od/applications/a/What-Is-The-787-
Dreamliner.htm

Kahan, Dan M.; Cantrell Dawson, Erica; Peters, Ellen; Slovic, Paul;
Motivated Numeracy and Enlightened Self-Government, Yale Law
School,
http://www.cogsci.bme.hu/~ktkuser/KURZUSOK/BMETE47MC15/2
013_2014_1/kahanEtAl2013.pdf

Kahneman, Daniel; Slovic, Paul; Tversky, Amos; Judgment under
uncertainty: heuristics and biases, Cambridge University Press,
Cambridge, 1982

Kahney, Leander; John Sculley On Steve Jobs, The Full Interview
Transcript, Cult of the Mac,
http://www.cultofmac.com/63295/john-sculley-on-steve-jobs-the-
full-interview-transcript/#miq7cArzCXBXIeiB.99, 18 December
2013

Kaplan, Marty; Scientists' depressing new discovery about the
brain, Alternet, Salon, 17 September 2013,
http://www.salon.com/2013/09/17/the_most_depressing_discove
ry_about_the_brain_ever_partner/

Kay, Alan; Wikiquote, http://en.wikiquote.org/wiki/Alan_Kay

Kealey, Terence; Sex, Science and Profits, William Heinemann: London, 2008

Keeley, Larry: The Greatest Innovations of All Time, Business Week, 16 February 2007

Kelly, Gavin; The robots are coming. Will they bring wealth or a divided society?, The Observer, 4 January 2014, http://www.theguardian.com/technology/2014/jan/04/robots-future-society-drones

Keohane, David; Ahhhh! No robots! Financial Times Alphaville http://ftalphaville.ft.com//2012/08/28/1134571/ahhhh-no-robots/, 18 December 2013

Keynes, John Maynard; Economic Possibilities for our Grandchildren (circa 1930) Aspenin Institute, http://www.aspeninstitute.org/sites/default/files/content/upload/Intro_Session1.pdf, 2 January 2014

Khosla, Vinod; Do We Need Doctors Or Algorithms?, TechCrunch 10 January 2012, http://techcrunch.com/2012/01/10/doctors-or-algorithms/
Khosla, Vinod; Technology will replace 80% of what doctors do, Fortune Magazine, 4 December 2012, http://tech.fortune.cnn.com/2012/12/04/technology-doctors-khosla/
Kioskea.net; WPAN (Wireless Personal Area Network), 2014, http://en.kioskea.net/contents/834-wpan-wireless-personal-area-network, 19 January 2014

Koff, William; Gustafson, Paul; 3D printing and the future of manufacturing, CSC, Fall 2012, http://assets1.csc.com/innovation/downloads/LEF_20123DPrinting.pdf

Kovach, Steve; Google bought a company that collects windpower from airborne turbines 2,000 feet above ground, Business Insider, 22 May 2013, http://www.businessinsider.com/google-buys-makani-power-2013-5

Kowalski, Richard; Robots Ahead, Five Technology Trends to Watch 2014, Consumer Electronics Association, p20,
http://content.ce.org/PDF/2014_5tech_web.pdf

Kruger, J.; Lake Wobegon be gone! The "below-average effect" and the egocentric nature of comparative ability judgments, Journal of Pers Soc Psychology, 7 August 1999,
http://www.ncbi.nlm.nih.gov/pubmed/10474208

Krugman, Paul; Here comes the sun, New York Times, 6 November 2011, http://www.nytimes.com/2011/11/07/opinion/krugman-here-comes-solar-energy.html?_r=0

Krugman, Paul; The Populist Imperative, New York Times, 23 January 2014,
http://www.nytimes.com/2014/01/24/opinion/krugman-the-populist-imperative.html?_r=0 24 April 2014

Kurzweil, Ray; The Law of Accelerating Returns, Kurzweil Accelerated Intelligence, http://www.kurzweilai.net/the-law-of-accelerating-returns, 2 January 2014

Lakeland; http://www.lakeland.co.uk/23969/iRobot-Roomba-630

Lamdany, Ruben; Wagner, Nancy, et al; IMF Performance in the Run-Up to the Financial and Economic Crisis IMF Surveillance in 2004–07, IEO-IMF, http://www.ieo-imf.org/ieo/files/completedevaluations/Crisis-%20Main%20Report%20(without%20Moises%20Signature).pdf, 27 May 2011

Lapore, Jill; The Disruption Machine, The New Yorker, http://www.newyorker.com/magazine/2014/06/23/the-disruption-machine?currentPage=all/, 23 June 2014

Lee, Timothy B.; How software-defined radio could revolutionize wireless, Arstechnica, 6 July 2012, http://arstechnica.com/tech-policy/2012/07/how-software-defined-radio-could-revolutionize-wireless/

Lockheed Martin; 3D Printing Drives Manufacturing Innovation at Lockheed Martin, 15 January 2014,
http://www.lockheedmartin.co.uk/us/news/features/2014/1-15-3dmanufacturing.html

Lomas, Natasha; Read The Sonnet Co-Authored By Shakespeare, An MIT PhD Student & A Machine-Learning Algorithm, Tech Crunch, 26 January 2014, http://techcrunch.com/2014/01/26/swift-speare/, 30 January 2014

London School of Hygiene & Tropical Medicine, The drugs don't work: the global threat of antimicrobial resistance, The Chariot, http://blogs.lshtm.ac.uk/news/2013/09/19/the-drugs-dont-work-the-global-threat-of-antimicrobial-resistance/ 18 December 2013

Lozano, Marina; Subirà, Maria Eulàlia; Aparicio, José; Lorenzo, Carlos, Gómez-Merino, Gala; Toothpicking and Periodontal Disease in a Neanderthal Specimen from Cova Foradà Site (Valencia, Spain), Plos One, 16 October 2013

Mackay, Charles; Extraordinary Popular Delusions and the Madness of Crowds, first published in 1841, Harriman House republished September 2003

Maddison, Angus; Contours of the World Economy 1-2040 AD, Oxford University Press, 2007

Mainstream Renewable Power; Why renewables, debunking the myth, http://test.mainstreamrp.com/why-renewables /debunking-the-myth/

Manyika, James; Chui, Michael; Bughin, Jacques; Dobbs, Richard; Bisson, Peter; Marrs, Alex; Advances that will transform life, business, and the global economy, McKinsey Global Institute Disruptive Technologies, May 2013

Mark Forged, The World's first 3D printer than print carbon fibre, http://markforged.com/, 31 January 2014

Markoff, John; Google Puts Money on Robots, Using the Man Behind Android, 4 December 2013, http://www.nytimes.com/2013/12/04/technology/google-puts-money-on-robots-using-the-man-behind-android.html?, January 31 2014

Marricchi, Ciara; Wanner, Brent; Wilkinson, David; World Energy Outlook 2012 Renewable Energy Outlook, International Energy Agency, 2012, http://www.worldenergyoutlook.org/media/weowebsite/2012/W

EO2012_Renewables.pdf

Martin, James; The Meaning of the 21st Century: A vital blueprint for ensuring our future, Transworld Publishers, London 2006

Masson, Gaetan; Latour, Marie; Rekinger, Manoel; Theologitis, Ioannis-Thomas; Papoutsi, Myrto; Winneker, Craig (Editor); Global Market Outlook for Photovoltaics 2013-2017, EPIA, 2013, http://www.epia.org/fileadmin/user_upload/Publications/GMO_2 013_-_Final_PDF.pdf

Matic, Aleksandar; Scrosati, Bruno; MRS Bulletin, Ionic liquids for energy applications,.Cambridge University Press: July 2013, http://journals.cambridge.org/action/displayFulltext?type=1&fid=8 952114&jid=MRS&volumeId=38&issueId=07&aid=8952092&bodyI d=&membershipNumber=&societyETOCSession=, 26 January 2013

McCrone, John; The Ape that Spoke: Language and the Evolution of the Human Mind, Picador, 1990, ISBN-10: 068810326X

Mearian, Lucas, AI found better than doctors at diagnosing, treating patients, Computer World, 12 February 2013 http://www.computerworld.com/s/article/9236737/AI_found_bet ter_than_doctors_at_diagnosing_treating_patients 12 May 2014

Mearian, Lucas; IBM claims spintronics memory breakthrough, Computerworld, http://www.computerworld.com/s/article/9230150/IBM_claims_s pintronics_memory_breakthrough, 30 January 2014

Mehen, Lori; Is the future of Pharma open source? Opensource.com, http://opensource.com/health/11/4/future-pharma-open-source, 21 April 2011

Meigs, James B, Inside the future – how popmech predicted the next 110 years, Popular Mechanics, http://www.popularmechanics.com/technology/engineering/news /inside-the-future-how-popmech-predicted-the-next-110-years-14831802

Memsnet; What is MEMS?, http://www.memsnet.org/mems/what_is.html

Mims, Christopher; 3D printing will explode in 2014, thanks to the expiration of key patents, Quartz, http://qz.com/106483/3d-printing-will-explode-in-2014-thanks-to-the-expiration-of-key-patents/, 21 January 2014

Mims, Christopher; Google engineers insist 20% time is not dead – it's just turned into 120% time, Quartz, 16 August 2013, http://qz.com/116196/google-engineers-insist-20-time- is-not-dead-its-just-turned-into-120-time/

MIO.com, History of GPS, http://www.mio.com/technology-history-of-gps.htm, 21 January 2014

MIT Technology Review, Graphene Supercapacitors Ready for Electric Vehicle Energy Storage Say Korean Engineers, 12 November 2013, http://www.technologyreview.com/view/521651/graphene-supercapacitors-ready-for-electric-vehicle-energy-storage-say-korean-engineers/, 30 January 2014

Mlodinow, Leonard; The Drunkard's Walk, Pantheon, 2008

Moscovici, S.; Zavalloni, M.; The group as a polarizer of attitudes, Journal of Personality and Social Psychology, 12, pp. 125-135,1969

Mullin, Joe; New study suggests patent trolls really are killing start-ups, Arts Technica, 12 June 2014, http://artstechnica.com/tech-policy/2014/06/new-study-suggests-patent-trolls-really-are-killing-startups/, 7 July 2014

Munoz, Claudia; Kim, Christina; Armstrong, Lucas; Layer-by-Layer: Opportunities in 3D Printing, MaRS, 16 December 2013, http://marscommons.marsdd.com/3dprinting/tech-trends-new-applications/#sthash.jP1I66mY.dpuf

Munsell, Mike; US Solar Market Grew 41%, Had Record Year in 2013, Greentechsolar, 7 March 2014, http://www.greentechmedia.com/articles/read/u.s.-solar-market-grows-41 has record-year-in-2013

Murnaghan, Ian; History of Stem Cell Research, http://www.explorestemcells.co.uk/historystemcellresearch.html, 21 January 2014

Naam, Ramez; Smaller, cheaper, faster: Does Moore's Law apply to solar cells?, Scientific American, 16 March 2011, http://blogs.scientificamerican.com/guest-blog/2011/03/16/smaller-cheaper-faster-does-moores-law-apply-to-solar-cells/

National Human Genome Research Institute, An Overview of the Human Genome Project, http://www.genome.gov/12011239, 21 January 2014

Natural History Museum, How long have we been here?, http://www.nhm.ac.uk/nature-online/life/human-origins/modern-human-evolution/when/index.html, 26 April 2014

Neven, Hartmut; Launching the Quantum Artificial Intelligence Lab. Research blog Google, http://googleresearch.blogspot.co.uk/2013/05/launching-quantum-artificial.html, 30 January 2014

New Energy Technologies; Solar Window, http://www.newenergytechnologiesinc.com/technology/solarwindow

Nguyen, Hanh; Stuchtey, Martin; Zils, Markus; Remaking the industry economy, McKinsey Quarterly, February 2014, http://www.mckinsey.com/Insights/Manufacturing/Remaking_the_industrial_economy?cid=manufacturing-eml-alt-mkq-mck-oth-1402http://hbr.org/2013/03/3-d-printing-will-change-the-world/

Nichols, Will; IEA: Expanding wind and solar does not mean additional costs, Business Green, 28 February 2014, http://www.businessgreen.com/bg/analysis/2331389/iea-expanding-wind-and-solar-power-does-not-mean-additional-costs

NME: Music streaming doubles in 2013, as album sales fall, 1 January 2014

Normal Deviate, The Future of Machine Learning and the End of the World?, http://normaldeviate.wordpress.com/2012/10/30/the-future-of-machine-learning-and-the-end-of-the-world/, 31 January 2014

NPD Group, Consumers now take more than a quarter of all photos and videos on smart phones, https://www.npd.com/wps/portal/npd/us/news/press-releases/pr_111222/ 18 December 2013

O'Connor, Eddie; How competitive is wind energy compared to the others?, O'Connor Online, 30 September 2013, http://eddie.mainstreamrp.com/how-competitive-is-wind-energy-compared-to-the-others/

O'Connor, Eddie; The CO_2 content of our atmosphere is at its highest point for 4 million years. Is this a coincidence?, O'Connor Online, 19 July 2013, http://eddie.mainstreamrp.com/the-co2-content-of-our-atmosphere-is-at-its-highest-point-for-4-million-years-is-this-a-coincidence/

Oculus Rift, http://www.oculusvr.com/, 1 February 2014

OECD/International Energy Agency; The Power of Transformation: Wind Sun and the Economics of Flexible Power Systems, 2014, http://www.iea.org/w/bookshop/add.aspx?id=465

Orcutt, Mike; Nanoparticle that mimics red blood cell shows promise as vaccine for bacterial infections, MIT Technology Review, 3 January 2014, http://www.technologyreview.com/news/522846/nanoparticle-that-mimics-red-blood-cell-shows-promise-as-vaccine-for-bacterial/

O'Toole, James; Musk says cheaper Tesla model 'about three years away', CNN, 14 January 2004, http://money.cnn.com/2014/01/14/autos/musk-tesla-cheaper/

O'Toole, James; Your new heat source: data centers, CNNMoney, 7 April 2014, http://money.cnn.com/2014/04/07/technology/innovation/data-centers-heat/index.html?iid=HP_River

Pariser, Eli.; The Filter Bubble: What the Internet Is Hiding from You, Penguin Press HC, 12 May 2011

Parsons, David; Chatterton, Julia, Brennan, Professor Feargal; Kolios, Dr Athanosios; Carbon Brainprint Case Study: Novel Offshore Vertical Axis Wind Turbines, Cranfield University, July 2011, http://www.carbonbrainprint.org.uk/pdf/CBrainprint-CS02-NOVA.pdf

Perella, Maxine; Brands look for greater ownership stake in sharing economy, Edie, 12 August 2013, http://www.edie.net/news/5/Brands-look-for-greater-ownership-stake-in-sharing-economy-/?utm_source=weeklynewsletter&utm_medium=email&utm_content=news&utm_campaign=weeklynewslettwe

Perry, Caroline; Robotic construction crew needs no foreman, Harvard School of Engineering and Applied Sciences, 13 February 2013, https://www.seas.harvard.edu/news/2014/02/robotic-construction-crew-needs-no-foreman

Phelps, Edmund S.; What has gone wrong up until now, Spiegel Online International, 12 November 2008, http://www.spiegel.de/international/world/edmund-s-phelps-what-has-gone-wrong-up-until-now-a-590030.html

Phillips, Matt and Ferdman, Roberto A.; A brief, illustrated history of Blockbuster, which is closing the last of its US stores, Quartz, 18 December 2013

Pickrell, Don; Pace, David; Has Growth in Automobile use ended?, Volpe, 8 August 2014, http://www.volpe.dot.gov/news/has-growth-automobile-use-ended

Piketty, Thomas; Capital in the 21st Century, The Belknap Press of Harvard University Press, 2014

Plus 500, Bitcoin (BTCUSD) CFD, http://www.plus500.co.uk/Instruments/BTCUSD?gclid=CObmqbndxr0CFernwgodDG4A9w

Powatag; http://www.powatag.com/page/powatag-transact-how-it-works

Power, Thomas; The future of social networks, TED, 22 October, https://www.youtube.com/watch?v=fVs6Zogzg4g

PwC; The new gold rush: Prospectors are hoping to mine opportunities from the health industry, PwC, May 2011, http://www.pwc.com/us/goldrush

Rabuck, Fran; Look – Up in the Air, It's a Bird, It's a Plane... No It's Just Another Drone, LIDAR News, http://www.lidarnews.com/content/view/9723/, 19 January 2014

Rachel Botsman; http://www.rachelbotsman.com/

Ramsey, Mike; Will Tesla's $5 Billion Gigafactory Make a Battery Nobody Else Wants?, The Wall Street Journal, 4 April 2014, http://blogs.wsj.com/corporate-intelligence/2014/04/04/will-teslas-5-billion-gigafactory-make-a-battery-no-one-else-wants/

Raptopoulos, Andreas; No roads? There's a drone for that, TED, http://www.ted.com/talks/andreas_raptopoulos_no_roads_there_s_a_drone_for_that.html

Ratti, Carlo; Claudel, Matthew; The driverless car, Project Syndicate, 2 January 2014, http://www.project-syndicate.org/commentary/carlo-ratti-and-matthew-claudel-foresee-a-world-in-which-self-driving-cars-reconfigure-urban-life#Xd6kiBrpydwmEq7C.99

Reisman, David A.; Schumpeter's market enterprise an evolution, Edward Elgar Publishing, 2004

RFID in Healthcare, RFID, http://www.rfidba.org/rhcc/rfid-healthcare, 12 May 2014

RFID Journal; From how far away can a typical RFID tag be read?, http://www.rfidjournal.com/faq/show?139

RFID Solutions for Healthcare Industry, RFID, http://healthcare.gaorfid.com/, 12 May 2014

Rikleen, L. (n.d.); Creating tomorrow's leaders: the expanding roles of Millennials in the workplace, Boston College Center for Work & Family, Chestnut Hill, MA

Riley-Smith, Ben; Britons lose five and a half days a year from slow computers, Telegraph, 18 December 2013

Riskin, Dan; The Next Revolution in Healthcare, Forbes, 10 January 2012, http://www.forbes.com/sites/singularity/2012/10/01/the-next-revolution-in-healthcare/, 12 May 2014

Road Transport Forecasts 2013; The National Transport Model, Department for Transport, https://www.gov.uk/government/uploads/system/uploads/attachment_data/file/212474/road-transport-forecasts-2013.pdf 7 April

2014

Robertson, Grant; How powerful was the Apollo 11 computer? Huffpost tech
http://downloadsquad.switched.com/2009/07/20/how-powerful-was-the-apollo-11-computer/ 30 December 2013

Rowe Price, T; Connections, A Brief History of 3D Printing,
http://individual.troweprice.com/staticFiles/Retail/Shared/PDF

RT.com; Giant 3D printer could build homes in under a day,
http://rt.com/usa/3d-printed-concrete-house-727/, 30 January 2014

Russon, Mary-Ann; 3D Printers Could be Banned by 2016 for Bioprinting Human Organs, IB Times, 29 January 2014

Sadoway, Donald; The missing link to renewable energy, TED, March 2012,
http://www.ted.com/talks/donald_sadoway_the_missing_link_to_renewable_energy.html, 30 January 2014

Samsung, Samsung Announces World's First 5G mmWave Mobile Technology,
http://global.samsungtomorrow.com/?p=24093#sthash.PIQ5h9jO.dpuf, 30 January 2014

Samuels, Jonathan; Australia: Sharks Use Twitter To Warn Swimmers, Sky News, 1 September 2014,
http://news.sky.com/story/1187066/australia-sharks-use-twitter-to-warn-swimmers/

SciTechStory; A Coming Marriage: Additive Manufacturing and Nanotechnology, 1 June 2010,
http://scitechstory.com/2010/06/01/a-coming-marriage-additive-manufacturing-and-nanotechnology/

Scott, Cameron; Delicate Eye Cells are Latest to be 3D Printed, Singularity Hub, http://singularityhub.com/2013/12/23/delicate-eye-cells-are-latest-to-be-3d-printed/, 30 January 2014

Scott, Cameron; Simple Method for Creating Stem Cells Promises Cheaper, Faster Therapies, Singularity Hub,
http://singularityhub.com/2014/01/30/simple-method-for-creating-stem-cells-promises-cheaper-faster-therapies/, 30 January

2014

Shahan, Zachary; Credit Suisse Projects ~85% Of US Energy Demand Growth Coming From Renewables Through 2025, Clean Technica, 1 January 2014, http://cleantechnica.com/2014/01/01/credit-suisse-projects-85-us-energy-growth-coming-renewables-2025/

Shahan, Zachary; Seven impressive solar energy facts, ABB, 2 December 2013, http://www.abb-conversations.com /2013/12/7-impressive-solar-energy-facts-charts/ 30 December 2013

Sherif, M.; A study of some social factors in perception, Archives of Psychology, 27, 1935

Slaus, Ivo; Jacobs, Garry; Human Capital and Sustainability, Sustainability Journal, Vol 3, Issue 1, 7 January 2011, http://www.mssresearch.org/?q=node/581

Smil, Vaclav. Creating the Twentieth Century: Technical Innovations of 1867-1914 and Their Lasting Impact, Oxford, Oxford University Press, 2005

Smith, Richard; Coast, Joanna; The true cost of antimicrobial resistance http://www.bmj.com/content/346/bmj.f1493?ijkey=gFj9fDOoZotH a9S&keytype=ref 18 December 2013

Southwest Center for Microsystems Education and The Regents of University of New Mexico, History of Micro-electro-mechanical Systems (MEMS), http://scme-nm.org/files/History%20of%20MEMS_Presentation.pdf, 19 January 2014

StarveTheSystem2, Everything Is A Remix, http://www.youtube.com/watch?v=coGpmA4saEk, 21 January 2014

Stem Cell Information, Stem Cell Basics, http://stemcells.nih.gov/info/basics/pages/basics1.aspx, 21 January 2014

Stiglitz, Joseph E.; Inequality Is a Choice, New York Times, 13 October 2013

Stinson, Liz; The Future of Prosthetics Could Be This Brain-Controlled Bionic Leg, Wired, 15 October 2013 http://www.wired.com/2013/10/is-this-brain-controlled-bionic-leg-the-future-of-prosthetics/

Stoffels, Bob; Kilby, Noyce; The Integrated Circuit, OSP Magazine, http://www.ospmag.com/issue/article/012009-Stoffels, 19 January 2014

Stone, James A. F.; Risky and cautious shifts in group decisions, Journal of Experimental Social Psychology, Volume 4, Issue 4, October 1968, pp. 442-459 Massachusetts Institute of Technology

Strauss, Karsten; The Secret Technology That Attracted $76 Million And Could Eat Amazon's Lunch, Forbes, 13 September 2013, http://www.forbes.com/sites/karstenstrauss/2013/09/13/the-secret-technology-that-attracted-76-million-and-could-eat-amazons-lunch/

Stringer, Chris; McKie, Robin; African Exodus, Jonathan Cape, London, 1996

Surowiecki, James; The Wisdom of Crowds: Why the Many Are Smarter Than the Few and How Collective Wisdom Shapes Business, Economies, Societies and Nations, Doubleday, 2004

Sutherland, Paul; Japan aims to beam solar energy down from orbit, Wired, 2 October 2013, http://www.wired.co.uk/news/archive/2013-10/02/japan-solar-energy

Svenson, Ola; Are we all less risky and more skilful than our fellow drivers?, Acta Psychologica 47 (1981), 143-148, North-Holland Publishing Company, Department of Psychology, University of Stockholm, Sweden, Accepted March 1980

Svitil, Kathy; The promise of stem cells, UCLA Newsroom, http://newsroom.ucla.edu/stories/the-promises-of-stem-cells-247547, 12 May 2014

Synthetic biology NCBI, http://en.wikipedia.org/wiki/Synthetic_biology

Takahashi, Dean; Our complete interview with IBM's Bernie Meyerson on the top five predictions for the next five years,

Venture Beat, December 19,
http://venturebeat.com/2013/12/19/our-complete-interview-with-ibms-bernie-meyerson-on-the-top-five-predictions-for-the-next-five-years/

Task Rabbit; https://www.taskrabbit.com/how-it-works

Tehrani, Rich; As We May Communicate, TMCnet.com, http://www.tmcnet.com/articles/comsol/0100/0100pubout.htm, 19 January 2014

Tesla Motors; Gigafactory, teslamotors.com, 26 February 2014, http://www.teslamotors.com/blog/gigafactory

Tett, Gillian; Can we avoid an antibiotic apocalypse?, Financial Times, 6 December 2013

The Economist, Pricing sunshine, 28 December 2012

The Economist; Print me a Stradivarius, 10 February 2011, http://www.economist.com/node/18114327

The Economist; The other-worldly philosophers, 18 July 2009, pp65–67

The Economist; Vertical Farming: Does it really stack up?, 9 December 2010

The Economist; The future of jobs: The onrushing wave, 16 January 2014, http://www.economist.com/news/briefing/21594264-previous-technological-innovation-has-always-delivered-more-long-run-employment-not-less
The Independent, Laser power beaming: A bright new idea for flight, 26 April 2011

The Verge Live from Yahoo's Flickr press event, http://live.theverge.com/yahoo-flickr-event-live-hlng-nyc-may 2013/, 18 December 2013

The Vertical Farm, http://www.verticalfarm.com/, 21 January 2014

Tarlton Law Library; Television History - A Timeline, 1878-2005, The University of Texas School of Law Tarlton Law Library 1878-2005. http://tarlton.law.utexas.edu/exhibits/mason_&_associates/documents/timeline.pdf 5 September 2014

Thompson, Derek; IBM's killer idea: The $100 DNA-sequencing machine, The Atlantic, 16 November 2011

Tibbits, Skylar; The emergence of 4D printing, TED http://www.ted.com/talks/skylar_tibbits_the_emergence_of_4d_printing.html, 30 January 2014

Toumazou, Christofer; Rapid DNA Test on a USB Stick, MDT Magazine, September 2014, http://www.mdtmag.com/news/2014/04/rapid-dna-test-usb-stick

Transparency Market Research; Wearable Technology Market - Global Scenario, Trends, Industry Analysis, Size, Share And Forecast 2012 - 2018, 14 January 2013, http://www.transparencymarketresearch.com/wearable-technology.html

Tristam, Pierre; Jericho, about news, http://middleeast.about.com/od/glossary/g/me090314.htm, 26 April 2014

Tucker, William; Paul Krugman Flunks Moore's Law, The American Spectator, 15 November 2011, http://spectator.org/articles/36579/paul-krugman-flunks-moores-law

UEA, Antibiotic research to find next-generation drugs unveiled in London, 30 Jun 2014. http://www.uea.ac.uk/mac/comm/media/press/2014/june/ants-royal-society, 7 July 2014

University of Manchester, Graphene: World-leading Research and Development, http://www.graphene.manchester.ac.uk/, 26 January 2014

University of Strathclyde; Catching up with the 'superbug', Prism, November-December 2004 http://www.strath.ac.uk/media/publications/prism/2004/media_77413_en.pdf, 7 July 2014

US Department of Energy; Additive Manufacturing: Pursuing the Promise, August 2012, https://www1.eere.energy.gov/manufacturing/pdfs/additive_manufacturing.pdf

Venter, Craig; Annual Richard Dimbleby Lecture for the BBC, December 2007, www.bbc.co.uk/pressoffice/pressreleases/stories/2007/12_december/05/dimbleby.shtml, 7 June 2011

Venter, Craig; Watch me unveil synthetic life, TED, http://www.ted.com/talks/craig_venter_unveils_synthetic_life.html, 21 January 2014

Vicarious, Vicarious AI passes first Turing Test: CAPTCHA, 27 October 2013, http://news.vicarious.com/post/65316134613/vicarious-ai-passes-first-turing-test-captcha

Virtual Reality (VR) in Healthcare in the U.S. (Markets for Surgery, Visualization, Rehabilitation and Training), 1 February 2011, http://www.kaloramainformation.com/Virtual-Reality-VR-6077260/, 12 May 2014

Virtual Reality, Developments In Virtual Reality, http://www.vrs.org.uk/virtual-reality/developments.html, 1 February 2014

Virtual Reality, When Was Virtual Reality Invented?, http://www.vrs.org.uk/virtual-reality/invention.html, 1 February 2014

Vlaskovits, Patrick Henry Ford; Innovation, and That "Faster Horse" Quote, Harvard Business Review Blog: http://blogs.hbr.org/2011/08/henry-ford-never-said-the-fast/, 28 December 2013

Walker, Professor A.; Dunstan, B.; A forecast for the composites industry 2012-2023, Vcamm, http://www.nccef.co.uk/Portals/0/Documents/Forecast%20for%20the%20Composite%20Industry%202011-2023.pdf

Weber, Max; The Protestant Ethic and the Spirit of Capitalism (published 1904-5 originally), Allen and Unwin, 1930

Weschler, Matthew; How Lasers Work, http://science.howstuffworks.com/laser.htm, 19 January 2014

Wikinvest, Apple http://www.wikinvest.com/stock/Apple_(AAPL)/Data/Market_Capi

talization/2003/Q3 18 December 2013

Wikipedia, Synthetic biology: promises and challenges, http://www.ncbi.nlm.nih.gov/pmc/articles/PMC2174633/, 12 May 2014

Wikipedia, World Wide Web, http://en.wikipedia.org/wiki/World_Wide_Web, 19 January 2014

Wikipedia, ZigBee, http://en.wikipedia.org/wiki/ZigBee, 19 January 2014

Wikipedia: Phaistos Disc, http://en.wikipedia.org/wiki/Phaistos_Disc, 31 December 2013

Wikipedia; George Gamow: DNA and RNA, http://en.wikipedia.org/wiki/George_Gamow

Wikipedia; http://en.wikipedia.org/wiki/Dodge_v._Ford_Motor_Company

Wikipedia; http://en.wikipedia.org/wiki/Emergence

Wikipedia; http://en.wikipedia.org/wiki/Hyperloop

Wikipedia; http://en.wikipedia.org/wiki/Wikipedia:Wikipedians

Wikipedia; http://en.wikipedia.org/wiki/Wikipedia_community

Wikipedia; National Maximum Speed Law, http://en.wikipedia.org/wiki/National_Maximum_Speed_Law

Wikipedia; Nov, Oded (2007)., "What Motivates Wikipedians?",. Communications of the ACM 50 (11): 60–64. doi:10.1145/1297797.1297798. Retrieved 11 August 2011.

William Lee; http://calverton.homestead.com/willlee.html, 5 July 2014

Wiltz, Chris; The Oculus Rift – Changing Virtual Reality for Healthcare, MDDI Medical Device and Diagnostic Industry News Products and Suppliers, 17 July 2013, http://www.mddionline.com/article/oculus-rift-%E2%80%93-changing-virtual-reality-healthcare, 12 May 2014

Wolfram-Alpha; http://www.wolframalpha.com/pro/problem-generator/

Wood, Daniel; Space-based solar power, energy.gov, 6 March 2014, http://energy.gov/articles/space-based-solar-power

Wood, Karen; Wind turbine blades: Glass versus carbon fiber, Composites Technology, 31 May 2012, http://www.compositesworld.com/articles/wind-turbine-blades-glass-vs-carbon-fiber

Woodcock, Jim; 3D printing don't believe the hype, Digital Innovation, 29 July 2013, http://diginnmmu.com/opinion/3d-printing-dont-believe-the-hype-704

Wrangham, Richard W.; Catching Fire: How Cooking Made Us Human, Basic Books, First Trade Paper Edition edition, 7 September 2010

Yamanaka, Shinya; Nobel Prizes Facts, http://www.nobelprize.org/nobel_prizes/medicine/laureates/2012/yamanaka-facts.html, 21 January 2014

Yang, Heng-Li; Lai, Cheng-Yu (November 2010). "Motivations of Wikipedia content contributors". Computers in Human Behavior 26 (6): 1377–1383. doi:10.1016/j.chb.2010.04.011. Retrieved 2 August 2011. cited at http://en.wikipedia.org/wiki/Wikipedia_community

Yang, Joy; The Human Microbiome Project: Extending the definition of what constitutes a human, Genome.gov, https://www.genome.gov/27549400, 12 May 2014

Index

438

CPSIA information can be obtained at www.ICGtesting.com
Printed in the USA
BVOW05s1020160615

404836BV00004B/105/P